# Documents in Contemporary History

*General editor*
Kevin Jefferys
Faculty of Arts and Education, University of Plymouth

## The Conservative Party since 1945

The Conservative Party has been the dominant force in post-war British politics, shaping and responding to fundamental changes in society, the economy, and Britain's place in the world. This book explores the fifty-two years from Winston Churchill's landslide defeat in 1945 to the long tenure of power under Margaret Thatcher and John Major which ended in 1997. Despite an impressive record of electoral success, the Conservatives have faced many difficulties since 1945, with divisions over leadership, crises in government, and frustrations in opposition.

The documents contained in this book illuminate the changing nature, outlook and policies of the Conservative Party. The themes and events of the period are brought vividly to life through the views and reactions of those involved, from the Party leaders to the local rank and file. The extracts have been selected from a wide range of sources, and include previously unpublished papers from the Conservative Party's own archive. The editor, a leading authority on the history of the Conservative Party, provides an introductory essay and sets each item in context.

This book provides a fresh insight into a key topic for all students of modern British history and politics, and will also appeal to anyone interested in the making of contemporary Britain.

Stuart Ball is Reader in History at the University of Leicester

MANCHESTER
UNIVERSITY PRESS

*Documents in Contemporary History* is a series designed for sixth-formers and undergraduates in higher education. It aims to provide both an overview of specialist research on topics in post-1939 British history, and a wide-ranging selection of primary source material.

*Already published in the series*

John Baylis  *Anglo-American relations: the rise and fall of the special relationship*

Alan Booth  *British economic development since 1945*

Stephen Brooke  *Reform and reconstruction: Britain after the war, 1945–51*

Steven Fielding  *The Labour Party: 'socialism' and society since 1951*

Sean Greenwood  *Britain and European integration since the Second World War*

Kevin Jefferys  *War and reform: British politics during the Second World War*

Scott Lucas  *Britain and Suez: the lion's last roar*

Ritchie Ovendale  *British defence policy since 1945*

Harold L. Smith  *Britain in the Second World War: a social history*

Chris Wrigley  *British trade unions, 1945–1995*

*Forthcoming*

Richard Aldrich  *Security, intelligence and assessment in Britain, 1945–1968*

Rodney Lowe  *The classic welfare state in Britain*

Ralph Negrine  *The British media since 1945*

# The Conservative Party since 1945

Edited by
## Stuart Ball
*Reader in History, University of Leicester*

Manchester University Press
Manchester and New York
*Distributed exclusively in the USA by St. Martin's Press*

The right of Stuart Ball to be identified as the author of this work has been asserted by him in accordance with the Copyright, Designs and Patents Act 1988.

*Published by* Manchester University Press
Oxford Road, Manchester M13 9NR, UK
*and* Room 400, 175 Fifth Avenue, New York, NY 10010, USA

*Distributed exclusively in the USA by*
St Martin's Press, Inc., 175 Fifth Avenue, New York, NY 10010, USA

*Distributed exclusively in Canada by*
UBC Press, University of British Columbia, 6344 Memorial Road, Vancouver, BC, Canada V6T 1Z2

*British Library Cataloguing-in-Publication Data*
A catalogue record for this book is available from the British Library

*Library of Congress Cataloging-in-Publication Data applied for*


ISBN   0 7190 4012 4   *hardback*
       0 7190 4013 2   *paperback*


First published 1998

02  01  00  99  98          10  9  8  7  6  5  4  3  2  1

Printed in Great Britain by Bell & Bain Ltd, Glasgow

# Contents

# Acknowledgements

I am most grateful to the Conservative Party for permitting extracts to be taken from material in its copyright, and in particular from unpublished manuscripts for the period 1945–75 which are held in the Conservative Party Archive at the Bodleian Library. I am especially indebted to Alistair Cooke, formerly the Director of the Conservative Political Centre, for his support not only of this project but of the work of all historians of the Conservative Party for the last two decades. I would also like to thank Martin Maw, the Conservative Party archivist at the Bodleian, for his cheerful and practical help on every occasion.

This project could not have been completed without the loving support of my wife, Gillian, to whom I am profoundly grateful.

# Chronology of events

See the Appendices for the dates of general elections, leadership ballots
and the appointments of Party Leaders, Chairmen and Chief Whips

*1945*
4 June            Churchill's 'Gestapo' general election radio broadcast
December          Conservative Political Centre established by R. A.
                  Butler
13 December       seventy-four Conservative MPs vote against terms of
                  loan from the United States, despite shadow cabinet
                  decision to abstain

*1947*
11 May            publication of the *Industrial Charter*

*1948*
17 March          success of Lord Woolton's 'Million Fund' appeal is
                  announced
19 April          Eden launches campaign to double membership to
                  two million
12 June           first Young Conservative conference held

*1949*
3 March           Churchill faces stormy 1922 Committee meeting,
                  after failure to win Hammersmith South by-election
15 July           Final Report of (Maxwell-Fyfe) Committee on Party
                  Organisation accepted

*1950*
13 October        Annual Conference insists on a target of building
                  300,000 new houses

*1953*
23 June           Churchill suffers a stroke, which is kept secret

# Chronology of events

**1955**

26 October     Butler increases taxation in a post-election supplementary budget

**1956**

3 January     *Daily Telegraph* attacks Eden as lacking the 'smack of firm government'

6 December     fifteen Conservative MPs abstain in vote of confidence over Suez invasion

**1958**

6 January     Chancellor of the Exchequer Thorneycroft and his Treasury team resign

**1959**

7 April     Budget cuts taxes by £350 million

**1960**

3 February     Macmillan's 'wind of change' decolonisation speech, in Cape Town

**1961**

25 July     introduction of the 'pay pause'

31 July     announcement of application to join the European Economic Community (EEC)

**1962**

13 July     'night of the long knives': Macmillan dismisses seven cabinet ministers

**1963**

14 January     application to join the EEC is vetoed by French President de Gaulle

3 April     Maudling's 'dash for growth' expansionist budget

17 June     twenty-seven Conservative MPs abstain over Profumo affair but the government survives

10 October     Macmillan's resignation announced at the start of the Annual Conference

**1964**

24 March     thirty-one Conservative MPs rebel over the abolition of Resale Price Maintenance

9 April     Home announces that the general election will be held in the autumn

# Chronology of events

**1965**

25 February — publication of the new rules for the election of the Leader of the Party

21 December — serious divisions in the Commons vote over sanctions against Rhodesia

**1968**

21 April — Powell is dismissed from the shadow cabinet after his 'river of blood' speech

**1970**

30 January — shadow cabinet policy weekend at the Selsdon Park Hotel, Croydon

20 July — sudden death of the Chancellor of the Exchequer, Iain Macleod

**1971**

28 October — Commons approves the terms for joining the EEC by 356 to 244, with Labour pro-Europe rebels outweighing the thirty-nine Conservative MPs who vote against

**1972**

1 May — publication of Industry Bill indicates a U-turn in government policy

6 November — announcement of a wage freeze and a statutory prices and incomes policy

**1973**

13 December — three-day working week introduced after miners' work-to-rule

**1975**

23 January — Heath announces a leadership ballot will be held on 4 February

**1976**

4 October — publication of free-market policy manifesto, *The Right Approach*

**1979**

28 March — vote of no confidence carried against the Labour government by 311 to 310

12 June — Howe's first budget cuts income tax and public spending, but raises VAT

# Chronology of events

**1980**

8 August — Housing Bill gives council tenants the 'right to buy' their homes

**1981**

10 March — Howe's budget increases excise duties and cuts public spending by £3.2 billion; 'wet' cabinet ministers critical but decide not to resign

14 September — leading 'wets' sacked or demoted in cabinet reshuffle

**1982**

3 April — Carrington resigns as Foreign Secretary after the invasion of the Falklands

6 May — boosted by 'Falklands factor', Conservatives make large gains in local elections

**1984**

12 October — IRA bomb narrowly misses Thatcher at the Party Conference in Brighton

**1986**

9 January — Michael Heseltine resigns as Defence Secretary over the Westland affair

15 April — liberalisation of Sunday trading is defeated after sixty-eight Conservative MPs rebel

**1987**

17 March — Lawson cuts the basic rate of income tax by 2p to 27p

6 October — Party Conference presses for immediate introduction of the 'poll tax'

**1988**

15 March — Lawson cuts higher tax band from 60p to 40p and lower rate to 25p; this stokes an inflation-led boom

25 April — 'poll tax' passes third reading in the Commons; seventeen Conservative MPs vote against

20 September — Thatcher's speech at Bruges on the future of Europe

**1989**

24 July — Howe moved from the Foreign Office in cabinet reshuffle

26 October — Lawson resigns over the role of Thatcher's advisor, Sir Alan Walters

# Chronology of events

| 28 November | 'stalking horse' challenge from Sir Anthony Meyer forces a leadership contest |

**1990**

| 18 January | 'poll tax' legislation comes into effect |
| 5 October | Chancellor John Major announces joining of the Exchange Rate Mechanism (ERM) |
| 1 November | Howe resigns, making his statement to the Commons on 13 November |

**1991**

| 10 December | Maastricht treaty agreed, Britain securing an 'opt-out' on the Social Chapter |

**1992**

| 16 September | 'Black Wednesday': government forced to withdraw from the ERM |

**1993**

| 16 March | Lamont's budget extends VAT to domestic fuel despite manifesto pledge not to do so |
| 6 May | Newbury by-election defeat and loss of control in all but one shire county (Bucks.) in the county council elections |
| 27 May | Lamont sacked as Chancellor and dropped from the government |
| 22 July | Government defeated (324 to 316) on motion to ratify the Maastricht Treaty after twenty-six Conservative MPs rebel; Major wins vote of confidence held the next day |
| 8 October | Major's 'back to basics' conference speech is taken to indicate a moral social agenda, after attacks on single mothers by Peter Lilley and other ministers |

**1994**

| 28 November | whip is withdrawn from eight Conservative MPs who abstained on the European Communities (Finance) Bill; one other resigns the whip |

**1995**

| 4 May | loss of over 2,000 seats in local elections, in worst election performance of the century |
| 22 June | Major announces an immediate leadership election, in order to reimpose his authority |

# *Chronology of events*

| | |
|---|---|
| 26 June | Welsh Secretary John Redwood resigns and stands against Major |
| 5 July | Heseltine appointed Deputy Prime Minister in cabinet reshuffle |
| 8 October | Alan Howarth MP defects to the Labour Party |
| 29 December | Emma Nicholson MP defects to the Liberal Democrats |

*1997*

| | |
|---|---|
| 27 February | defeat in Wirral South by-election causes loss of overall majority in the Commons |
| 9 March | Sir George Gardiner MP, previously de-selected by the Reigate association, announces he has joined the Referendum Party |
| 17 March | Major announces that the general election will be held on 1 May |
| 2 May | After worst result since 1906 (with loss of 178 seats, including seven cabinet ministers), Major announces that he will be standing down as Leader |

# Introduction

The importance of the Conservative Party in contemporary British history needs no explanation. The measure of its dominance is not just that it was in office for nearly thirty-five of the fifty-two years from 1945 to 1997, twice as long as its opponents. The Conservatives were able to use their time in government more effectively, as their position was normally secure. They enjoyed two long spells of power, winning three consecutive elections and governing for thirteen years from 1951 to 1964, and four elections and governing for eighteen years from 1979 to 1997. There was only one single-term Conservative ministry, the troubled Heath government of 1970–74, and even here many felt that its narrow loss in February 1974 could have been prevented if the election had been called two weeks earlier. Before the 1997 landslide the Labour Party had secured an effective governing majority only twice, in 1945 and 1966. The Conservatives, on the other hand, won such majorities on seven occasions from 1951 to 1987; only in 1992 was their margin so thin that it was eroded during the life of the Parliament, leaving them in difficulty in its last few months.

Their two long tenures of power enabled the Conservatives to leave an established framework of policy and legislation, much of which the following Labour government had to accept. In the 1950s the Conservatives presided over the transition from the 'austerity' of wartime controls to the spread of 'affluence' and the increased sense of personal freedom and opportunity which burgeoned in the early 1960s. Between 1979 and 1997 the governments of Margaret Thatcher and John Major set in motion significant changes in the economy, the structure of society and popular attitudes. Since 1951, most of the important decisions affecting Britain's position in the world have been taken by Conservative governments: over decolonisation in the late 1950s and early 1960s; over nuclear integration with the United States with Polaris, cruise missiles and Trident; over moves towards détente in the Cold War by Churchill, Macmillan and Thatcher (in response to the emergence of Gorbachev); and above all over Europe. It was the Conservatives who stood aside when the European Community was formed in 1955–57 and then first applied to join in 1961, who took Britain in under Heath in 1971, signed the Single European Act in 1986, negotiated the Social Chapter 'opt-out' of the Maastricht Treaty in 1991, and joined and then crashed out of the Exchange Rate Mechanism (ERM) in 1990–92.

To the public, the Conservatives nearly always appeared to be the competent party of government, with a cohesive and experienced leadership and a disciplined and united Parliamentary Party. Electoral defeats followed from the loss of this prestige – at each end of this period, in 1945 and 1997, and in between in 1964 and 1974. The Conservative Party has always had an appetite for power and it has been hard to dislodge, as demonstrated by the narrowness of defeat in 1964, the unexpected victory snatched at the last moment in 1992, and the manoeuvres which kept it in office for the full life of the following Parliament until 1997. When in opposition, the Conservatives have been resilient and adaptable, moving swiftly to review both their policies and their organisation. On each occasion they have pioneered new campaigning methods, devised effective propaganda, and mounted a confident challenge. Even after the heaviest defeats of 1945 and 1966, they were able to recover ground in the next election and to come either to the brink of power (in 1950) or to return to office (in 1970). Labour's huge victory of 1997 was a shock for the Conservatives and recovery may be a long and uphill task, but it is taken for granted on all sides that it will eventually take place.

There is not space here for a detailed history of the Conservative Party since 1945; if required, such accounts can be found at varying lengths in several other works.[1] The purpose of this introduction is to provide an outline of the existing historical work on the topic, and an explanation of the nature of the sources from which the documentary

1   Anthony Seldon, 'Conservative century', in Anthony Seldon and Stuart Ball (eds), *Conservative Century: The Conservative Party since 1900*, Oxford, 1994, pp. 41–65; Philip Norton (ed.), *The Conservative Party*, Hemel Hempstead, 1996, pp. 43–67; John Charmley, *A History of Conservative Politics 1900–1996*, Basingstoke, 1996; for other surveys, see the section on Further Reading.

extracts have been drawn. The introduction is followed by the six main chapters of the book, each of which examines a particular aspect of the Conservative Party between the general election defeats of 1945 and 1997. The first three chapters survey its structure; the last three focus upon its conduct of events, and its programme and ideas.

The first chapter deals with the key position of Party Leader, concentrating upon the personalities of the holders of that post and upon the crises and changes of leadership. The operation of both the 'informal' selection process which was used up to 1963, and the electoral ballot system introduced in 1965, are observed, and the extracts include the rules which applied at the time of John Major's re-election contest of 1995 and after his retirement in 1997. The second chapter looks at the Parliamentary Party, including the role of the Whips, the backbench committees and the 1922 Committee. It deals also with aspects of parliamentary life, from the rules governing candidate selection to the work of an MP and the slippery path of promotion to ministerial office. The third chapter provides an anatomy of the Party organisation outside Parliament. After examining the role and authority of the Party Chairman and Central Office, it ranges widely over various aspects of the Conservative grass-roots, from the local association chairman and agent to fund-raising in the branches.

Chapter 4 surveys the core area of domestic politics. It opens with three extracts which examine how Conservative policy is made, before moving through the main events and issues since 1945: the winning and losing of general elections, the content of the Party programme, and the difficulties of government. Chapter 5 reviews the most important aspects of external affairs in a similar way; both of these chapters should be used in close conjunction not only with each other, but also with the aspects of leadership covered in the first chapter. It is not always easy to draw a clear line between policy and leadership, and decide where a document should be placed: Michael Heseltine's resignation speech over the Westland affair in 1986, which shook the leader's position but did not cause her downfall, will be found in Chapter 5, as it sheds light on attitudes to Europe; whilst Sir Geoffrey Howe's resignation statement of 1990, which did precipitate the fall of a leader, is for that reason located in Chapter 1. Finally, Chapter 6 explores an important area which is sometimes neglected in the case of the Conservative Party: the principles and attitudes which draw people to Conservatism, and upon which the outlook and programme of the Party is founded.

Each chapter begins with a brief discussion of its topic and principal themes. After this, the extracts are arranged in chronological order; the context of each item is explained by a short introductory paragraph, and its source is given at the end of the entry.

## The context

The history of the Conservative Party since 1945 is only now beginning to be widely explored. Until recently most of the discussions were by political scientists, and so tended to focus upon the current position or the immediate past. Historical investigations were handicapped by a lack of sources, as few of the personal archives of the leading figures were open to research. This was the result partly of the longevity of the individuals themselves, and partly of the posthumous closure of collections whilst an official biography was being written – a process which could take many years. The first major collection to be opened to research was the papers of R. A. Butler in the early 1980s, but a decade was to follow before access became possible to the papers of Winston Churchill, Anthony Eden and Selwyn Lloyd. The papers of Harold Macmillan, now at the Bodleian Library in Oxford, should be open soon and his diary is being edited for publication. The advance of the official thirty-year rule has meant that government files for the whole of the Conservative ministries of 1951–64 are now accessible, and the holdings of the Public Record Office have been used in several recent studies.[2]

The archive of the Conservative Party itself has been a major source for the post-war period, although inevitably it sheds most light upon the institutional aspects of the Party: its organisation, campaigning and propaganda, and the processes by which policies are developed. The archive has been located at the Bodleian Library since it was first established in the late 1970s, and its holdings are constantly being augmented. Although the pre-1945 records are limited in scope, a huge range of material for the period from 1945 to 1975 is available for research (permission must be sought for access to documents from

2   Richard Lamb, *The Macmillan Years 1957–1963: The Emerging Truth*, London, 1995; Henry Pelling, *Churchill's Peacetime Ministry 1951–1955*, Basingstoke, 1996; Kevin Jefferys, *Retreat from New Jerusalem: British Politics 1951–1964*, Basingstoke, 1997.

1965 to 1975).[3] The one exception is information relating to the national Party funds, about which there is great sensitivity. The archive does not reflect every aspect of the Party, for it contains mainly the papers of the central organisation (Central Office) and of the national and regional levels of the voluntary membership (the National Union). It does not hold constituency records; in most cases, material for the period since 1945 remains with the local association, although the practice of depositing the older post-war minute books in a local Record Office is becoming more prevalent. More importantly, the archive contains little relating to the third main component of the Conservative Party – the Parliamentary Party. There are a few minute books of backbench subject committees, but nothing of significance from the Whips Office. The older minute books of the 1922 Committee are also at the Bodleian Library, but the record of each meeting is skeletal and uninformative.

This pattern of sources has led to a divide in the nature and extent of scholarly work on the modern Conservative Party. Topics in the period up to 1975 are being explored with the use of a widening range of sources, and several major works have appeared in the mid-1990s. The most significant were two books by John Ramsden which drew extensively on the Party Archive: *The Age of Churchill and Eden 1940–1957* and *The Winds of Change: Macmillan to Heath, 1957–1975*.[4] These completed an authoritative six-volume series on the history of the Conservative Party from 1830 to 1975, the first instalments of which had been published in the late 1970s. The other major study, Anthony Seldon and Stuart Ball (eds), *Conservative Century: The Conservative Party since 1900*, used the available private papers and the Party Archive for the period up to 1975, together with other sources, such as interviews and published documents, for the Thatcher and Major years.[5] Studies which deal with the period after 1975 have had to depend solely upon publicly available material: speeches, pamphlets, manifestos and the coverage in the more dependable newspapers, supplemented where possible by interviews or mem-

3    For more information, see Sarah Street, 'The Conservative Party Archives', *20th Century British History*, 3, 1992, and the entry in Chris Cook and David Waller (eds), *The Longman Guide to Sources in Contemporary British History: Volume 1, Organisations and Societies*, London, 1994.
4    John Ramsden, *The Age of Churchill and Eden 1940–1957*, London, 1995; *The Winds of Change: Macmillan to Heath, 1957–1975*, London, 1996.
5    Seldon and Ball (eds), *Conservative Century*.

oirs. Most of this work has been written by and for political scientists, and has dealt with the immediate context. The lack of perspective which inevitably follows from writing hard on the heels of events, as well as the restricted range of sources, means that such works are valuable and ground-breaking, but cannot be definitive. To take just one example, views of Conservative economic success in the Lawson era have changed considerably in the course of the decade from 1987 to 1997.

Given the emphasis in the Conservative Party upon the Leader, and the importance of the leading frontbenchers, it is not surprising that biographies are heavily represented in the published work on both periods. Even here, however, the divide is still apparent: whilst there are several detailed 'authorised' lives for the period 1945–65, studies of later figures have to depend upon journalistic rather than historical investigation. Many of these are interim and contemporary works, although the best – most notably John Campbell on Edward Heath, Hugo Young on Margaret Thatcher, Michael Crick on Michael Heseltine and Anthony Seldon on John Major – are pioneering studies which have used extensive interviewing of the subject's friends and colleagues (only Seldon had any co-operation from his actual subject, but it was not an authorised biography).[6]

Because it is still very much a fresh field, the history of the Conservative Party since 1945 is marked less by debates than by areas of interest. This does not, of course, mean that there is some strange unanimity amongst those who have studied the post-war Party, but whilst there are certainly differences of interpretation, these have not formalised into contending schools of thought. The situation is similar with questions of topic and approach. There has been a recent criticism by some scholars that previous works had been too much concerned with the Party as an institution: its structure, its organisation, and even the way in which it developed its policies. In place of this, they argued that more attention should be given to the sources of support and how these are harnessed, and so to such matters as the Party's public image and its underlying principles.[7] However, these approaches are not alternatives, but rather two halves of the same

6   John Campbell, *Edward Heath*, London, 1993; Hugo Young, *One of Us: A Biography of Margaret Thatcher*, London, 1991; Michael Crick, *Michael Heseltine*, London, 1997; Anthony Seldon, *Major: A Political Life*, London, 1997.
7   See the introduction to Martin Francis and Ina Zweiniger-Bargielowska (eds), *The Conservatives and British Society 1880–1990*, Cardiff, 1996.

whole which need to be put together to obtain a fully rounded picture. The composition and organisation of the Party reflect its sources of support and the areas where it is seeking to gain support, as does its ideology and the specific proposals for action in government which follow from this. The language used – whether verbal in speeches and leaflets, or visual in posters, advertisements and television broadcasts – flows from this hinterland, and in so doing reveals its contours.

The greatest attention has been given to explaining the gaining and losing of power. The first period to be explored was the recovery from the 1945 defeat and the reshaping of policy which accompanied it. Within the Party itself this was an era which rapidly became encrusted with mythology, as a heroic age crowned with virtuous triumph in 1951. It was also widely regarded as the time when the founding tablets of post-war Conservatism were established, symbolised on the organisational side by the Maxwell-Fyfe Report and in policy and outlook by the *Industrial Charter*. The opposition years of 1945–51 were formative in the emergence of three of the most influential figures of post-war Conservatism: 'Rab' Butler, Harold Macmillan and Iain Macleod. The period bulked large in memoirs and journalistic allusions, and was more soberly analysed in J. D. Hoffman's pioneering study of 1963. The points which the latter made about the degree of continuity between the Party of the 1930s and wartime years and the supposedly transformed post-war Party were taken further in an important article by John Ramsden over two decades later.[8]

The second area of interest follows from the post-1945 recovery, and is the years of power from 1951 to 1964. There have been many studies concentrating upon aspects of government policy – economic, social, diplomatic, imperial and defence – which lie outside the remit of this short work. The Cold War, the development of nuclear weapons and the 'special relationship' with the United States, the Suez crisis, decolonisation, and the application to join the European Economic Community (EEC), all had an impact upon the health and fortunes of the Conservative ministries. Of most direct relevance, however, was the domestic economy and the changes in society. The dominating theme of this period has been the growth of 'affluence', with rising

8    J. D. Hoffman, *The Conservative Party in Opposition 1945–1951*, London, 1964; John Ramsden, '"A Party for owners or a Party for earners": how far did the British Conservative Party really change after 1945?', *Royal Historical Society, Transactions*, fifth series, 37, 1987.

living standards and a broadening middle class, and the part which this played in Conservative electoral success in the 1950s. Other issues were welfare policy, methods of economic management and relations with the trade unions, all of which have been bound up in the notion that a 'consensus' existed between the main parties. The question of 'consensus' has been controversial ever since Norman Macrae of *The Economist* conjured up the figure of 'Mr Butskell' – a fusion of the former Labour Chancellor of the Exchequer Hugh Gaitskell and his Conservative successor R. A. Butler – in the early 1950s. Contemporary historians have debated the extent to which a 'consensus' actually existed, and the causes and timing of its rise and decline.[9] In the case of the latter, two periods of troubled Conservative government have stood out: the later Macmillan Premiership of 1960–63 and the Heath ministry of 1970–74.

The Heath government was the only single-term Conservative ministry of the post-war era, but its electoral record was not the main reason why most Conservatives came to regard it with embarrassment and even hostility. The cause of this was the belief that the government had set out on a vigorous new direction, but on encountering difficulties had suffered a loss of nerve and had abandoned its principles in a series of 'U-turns'. Its hallmark appeared to be not pragmatism but impotence; it seemed to have accepted a political culture defined by the values of interventionism and state regulation – effectively, of Socialism, as the Chairman of the 1922 Committee was unhappily to stigmatise the key measure of the Industry Act in 1972.[10] This critique was to emerge most strongly from the Conservative right, as justification for the changes in policy after 1975 and the refusal to compromise when in office from 1979 to 1990. The forbidding personality of Heath himself, and his failure to set out his own case in print, left this analysis largely unchallenged. There is no doubt that the Heath government was buffeted by difficulties on almost every side, and in retrospect it stands out as a turning-point in post-war British history. It has been argued that it marked the collapse of the 'consensus' in domestic politics, and certainly under Thatcher's leadership the term was used only with derision and contempt. The Heath

9    For a recent review of this topic, see Harriet Jones and Michael Kandiah (eds), *The Myth of Consensus: New Views on British History 1945–1964*, Basingstoke, 1996.
10   See document 4.20.

government's enduring legacy in external affairs, the entry into Europe, was also both significant and controversial. Although the government files remained unavailable under the thirty-year rule, the mid-1990s have seen the emergence of more scholarly and dispassionate studies of the Heath era. The first and path-breaking contribution was the substantial biography of Heath by John Campbell which appeared in 1993. This was followed three years later by two accounts which used the resources of the Party Archive: John Ramsden's final volume in the Longman history of the Conservative Party, and the wide-ranging reappraisal of the Heath government's policies and fortunes in the volume of essays edited by Stuart Ball and Anthony Seldon.[11]

Without doubt, the largest area of writing on post-war Conservative politics concerns the phenomenon of Thatcherism and the Conservative dominance of the 1980s. Much of this discussion has been contemporary, and it emerged most strongly in the wake of the third election victory of 1987. It is a striking sign of the different face presented by Conservative politics in this period that ideology has been at the forefront of attention, with the Party itself relegated furthest into background obscurity. Even though the personality of Margaret Thatcher was the driving force behind her governments and the '-ism' coined from her name, the focus was not biographical but intellectual. Against the two or three serious journalistic lives written during her long tenure of the Premiership can be set more than twice that many scholarly tomes addressing the nature and impact of Thatcherism.[12] The reasons for this are not hard to see. Firstly, the Conservative electoral record of 1979–92 broke all precedents, and the cause of these triumphs was clearly in need of explanation. Still more, it seemed – and its adherents strenuously claimed – that there had been a clean break with the past, and that Britain itself had been profoundly changed as a result. This was more than just economic policy or even taxation; it was a matter of ethics, values and the national culture. Nor did the process have an end in sight: Thatcherism was to be a permanent revolution, seeking new fields to conquer. With the

11   John Campbell, *Edward Heath*, London, 1993; Ramsden, *Winds of Change*; Stuart Ball and Anthony Seldon (eds), *The Heath Government 1970–1974: A Reappraisal*, London, 1996.
12   Young, *One of Us*; Kenneth Harris, *Thatcher*, London, 1988; Bruce Arnold, *Margaret Thatcher*, London, 1984; for Thatcherism, see the works listed in the Further Reading section.

collapse of Marxism and the end of the Cold War, free-market Conservatism of the Thatcher–Reagan imprint had become the unchallenged colossus upon the world stage, a new orthodoxy and the point in relation to which all others were defined. Finally, there was the temper of the beast: Thatcherism was vibrant with energy and intellectual confidence (interpreted by its critics as arrogance and hubris). It was avowedly confrontational and controversial, and aroused strong passions both for and against.

For all these reasons, it was inevitable that much attention would be given to exploring and defining Thatcherism. Perhaps the only surprise is that the mountain of books is not higher, but it is certain that it will continue to grow.[13] The problem of reconciling a radical and populist stance with Conservatism caused particular tensions, to which two main responses can be detected. The first was that the continuity with previous Conservative ideas had been understated beneath a smokescreen of rhetoric; from this viewpoint it could be said either that Thatcher was returning to the Conservatism of Bonar Law or Neville Chamberlain after the aberrant lurch into Keynesian 'consensus' from 1945 to 1975, or that Heath – in his 1970 'Selsdon' incarnation – had been a kind of John the Baptist precursor, pointing the way but being decapitated in the process. The alternative response – the refuge of Mrs Thatcher's critics within the Party – was that the traditional good-natured paternalist 'one nation' party of Butler, Macmillan, Macleod and Heath had been hijacked in 1975, captured in a right-wing coup by neo-liberal free-market ideologues whose inspiration was Adam Smith and whose methods and cast of mind were utterly un-Tory. It was this debate which focused upon the question of whether Thatcher herself – and therefore Thatcherism – was or was not Conservative.[14]

If the development and nature of Thatcherism was one matter of fascination, the downfall of its progenitor was another. The combination of compulsive human drama and historical significance made the leadership crisis of 1990 an irresistible subject. Some of these investigations concentrated upon reconstructing the events of November 1990, whilst others looked at the problems and issues which in the

---

13 The next major contribution is likely to be John Campbell's biography of Thatcher, to be published in the late 1990s.
14 Daniel Wincott, 'Thatcher: ideological or pragmatic?', *Contemporary Record*, 4, 2, 1990; Christopher Barder, 'Thatcher *was* a Conservative', *Contemporary Record*, 4, 3, 1991.

longer term had led up to them.[15] The focus was upon Margaret Thatcher's loss of the Premiership, rather than the emergence of her successor.

There has not yet been enough time for much considered work to appear on John Major's period as Prime Minister and Leader of the Conservative Party. However, one theme which is certain to be prominent surfaced repeatedly from the moment of his anointment by Thatcher in 1990 as her chosen heir until the general election of 1997. This was the question of where Major really stood within the spectrum of the Conservative Party: was he – as Thatcher had initially believed but later came bitterly to doubt – on the right, or was he instead a conciliator and party manager by instinct, whose true home lay in the pragmatic centre. Three themes or events stand out from the Major governments, and have already received some attention. They all concern relations with the European Union (EU): the economic and political effects of Britain's membership of the ERM and the collapse of that policy on 'Black Wednesday' in September 1992; the issues of federalism and sovereignty from the Maastricht Treaty to the single currency; and the debilitating disunity over Europe within the Parliamentary Party.[16] They are likely to be joined by one other: the extent and effects of what became popularly known as 'sleaze' – the sexual scandals and allegations of financial corruption which embroiled a succession of Conservative ministers and backbench MPs, and which were to dominate the headlines during the first weeks of the 1997 election campaign.

## The documents

This volume has been prepared primarily for the use of students who are following courses in recent British history and politics, either in

15  Alan Watkins, *A Conservative Coup: The Fall of Margaret Thatcher*, London, 1991; Robert Shepherd, *The Power Brokers: The Tory Party and its Leaders*, London, 1991; David Butler, Andrew Adonis and Tony Travers, *Failure in British Government: The Politics of the Poll Tax*, Oxford, 1994.
16  Philip Stephens, *Politics and the Pound: The Tories, Sterling and Europe*, London, 1995; Helen Thompson, *The British Conservative Government and the European Exchange Rate Mechanism 1979–1994*, London, 1996; M. Sowemimo, 'The Conservative Party and European integration 1988–1995', *Party Politics*, 2, 1, 1996; D. Baker et al., 'Backbench Conservative attitudes towards European integration', *Political Quarterly*, 66, 2, 1995; Steve Ludlam and Martin Smith (eds), *Contemporary British Conservatism*, Basingstoke, 1996.

the sixth form or in higher education. Its aim is to deepen their understanding and knowledge of the topic, by making available an illustrative and representative range of primary source material within the compass of a single book of reasonable length and price. The documents are drawn from a wide range of sources, many of which are not otherwise readily accessible. They include previously unpublished internal papers and memoranda of Conservative Central Office and the Party's policy-shaping bodies, drawn from the huge quantity of documents deposited in the Conservative Party Archive. However, it must be appreciated that a compilation of this nature cannot be exhaustive, and the reader has to depend upon the editor's familiarity with the topic and sources, and the judgements which have been made in the selection of the material used.

A collection of primary sources can fulfil many useful roles. A documentary extract – even if it is a passage from a later memoir – can take the reader to the heart of a topic with a directness and brevity which cannot be matched by passages of commentary. The items presented are intended to give a sense of immediacy, and to convey the flavour of the times. Primary sources help us to shed the blinkers imposed by hindsight and to avoid the distorting views and assumptions of our own times – temptations which are at their most insidious when dealing with the recent history of one's own country. The documents enable us to see through the eyes of the participants, and at their best can vividly communicate their priorities, expectations and concerns. The extracts can be utilised not only on the surface level of the information which they give about events or viewpoints, but also in many cases as texts which will repay close analysis. The emotional content can be as important as the actions described; the assumptions made and the language used can be very revealing, and what is left out is sometimes as significant as what is put in. When looking at the extracts, students should read between the lines, looking out for the unspoken attitudes and values which throw into relief the subjects' view of the world around them.

These purposes have shaped the nature and sources of the documents chosen. In order to show the workings of the Party from the inside, they are drawn as much as possible from those most closely involved in each aspect. For this reason, as well as practical limitations of space, the selection does not include the views of political opponents or of commentators in the press and academia. Valid though those perspectives are, they tell us only about the public image and

# Introduction

reception of the Party, an area which can also be pursued through other volumes in this series. The aim of this collection is to show how the Conservatives themselves have acted, organised, planned and thought. Contemporary material is most revealing in this respect, and so has been used wherever possible. There are three main types of contemporary sources: speeches, published pamphlets, and internal confidential documents and reports from the files in the Party Archive. The latter was available for the period up to 1975, whilst the first and second categories have been used throughout. Most of this material, whether published or unpublished, falls within the Conservative Party's copyright control. It is important in this respect to acknowledge that the Party placed no restriction upon the editor's consultation of documents in the Party Archive (apart from the standing exclusion of material relating to the central funds), and raised no objection to the selection or presentation of the extracts used. They have been chosen solely for their historical merit and interest, and according to the judgement of the editor.

Each of the three categories has its own particular characteristics. Material which is presented in public, even when aimed at a Conservative audience, will normally seek to avoid anything which political opponents could use to their advantage: nothing too extreme, nothing which indicates or would provoke disunity within the Party. There is an element of reflection and polish in such utterances, whether spoken or written. Of the two, oratory will be more affected by the context of its delivery and more spontaneous, although ministerial and Leaders' speeches are heavily scripted in advance. So too are resignation or personal statements delivered in the House of Commons, but contributions from backbenchers in debate will be less so. Speeches delivered at the Party Conference – and especially the Leader's address to the closing rally – are designed to rally the rank and file and to rouse the enthusiasm and commitment of the voluntary membership. The rhetoric which is used is likely to draw stark, indeed exaggerated, contrasts between Conservative virtues and achievements and the follies and failures of their opponents. These speeches can be revealing and indicative, partly by reducing the Party's position to its essence, and partly by the choice of images and language – the buttons which it seeks to push say much about the Conservative frame of mind.

The contemporary published material takes two forms. Firstly, there are official statements of the Party's policy, the most important – and

13

for that reason often the blandest – of which is the manifesto produced for each general election. In more recent years these have sought to avoid specifics, in order to present less of a target for opposition attacks and to avoid tying the hands of the government when in office. The problems which could result were shown by the damage done to the Major government's standing by the introduction of VAT on domestic fuel and power in Norman Lamont's 1993 budget, despite a pledge not to do so given in the 1992 manifesto. Linked to this first category are the constitutions which regulate the composition and procedure of various Party bodies. These range from the ballots by which the Party Leader has been chosen since such a scheme was first introduced in 1965 to the model rules which local constituency associations are encouraged to adopt and follow. Less mandatory, but still official in origin, are the various leaflets on organisational matters which have been produced to educate local party volunteers and encourage greater activity and efficiency. So far as the Conservative Party has ever had internal newspapers, they have had a similar function. They have always avoided controversy, and have never had a political significance either inside or outside the Party. Some of these have been linked to particular sections of the organisation, such as the Young Conservatives or local government. More independent, and occasionally more controversial within its particular remit, is the *Conservative Agents' Journal*, the periodical of the professional agents' national society.

The second form of published material is the independently authored pamphlets, most of which deal with Conservative principles and with questions of policy. Very many of these are published by the Conservative Political Centre, an important part of the Party's internal education and communication since it was established by R. A. Butler after the 1945 election defeat. It is perhaps surprising how large a literature exists in this form, especially on the more esoteric topic of Conservatism itself. There was a particular flowering of books, pamphlets and lectures in this area in the immediate post-war decade of 1945–55, as the Conservatives sought to find and present a new identity in response to the 1945 defeat and the measures of the 1945–51 Labour government. A further striking feature is the extent to which these discussions of ideology have been penned by active Conservative politicians. In many cases they have been MPs, and though often still in the earlier stages of their careers their number has included a high proportion who have risen to ministerial and cabinet office, such

14

as Quintin Hogg (Lord Hailsham), Enoch Powell, Ian Gilmour, Nigel Lawson, David Howell, Chris Patten and David Willetts.

The documents which are held in the Party Archive are of a different nature, having been produced for a specific and private audience. Being internal and confidential they can be franker in discussing the weaknesses and problems of the Party's position, although within certain limitations. The picture which they present is mainly that seen from the upper echelons: the regional grandees of the National Union executive committee, and the professional bureaucracy in Smith Square. Central Office is the machine of the Party Leader, and will not critically review his or her performance or debate the matter of possible replacements. There is more of a role in policy-making, but even here the functions are mainly those of acting as advisory sounding-boards or furnishing clerical support, collecting information and carrying out detailed drafting. The documents which have been drawn from the Party Archive reflect its contents. On the organisational side, they mainly consist of memoranda circulating between senior figures such as the Party Chairman, Deputy Chairmen and Vice-Chairmen, and the experienced professionals: the General Director, the Chief Organisation Officer, and so on. There are also extracts from internal papers which review the state of affairs within the organisation or the electoral and tactical position. A wealth of information about the working of the Party organisation can be found in the papers of the committees of inquiry which were set up from time to time. Some of these examined the whole picture, such as the Maxwell-Fyfe Committee of 1948–49 and the Fowler review of 1993, whilst others were the response to the problems affecting particular sections, such as the trade unionists in 1952 or the agents, the Young Conservatives, and the organisation in the cities in the 1960s.[17] Their utility lies not just in their reports, which were often published and could be vague and bland, but in some cases even more in the evidence which they collected in the course of their work.

The extracts from the Party Archive which relate to the making of Conservative policy are drawn mainly from the files of the three most influential committees. The Advisory Committee on Policy (ACP), founded in 1946, is a forum for the discussion of policies and strategy which brings together representatives of the National Union and the

17  For further details, see the essays on the Party organisation in Seldon and Ball (eds), *Conservative Century*.

Parliamentary Party. Whilst it does not have executive authority, it has normally been chaired by the second most powerful figure in the Party leadership. It received written memoranda on various issues and its discussions were attended by the appropriate cabinet minister or (when in opposition) frontbench spokesman. Its deliberations tested the climate of opinion in the Party and so carried weight, and its records are of value for both the papers which were circulated for discussion and the comments recorded in the minutes of its meetings. The Leader's Consultative Committee (LCC) is the name given to the 'shadow cabinet' when the Party is in opposition. During the two periods of 1964–70 and 1974–79 it not only held regular meetings to deal with day-to-day tactics, but also oversaw the framing of the Party's programme. The extensive records of the LCC contain its minutes, a wide range of confidential memoranda, and in the 1964–70 period the meetings and reports of the policy groups which were established to undertake detailed work on each area. The third body was the Steering Committee (SC), an inner group of senior cabinet ministers chaired by the Leader which framed the manifesto for the next general election. It was first established by Macmillan in 1957 and continued under this name until the early 1980s; it was not a standing body, and normally began its work one or two years before the anticipated election. Like the other two committees, it held meetings and received memoranda on various topics.

The work of all these committees was supported by the staff of the Conservative Research Department (CRD), who were responsible for drafting many of the discussion papers. One of the most important of the senior officials was Sir Michael Fraser, who was Chairman of the CRD from 1951 to 1964 and then Deputy Party Chairman from 1964 to 1975. In 1967 Fraser added a further element of co-ordination and support by establishing the Official Group (OG), a regular meeting of the key staff in the CRD, Central Office, the Leader's private office, and so on. The minutes and papers of the OG and the extensive files of the CRD are also housed in the Party Archive. As with all of the documents deposited there, it must be remembered that they were originally written not for historians but for the immediate and practical needs of a working organisation. Most of the memoranda have a limited horizon, being concerned only with the recent past and the immediate prospect of the next general election.

This is a truth of political life which most politicians' memoirs prefer to disguise, although a tendency to pomposity is not their only

16

limitation as a historical source. Even if there is no conscious effort at self-justification, the element of hindsight means that these later recollections must be handled with caution. The perspective of the author will have changed with the passage of time, and memory is not always reliable. In some cases the book has been written partly or mainly by other hands, assistance which usually is not disclosed on the title page or even in the acknowledgements. The overrated *Art of the Possible* which bears R. A. Butler's name is just one example, whilst the bulky volumes churned out by Harold Macmillan and Margaret Thatcher were constructed from the work of a team of assistants.[18] Whilst some leading figures of the period from 1945 to 1964 published their memoirs, it is since 1979 that the number has increased to avalanche proportions. During this time the writing of memoirs became more financially rewarding, and this was one reason for the promptness with which they now appeared after their author's retirement. In one sense this made them more immediate, but as the writers were still only a step removed from power, and often engaged in business careers in which their political weight and connections were their main asset, it tended to foster caution and dullness. The primary object was to bolster the bank balance, rather than to put the record straight or even to settle old scores – a rare exception being the Tebbit–Young spat over the conduct of the 1987 election campaign. If it were possible, the memoirs of MPs are still less rewarding; even a colourful character such as Steven Norris, best known for his five mistresses and folksy style, hid his light under a bushel – though he at least openly credited his assistant.[19] Only Julian Critchley, whose long sojourn in the cold during the Thatcher years left him little else to do but sharpen his pen, offered both entertainment and insight.

The greatest deficiency of modern political memoirs is not dishonesty, but discretion. They are solemn and industrious, treading a dull and worthy path, and worshipping at the shrine of consistency. They may be about a life, but all too often they lack life. One of Thatcher's circle, presumably in a position to know, remarked on the 'unconvincing decorousness' of Cecil Parkinson's memoirs, which conveyed nothing of the 'reckless conviviality' of the man overheard 'singing "The working class can kiss my arse" with his cronies in the Garrick

18  For details, see the Further Reading section.
19  Steven Norris (with Tony Austin), *Changing Trains*, London, 1996.

Club'.[20] Not just frankness is absent, but passion as well; in their stead is a colourless recitation of meetings attended, legislation overseen, speeches delivered and official visits. There is little flavour of the raw realities of political life: the personal dislikes and the pettiness, the ambition and the frustration, the heady excitement of office and the moments of sudden vertigo as the winds of fortune and favour veer to a different quarter. The contrast with Alan Clark's *Diaries* is acute and revealing, and goes far to explain the latter's runaway commercial success.[21] A few of the memoirs have been based upon personal records kept at the time, of which diaries are the most helpful. This was the case with Macmillan, who quoted selected passages, and later with Kenneth Baker and Douglas Hurd.[22]

However, whilst their deficiencies must be understood, memoirs can be of value in several ways. Firstly, they can shed some light on those incidents and private discussions for which no other source exists. At present and for some time to come, our knowledge of crises at leadership and cabinet level depends mainly on the accounts given in memoirs. Secondly, they can report on atmosphere, emotions and motivations: the intangibles which due to their more formal nature other documents – especially official or party memoranda – will not catch. Thirdly, most memoirs include descriptions of the characters of the prominent figures with whom the writer was closely engaged. Here the element of hindsight can be a positive virtue, providing the stimulus for an analysis of the individual which the author might otherwise either not have made or not have put on paper. In particular, memoirs are the main repository of the anecdotes and vignettes which can throw a personality into sharp relief and provide that invaluable sense of immediacy and proximity. Finally, for some periods and important incidents, there are now several published commentaries which to some extent can be checked and balanced against each other. This is particularly true of leadership changes, especially in 1963, 1975 and 1990, and also of some of the other events which have shaken governments, such as the Suez crisis, the Profumo affair, the downfall

---

20  Ferdinand Mount's review of Parkinson's memoirs, *Times Literary Supplement*, 9 October 1992.
21  Alan Clark, *Diaries*, London, 1993.
22  Kenneth Baker, *The Turbulent Years*, London, 1993; Douglas Hurd, *An End to Promises: Sketch of a Government 1970–1974*, London, 1979; Hurd's memoirs are forthcoming.

of the Heath government, the cabinet wrangles of 1981, the invasion of the Falklands, and the poll tax.

The nature of the sources used varies from chapter to chapter, and to some extent with time. Memoirs are inescapably the main source for Chapter 1, on leaders and leadership, and to a lesser extent for Chapter 2, on the Parliamentary Party. The review of the organisation in Chapter 3 draws mainly on papers from the Central Office sections of the Party Archive, together with reports and instructional leaflets. Local association records have not been used here, as they do not tend to provide passages which are suited to reproduction in this format. Post-war regional and local records are more professionally produced than was sometimes the case in earlier periods, and their greater brevity and more formal nature means that they are less revealing. There are two principal types of material used in Chapters 4 and 5, which deal with policies and events in domestic politics and external affairs. These are, firstly, contemporary documents from the policy-making sections of the Party Archive (for the period up to 1975), and, secondly, speeches or published policy statements (for the whole period). The final chapter, on Conservative ideas, contains some extracts from speeches, but draws mainly on contemporary publications in pamphlet form, many of which were produced under the imprint of the Conservative Political Centre.

# 1

# Leaders and leadership

The position of Leader of the Conservative Party is one of great power, both in theory and in practice. The Leader has complete authority over the programme of the Party, and he or she decides who is appointed to the cabinet (or to shadow posts when in opposition). When – as for most of this period – the Conservatives are in power, the Leader also enjoys the powers and patronage available to the Prime Minister, including the resources of No. 10 and the Cabinet Office. The Leader alone appoints the Chief Whip and the Chairman of the Party, and through the latter controls Conservative Central Office. However, it has been observed that the position of Leader is a leasehold and not a freehold: it is conditional upon maintaining the confidence and support of the Parliamentary Party, and therefore upon the Party's electoral fortunes or likely prospects. Churchill in 1949 and Macmillan in 1962–63 were faced with serious criticism, whilst the leaderships of Home, Heath and Thatcher all came to end due to their losing support amongst Conservative MPs. In 1993–95 John Major's authority was eroded by continual rumours of a leadership challenge, until he decided to force a showdown and initiated a contest himself in June 1995.

This chapter surveys the Leaders of the Conservative Party since 1945; it focuses upon their different characters and methods, and the factors which shaped their rise and fall. During this period the informal system by which Leaders 'emerged' was replaced, after the controversy over the choice of Home in 1963, by an electoral system. This changed the locus of power within the Party. Previously, whilst the choice of Leader in theory rested with Conservative MPs, in practice the cabinet leadership had normally settled the matter privately amongst themselves. The electoral system introduced in 1965 established that Leaders were made and unmade by a secret vote of Conservative MPs, and it played a key role in the downfall of Heath in 1975 and of Thatcher in 1990.

### 1.1 **Churchill as Leader in opposition, 1945–51**

Churchill's position as Party Leader was not affected by the landslide election defeat of 1945, but his detachment and preference for avoiding detailed commitments caused some restiveness during the next few years, as Harold Macmillan recalls.

[Churchill] was the undoubted and undisputed head of the party. He had led the country to victory out of the jaws of defeat. He was a supreme national and international figure. Yet at the end of the war the people, who felt a deep sense of gratitude to him, would have done anything for him except return him to power as a Tory Prime Minister. ... in the post-war mood they did not want him, and still less his political friends. It was clear to an unbiased observer that it was not Churchill who had brought the Conservative Party so low. On the contrary it was the recent history of the party, with its pre-war record of unemployment and its failure to preserve the peace. These memories had fatally, although unfairly, impaired Churchill's chances of electoral success.

The question of leadership, therefore, did not arise. It is true that as the years passed there were murmurings both in the Parliamentary Party and among his colleagues. There were even meetings of ex-Ministers to voice their complaints to the Chief Whip. Sometimes the 1922 Committee, the most influential body of Private Members in the House of Commons, became restive. Sometimes there was the feeling that the leader of the Opposition devoted too much of his time to writing history and travelling about the world making speeches of international importance, and too little attention to home politics. All this, of course, arose mainly from the frustrations of our apparent failure to make any progress in the House of Commons or in the country. These murmurings were serious in 1947, but were quieted without much difficulty. Early in 1949, after our failure to win a by-election in South Hammersmith of which we had high hopes, they were heard again. But after the successes in the spring in local elections, both for the boroughs throughout the country and for the London County Council, which were the first fruits of Woolton's[1] practical work, they were silenced for good.

Harold Macmillan, *Tides of Fortune 1945–1955*, London, 1969, pp. 286–7.

## 1.2 Churchill's reluctant departure

Churchill returned to the Premiership in October 1951 but suffered a serious stroke in June 1953, although this was hidden from the public. The vexed question of when he would hand over to his designated successor, Anthony Eden, dragged on for nearly two more years. 'Rab' Butler, Chancellor of the Exchequer and by this time the third most important figure in the cabinet, describes Churchill's reluctance to retire.

By this time the reconstitution of the government was under very active discussion and it remained so until Churchill's retirement in April 1955. For more than a year the leading figures in the Conservative Party had their gaze diverted from the more pressing executive problems by his long-drawn-out hesitation. As early as 11th March 1954, I recorded the Prime Minister telling me over dinner: 'I feel like an aeroplane at the end of its flight, in the dusk, with the petrol running out, in search of a safe landing.' The only political interest he had left, he said, was in high-level conversations with the Russians. He would then be glad to retire ... I was continually brought in to witness this distressing and distracting transition. The first crunch came in August when, after successive visits to Chartwell,[2] I warned Anthony, 'Winston is writing to you. He doesn't feel the world situation makes it right for him to move at present. There was little of the Russian visit talk. He rejected calmly but firmly ideas of being an Elder Statesman, or of being Lord President in a Cabinet of which he was not P.M. He acknowledged the need for a reconstituted government and wants to do this *with* you. He registered but was unmoved by my opinion that he would shock you and get opposition if he stayed on. It is all very difficult since in the best interests of the party and the coun-

1  Lord Woolton, Chairman of the Party since 1946.
2  Churchill's country home.

try we must move forward with the minimum of defections. His deep obsession with the gravity of the international situation, and what seemed his determination that his mission is not yet done, are factors to which evidently we had not given sufficient weight. He had registered your wish for a year in which to consolidate, but has his own views based on precedent and history about the best way to handle successor governments.' ...

A week later the Prime Minister sent me a copy of what he called 'the final edition' of his letter to Anthony. It covered what by now was well-trodden ground. ... It was not so much a decision as a further postponement of decision. ...

I calculate that during the period between Winston's 80th birthday on 30th November [1954] and the following April when he retired I had no less than eight gargantuan dinners with him alone; the dinners being followed by libations of brandy so ample that I felt it prudent on more than one occasion to tip the liquid into the side of my shoe. The subjects discussed were always the same: his retirement and the succession, the fag-end government syndrome, a Russian summit and, strange to relate, space travel. ...

At the end of March [1955] Anthony and I were invited into the Cabinet room. Winston made a slip by asking me to sit on his right, but then corrected himself and beckoned to Anthony. We all gazed out over Horse Guards Parade. Then Winston said very shortly, 'I am going and Anthony will succeed me. We can discuss details later.' The ceremonial was over. We found ourselves in the passage where Anthony and I shook hands.

Lord Butler, *The Art of the Possible*, London, 1971, pp. 173–7.

### 1.3 **The failings of Eden**

> Despite all his charisma and promise, Eden's tenure of the Premiership proved to be a short and unhappy one. As a rising junior minister of the period recalls, the Prime Minister was living on his nerves even before the Suez crisis brought about the collapse of both his health and his reputation.

He was a good politician, with a flair for understanding how the voters felt. He handled the General Election of May 1955, which closely followed his appointment, with skill and judgement. Women voters were particularly susceptible to his appeal and good looks. He succeeded in trebling the slim majority which Churchill had won in 1951. But he had no understanding of economics and finance. And even less knowledge of or interest in the social services. He seemed to feel that these were hardly subjects with which gentlemen should concern themselves. He was absorbed in the great issues of foreign and imperial affairs played out on the world stage on which he knew personally all the chief actors. So marked was his detachment in such wide areas of the business of Government that it provided occasion for one of R.A. Butler's highly entertaining indiscretions. He had been good enough to come and speak for me in Kingston – my constituency. ... The date was early in 1955, with Eden's succession imminent, though not yet actual. Rab commented in his discursive way about the next Prime Minister's limitations. But ... these would not matter because at least in home affairs he (Rab) would 'manage him from behind'.

Eden also had personal characteristics which became significant only in the highest office. ... Eden worried. He worried at his Ministers, ringing them up with enquiries about matters which either were not ready for submission to him or indeed were not of sufficient importance to bother a Prime Minister. Far worse, he worried himself. He had a feminine streak of sensitivity. By this I do not mean he was effeminate. On the contrary he was a man of high courage, as his First War record as an infantry officer and M.C. demonstrated. But he had a strong desire for admiration. When he entered a room he looked round to try to see people's expressions. If there was not a look of enthusiasm he could be hurt and sulky. For all his social charm, and agreeable behaviour as a host, he only felt at ease among a small coterie of friends, mostly younger than himself but with the same background. He was not too difficult a target for toadies. He disliked people who did not openly admire him.

John Boyd-Carpenter, *Way of Life*, London, 1980, pp. 123–4.

### 1.4 The cabinet choose Macmillan, 1957

When Eden's ill-health led to his sudden resignation in January 1957, in the wake of the Suez crisis, the choice of successor

lay between Harold Macmillan and 'Rab' Butler. The proce-
dure was managed by the two senior cabinet ministers in the
House of Lords, Lord Salisbury (the Lord President) and Lord
Kilmuir (the Lord Chancellor).

On Wednesday, January 9th, Bobbety Salisbury came to see me at 3
o'clock and told me ... that Anthony could definitely not carry on as
Prime Minister. He would, therefore, communicate his resignation at
our [cabinet] meeting at 4. We then discussed the future, as we were
the senior members of the Cabinet whose position in the Lords left us
unconcerned in the succession.

Having considered the constitutional position very carefully I had
come to the conclusion that the Queen was entitled to ask for advice
from anyone she chose in order to discover who would command the
support of a majority in the House of Commons. I took the view very
strongly that she need and ought not to wait for a party meeting. ...
We therefore agreed that we would consult all Cabinet Ministers one
by one and get their views as between Harold Macmillan and Rab
Butler. We then went to Downing Street and Anthony announced his
resignation ...

Thereafter Bobbety and I asked our colleagues to see us one by one
in Bobbety's room in the Privy Council offices, which could be reached
without leaving the building. There were two light reliefs. Practically
each one began by saying, 'This is like coming to the Headmaster's
study.' To each Bobbety said, 'Well, which is it, Wab or Hawold?' As
well as seeing the remainder of the ex-Cabinet, we interviewed the
Chief Whip and Oliver Poole, the Chairman of the Party. John
Morrison, the Chairman of the 1922 Committee, rang me up from
Islay the next morning. An overwhelming majority of Cabinet Ministers was in favour of Macmillan as Eden's successor, and back-bench
opinion, as reported to us, strongly endorsed this view. Party feeling
in the House of Commons was running very strongly against Butler at
this time, and at one point there was even a serious proposal by a
number of Conservatives to walk out of the Chamber when Rab
entered it. For this sharp decline in his personal fortunes Rab had no
one to blame but himself. Many at the time considered that his habit
of publicly hedging his political bets was too great a weakness and
this had accordingly damaged his position both in the Conservative
hierarchy and in the parliamentary party. I have no doubt that a straight

vote between the two either in the Cabinet or in the party would have left Rab in a very small minority.

Earl of Kilmuir (David Maxwell-Fyfe), *Political Adventure*, London, 1964, pp. 285–6.

## 1.5 **Supermac**

Macmillan skilfully rallied the Party after the Suez crisis. His style was detached and debonair, and the combination of his 'unflappability', his patrician image as the 'last of the Edwardians' and the delivery of rising affluence made him the dominant figure in British politics by 1959. Although intended as satire, his cartoon image as 'Supermac' seemed to capture the reality.

Harold Macmillan ... managed to make the conduct of government interesting, agreeable and entertaining. He would enquire of Ministers how things were going from time to time, but would seldom interfere. If he wanted some course of action he would say so, and expect it to be done without constant supervision. He was easy to reach, and easy to talk to freely. We would therefore go to him for advice only when we really needed it, and we were sure of a ready and understanding hearing. ...

In Cabinet he deliberately used to illustrate his points with analogies from the shooting-field, which he knew nine-tenths of the members would not understand. I remember one such beginning, 'Of course, if you brown into a covey of partridges –'. He took an impish delight in the general bewilderment. ...

The secret of Macmillan's political success was his absolute mastery of every parliamentary occasion. It involved a lot of preparation, but it paid a high political dividend. As an historian, too, he had a finely developed sense of perspective. ...

He was, apart from his great ability, a supremely successful showman. Years later, in a private house, when he was discussing politics among a group of friends, he said musingly, 'Of course, when a man becomes Prime Minister, he has to some extent to be an actor.'

Lord Home, *The Way the Wind Blows*, London, 1976, pp. 191–2.

## 1.6 **The decline of Macmillan's leadership**

The fortunes of the Macmillan government declined from 1960 onwards, with economic problems and the failure of the attempt to join the European Community. Confidence in Macmillan himself was shaken by his sweeping cabinet reshuffle of July 1962, the 'night of the long knives', and still more by his handling of the Profumo affair. The debate on this saw a devastating attack from a former minister, Nigel Birch, and ended with the abstention of 27 Conservative MPs.

What is to happen now? I cannot myself see at all that we can go on acting as if nothing had happened. We cannot just have business as usual. I myself feel that the time will come very soon when my right hon. friend [Macmillan] ought to make way for a much younger colleague. I feel that that ought to happen. I certainly will not quote at him the savage words of Cromwell,[3] but perhaps some of the words of Browning might be appropriate in his poem on 'The Lost Leader', in which he wrote:

'let him never come back to us!
There would be doubt, hesitation and pain,
forced praise on our part – the glimmer of twilight,
never glad confident morning again!'

'Never glad confident morning again!' – so I hope that the change will not be too long delayed.

Ahead of us we have a Division. We have the statement of my right hon. and noble friend Lord Hailsham, in a personal assurance on television, that a Whip is not a summons to vote but a summons to attend. I call the Whips to witness that I at any rate have attended.

Nigel Birch, *House of Commons Debates*, fifth series, vol. 679, cols 98–9, 17 June 1963.

## 1.7 **Macmillan the manipulator: the leadership struggle of 1963**

When Macmillan suddenly resigned on health grounds in October 1963, his role was critical in blocking the succession

3 A reference to Leo Amery's denunciation of Neville Chamberlain in May 1940.

of the Deputy Prime Minister, R. A. Butler, and promoting instead the unexpected figure of the 14th Earl of Home. Two cabinet ministers, Iain Macleod and Enoch Powell, refused to serve under Home and the leadership crisis left the Party unsettled and divided. A few weeks later Macleod wrote a sensational article, in which he also coined the phrase 'the magic circle' to describe the small inner group who had determined the outcome.

The truth is that at all times, from the first day of his Premiership to the last, Macmillan was determined that Butler, although incomparably the best qualified of the contenders, should not succeed him. Once this is accepted, all Macmillan's actions become at least explicable. He thought that three of the members of his cabinet who were in the House of Commons, apart from Butler, were *papabile*[4] and of sufficient seniority to be considered: Maudling, Heath and myself. ... Macmillan's private preference between the three of us is known to have varied, but when the time came he was clear that none of us had emerged with the necessary decisive lead. ... Home at this stage and for some time to come had ruled himself out. Only Hailsham could stop Butler. And when Hailsham failed to gather enough support, then Macmillan still refused to accept Butler. He turned to Home. ... He thought, and it is only honest to admit that many others shared his view, that Butler had not in him the steel that makes a Prime Minister, nor the inspiration that a Leader needs to pull his party through a fierce general election. I did not agree. That Butler is mystifying, complex and sometimes hard to approach I would concede. But, on the other hand, he has the priceless quality of being able to do any job better than you think he will, and of attracting to himself wide understanding support from many people outside the Tory Party. And without such an appeal no general election can be won. ...

The decisive roles in the selection of Lord Home as Prime Minister were played by Macmillan and Redmayne.[5] I am certain that they acted at each stage in the interest as they saw it of the sort of Tory Party in which they believe. So did I.

Iain Macleod, 'The Tory leadership', *Spectator*, 17 January 1964.

4   That is, credible as potential leaders (the term comes from elections to the Papacy).
5   The Chief Whip; Redmayne not only collected the views of Conservative MPs but also encouraged support for Home.

## 1.8 **The introduction of leadership elections**

The unwritten system by which Conservative Leaders had 'emerged' was discredited by the controversy in 1963. In the formal election procedure which was devised after the 1964 defeat, the previous 'soundings' were replaced by a secret ballot of MPs. The new system introduced a change of methods, but the aims were still the same.

Objects to be achieved.

(a) The predominant voice in the selection must be that of the House of Commons since the Leader's position ultimately depends more on his ability to command the support of the Party in the Commons than on any other single factor.

(b) The choice of the Commons must be clear beyond reasonable doubt. Ideally the chosen candidate should receive such overwhelming support as to preclude the emergence of factions of determined opposition to his leadership.

(c) While in many ways the present procedure is admirably suited to the characteristics of the Conservative Party, a more open and obvious procedure would be more readily intelligible to the Party and the public.

(d) As the leader is not only the leader of the Parliamentary Party in the Commons but is also the leader of the whole Party in both Houses and in the country, it is necessary to associate in the election procedure representatives of other sections of the Party.

(e) The procedure must be capable of operating quickly.

'Possible methods for selecting a Leader of the Party', memorandum by Douglas, 20 November 1964, Conservative Party Archive (CPA), CRD/3/22/10.

## 1.9 **Edward Heath**

Heath was a dominant figure as Leader, especially after the sudden death of Iain Macleod only a month after the 1970 victory. Relations within the cabinet were generally good and Heath attracted the loyal support of his closest colleagues – but to others, and especially backbench MPs, he often seemed awkward and abrasive. As Attorney-General from 1970 to 1974, Peter Rawlinson observed his Leader's character.

He was not easy. He had built for himself that outer carapace inside which lived the very private and sensitive person who was ever struggling to get out. He found the small change of social life truly difficult. He could not flirt with women or tease men. So he brushed all that aside as being unimportant and trivial and a waste of precious time. But in reality a part of him was longing to carry off all those things which a man of the world finds so easy. It would have helped him very much if he could have acquired that comfortable facility. Not that he was ever a bad host. His houses were graceful; the flowers abundant, the food and drink excellent. But an easier air could have helped his commerce with his colleagues, none of whom at the end of his time in the leadership ever approached his political stature or rivalled those tastes of the cultivated man which he so conspicuously demonstrated. ... What is true is that if Ted could have acquired a more cosy, comfortable style, he would not have lost the leadership of the Party.

I found him always impressive and I liked him personally. His loneliness, somehow epitomized by the solitary hours which he spent at his piano, and that hidden but nevertheless real longing to be accepted as one of 'the Club', aroused affection in those who had the lesser, easier talents but who lacked the greater which he so obviously possessed. I certainly had my differences with him in government, but it was easier for me than for some to be independent. I was in a sense a technocrat. ... But with many colleagues Ted was brusque and all too blunt. When Margaret Thatcher was a member first of his Shadow and then of his real Cabinet, he did not treat her well. Or, more exactly, he did not treat her right. ... For him she was neither sensitive nor clever enough.

Peter Rawlinson, *A Price Too High*, London, 1989, pp. 244–6.

### 1.10 **The fall of Heath**

The fall of Heath after the second election defeat of October 1974 is remembered by Jim Prior. A rising figure in the 1970–74 cabinet and a strong supporter of Heath, Prior entered the

leadership race after Heath's defeat in the first ballot – but by
then Thatcher's bandwagon had gained critical momentum.

Our defeat was nothing like as heavy as most of us had feared. But
within twenty-four hours I told Ted that his only chance of carrying
on as Leader was if he submitted himself to an early election through
the 1922 Committee. He replied that he didn't intend to submit himself to a leadership election because he was determined to fight the
right wing ... My impression was that Ted by then was only hearing
the advice he wished to hear, including some from sources to which
previously he had paid scant attention.

I was surprised by the number of people who were saying that they
disliked him, and by the degree of bitterness and the spiteful determination that he had to go. The executive of the 1922 Committee met at
the home of its chairman, Edward du Cann, on October 14, and
decided to press for a leadership election. ...Again Ted demurred, but
the Parliamentary Party's unease over the procedure for new leadership elections caused him to set up a review committee under Alec
[Douglas-]Home. The conclusions of Alec's review committee, however, were not at all helpful to Ted. There should be a provision for
annual leadership elections in the Parliamentary Party. If there was a
second ballot, new candidates could stand at that stage.

The most likely of Ted's challengers was Keith Joseph, the most
senior 'dissident' who had been in Ted's Cabinet. No one had then
realised that, however decent the man, his political antennae were too
insensitive. ... he realised very quickly that he lacked the requisite
qualities and threw in the towel. This posed the dissidents with quite
a problem. ... But we reckoned without the persistence and almost
obsessive scheming of Airey Neave.

Airey was a man of great courage – he had escaped from Colditz –
and bitter determination. He was an implacable enemy of Ted's, from
the 1950s when Ted had been Chief Whip, and they had a great row.
Someone who had been determined enough to escape from Colditz
was unlikely to be put off by losing a couple of potential candidates,
so the next in line was pushed forward. This was Margaret Thatcher.

Up to that time, I do not believe that she had thought of herself as
a candidate for the Leadership. My conversations with her gave me
no inkling to that effect, and, although she was ambitious, I do not
think she felt that her time had come. However, Airey ran a brilliant
campaign ... There was a constant flow of MPs to see them, and I

began to realise that these were drawn from a wide cross-section of the Party. ...Airey Neave's exercise was carried out by a combination of promises and flattery, and was brilliantly masterminded. Margaret's stature in the Party had been enhanced by her performances at the despatch box as Robert Carr's deputy opposing Labour's Finance Bill. Her courage in opposing Ted went down well in the Party and in much of the press. Other potential candidates, who were remaining loyal to Ted but who it was known would come in on the second ballot if Ted were defeated, were quietly being accused of cowardice by the Neave camp. The fact that a vote for Margaret was the only way to secure a second ballot was also turned to advantage.

Jim Prior, *A Balance of Power*, London, 1986, pp. 98–100.

### 1.11 **The new style**

Thatcher's advent as Leader led to a shift in the policies and outlook of the Party; not only did she draw her support from the right, but her instincts were confrontational and hostile to the establishment. After 1975 new figures rose at the expense of the old guard – apart from Whitelaw, who served loyally as her Deputy. Prior, one of the despised 'wets', recalls the change.

I had been at the centre of Tory Party politics for almost ten years, since Ted had appointed me as his P[arliamentary] P[rivate] S[ecretary], but once Margaret Thatcher took over it all altered. It may seem hard to understand why I experienced so great a change – after all, I was in Margaret's Shadow Cabinet and then her Cabinet continuously until September 1984: surely that is being at the centre of things, or 'on the inside track'.

But in any Party, and in any Government, the Leader, or Prime Minister, inevitably relies on a very few trusted colleagues – usually a few ministers and perhaps two or three aides. With Ted as Leader and Prime Minister, I was right on the inside. But, when Margaret became Leader, I became one of the outsiders, saying my piece, at times able to exert some influence, but all the time aware that the centre of decision-making and weight of the Party and Government machine lay with others.

Yet curiously Margaret was a Leader and a Prime Minister who in some ways remained on the outside herself. She felt able to divorce herself from decisions which she did not like, as if at times the Party, or her Government, were nothing to do with her.

Partly as a result of her approach as Leader, and partly due to the changes in the Party since the early 1960s, the traditional ways in which the old 'inner circle' used to organise the Party – informally and discreetly, born of the values of duty and loyalty – could no longer work. Whenever Willie Whitelaw and Francis Pym used to get together, they still seemed to think that the Party could be run as they had run it ten or fifteen years earlier. Although they undoubtedly could wield some power and used all their skill to keep Margaret's Shadow Cabinet reasonably cohesive, it could never be the same again. ... It was not only the political personalities and methods of Party management which were altering: the philosophy was changing also; and by the mid-1970s, the economic argument was shifting perceptibly too – to the right. Inflation had become a bigger enemy than unemployment.

Jim Prior, *A Balance of Power*, London, 1986, pp. 103–4.

### 1.12 'Conviction' politics and the role of Whitelaw

Despite declaring that she needed a 'conviction' cabinet, throughout her Premiership Thatcher gave office to the most able and effective figures from the centre and left of the Party. The fact that her strong supporters were in the minority led to difficulties, especially in 1979–81 and when she fell in 1990. However, until his retirement in January 1988, the loyal and supportive role played by her Deputy, William Whitelaw, was vital: as Thatcher herself remarked, 'Every government should have a Willie'.

Any new leader, especially a newly elected first woman leader, needs to unite the party behind him or her, and Margaret Thatcher was no exception. What one expected was that over a period the new leader would gradually introduce new people into the team who shared her sense of purpose and commitment. She recognized that this was necessary in an interview she gave to Kenneth Harris in February 1979. 'As Prime Minister I couldn't waste time having any internal arguments ... When the time comes to form a real Cabinet, I do think I've got to have a Cabinet with equal unity of purpose, and a sense of dedication to it. It must be a cabinet that works on something much more than pragmatism, or consensus. It must be a "conviction" Government.' Yet having identified the need she failed to meet it. The solid central core of the Cabinet – Carrington, Soames, Pym, Prior, Walker, Heseltine – tolerated her views, they did not share them. Of the leading figures in the Cabinet only Geoffrey Howe and Keith Joseph met the 'conviction' criterion. Willie Whitelaw was in a special category of his own. Whether he shared her convictions I do not know. But he saw it as his duty to give her his total loyalty and support, and this he did to such a degree that he forfeited in part the friendship of some of his colleagues and natural allies. They felt he had let them down. He believed he owed it to the party and the country to support the person who had beaten him in the contest for the leadership and who had subsequently won, not just one, but three general elections. He was unswerving in his support and she benefited enormously from this. Time after time, even after 1981, when she finally got a majority in her own Cabinet, Willie's interventions eased the doubts of those who had them, and united the Cabinet. In those early years when she was in a minority his support must have been priceless. Although she never felt at ease with what she called the grandees, Willie was a grandee whom she did trust.

Cecil Parkinson, *Right at the Centre*, London, 1992, p. 8.

### 1.13 Cabinet government under Thatcher

Thatcher's conduct of cabinet government was a constant source of controversy during her Premiership.[6] Nicholas Ridley, one of her staunchest supporters and a cabinet minister from 1983 to 1990, discussed the issue in his admiring memoirs.

Margaret Thatcher saw the Cabinet as very much a formal body. She did not see it as a body to take decisions, except for decisions of the very greatest importance. She saw it as the forum in which all important activities of government were brought together and reported upon.

6 See also document 4.23 for the 1981 cabinet crisis, and document 4.25 for the 1986 Westland crisis.

She saw it as the body to approve individual ministers' policies. She used it as a tactical group to discuss the immediate problems of the day. ... Margaret Thatcher was going to be the leader in her Cabinet. She wasn't going to be an impartial chairman. She knew what she wanted to do, and she was not going to have faint hearts in her Cabinet stopping her. ...

The Cabinet is also the forum to which the structure of Cabinet Committees reports. There are large numbers of these – some permanent, and some ad hoc, set up to consider certain transient problems and then stood down. The permanent Cabinet Committees deal with the main aspects of policy – like defence and overseas policy, home affairs, legislation, and economic policy. ... Margaret Thatcher extended the Cabinet Committee system by setting up small groups consisting of those ministers most closely concerned. The composition of each group depended on the subject, but on the whole she preferred the least possible number of ministers to be present. When the decision concerned spending money, it was usually the Prime Minister, the Chief Secretary and the spending minister only who attended. ... All decisions of importance were reported to the Cabinet, except those which were market sensitive, or just plain 'sensitive'. There was thus an opportunity for anyone who wanted to do so to reopen a question if he didn't like a decision. It did sometimes happen, but only rarely. ...

She disliked having votes in Cabinet. She didn't see it as that sort of body. ... She carried the responsibility, so she was going to be in a position to discharge it. That was why she disliked Royal Commissions; she never appointed a single one. She was not going to be put in the position where someone else was given an official licence to tell the elected head of the Executive what the policy was going to be. ...

There is a feeling in the Tory Party that each strand of opinion in the Party should be represented at Cabinet. This feeling is magnified into the proposition that such representatives should be in Cabinet almost as of right, as leaders of some important group or faction, and that they have a political position of their own, as a result of their powerbase in the Party. This feeling gave some a sense of being more important than they were. It also made them harder to dispense with, lest they go back to their powerbase on the backbenches and cause real trouble. Although I believe such people greatly overestimate their power, it always caused Margaret Thatcher much concern.

Nicholas Ridley, *My Style of Government: The Thatcher Years*, London, 1991, pp. 28–31.

### 1.14 **Thatcher's character and methods**

The way in which Thatcher conducted and dominated her governments was observed at close quarters by Nigel Lawson, a close supporter in the early 1980s and her Chancellor of the Exchequer from 1983 until rifts between them led to his resignation in 1989.

Whether before Cabinet or the more effective smaller meetings, Margaret, who appeared to need only four hours' sleep a night, always did her homework on the subjects for discussion, almost as if she were about to sit an examination. In general this was a desirable characteristic, but it could lead to time-wasting attempts to show off her mastery of detail, at the expense of the main business in hand. ... Her conduct of meetings also became increasingly authoritarian. Some of her predecessors, such as Harold Macmillan, would allow other colleagues to have their say before summing up and stating a conclusion. Margaret on the other hand, when there was an issue upon which she had already formed a firm view, would start with an unashamedly tendentious introduction of her own, before inviting the responsible and sometimes cowed Minister to have his say. Thus what began as a method for the most expedient conduct of business ended as a means of getting her own way irrespective of the merits or political costs.

Why did the colleagues allow her to govern in the way she did? While spinelessness or careerism may be adequate explanation in the case of some, it will not do for all. And belief in her infallibility was even more narrowly shared. Of course all Prime Ministers are in a position of great power, so long as they can retain the office; and she was a particularly formidable Prime Minister who ... had acquired considerable experience. But beyond this, her method of Cabinet Government was accepted because in many ways it was highly convenient to her colleagues. Most Cabinet Ministers, particularly after a longish period in government, tend to be preoccupied with fighting their own battles and pursuing the issues that matter within their own bailiwick, and lose interest in the wider picture. Most of the time it is comforting for them to feel that all they need to do is strike a deal with the Prime Minister, and not have to bother overmuch about persuading their other colleagues. ... Finally, if less important, was the fact that she was in practice at her best in bilaterals and other small gatherings. The larger the numbers, the greater her tendency to play to the gallery, either showing off her own knowledge on the subject or rounding, in a profoundly embarrassing way, on some hapless colleague whom she felt either bullyable by nature or objectively in a weak position at a particular time. Geoffrey Howe was a favourite victim.

Nigel Lawson, *The View from Number 11*, London, 1992, pp. 127–9.

## 1.15 **The resignation of Sir Geoffrey Howe**

As Chancellor of the Exchequer in 1979–83 Sir Geoffrey Howe had been Thatcher's key supporter, but after he became Foreign Secretary in 1983 their views diverged, especially over Europe. In July 1989 Howe was switched to being Leader of the House, but the following unhappy year of petty humiliations and widening rifts over Europe ended with his sudden resignation, at the time of year when the rules allow a leadership contest. Howe's attack on the Prime Minister in his resignation speech had a devastating effect, and set in motion the events which ended with Thatcher's departure.

It has been suggested – even, indeed, by some of my right hon. and hon. friends – that I decided to resign solely because of questions of style and not on matters of substance at all. Indeed, if some of my former colleagues are to be believed, I must be the first Minister in history who has resigned because he was in full agreement with Government policy. The truth is that, in many aspects of politics, style and substance complement each other. Very often they are two sides of the same coin. ...

I do not regard it as in any sense wrong for Britain to make criticisms of that kind [of EEC proposals] plainly and courteously, nor in any sense wrong for us to do so, if necessary, alone. ... But it is crucially important that we should conduct those arguments upon the basis of a clear understanding of the true relationship between this country, the Community and our Community partners. And it is here,

I fear, that my right hon. friend the Prime Minister increasingly risks leading herself and others astray in matters of substance as well as of style. ...

We must at all costs avoid presenting ourselves yet again with an over-simplified choice, a false antithesis, a bogus dilemma, between one alternative, starkly labelled 'co-operation between independent sovereign states' and a second, equally crudely labelled alternative, 'centralised federal super-state', as if there were no middle way in between. We commit a serious error if we think always in terms of 'surrendering' sovereignty and seek to stand pat for all time on a given deal – by proclaiming, as my right hon. friend the Prime Minister did two weeks ago, that we have 'surrendered enough'. The European enterprise is not and should not be seen like that ... the nightmare image sometimes conjured up by my right hon. friend, who seems sometimes to look out upon a continent that is positively teeming with ill-intentioned people, scheming, in her words, to 'extinguish democracy', to 'dissolve our national identities' and to lead us 'through the back-door into a federal Europe'. What kind of vision is that for our business people, who trade there each day, for our financiers, who seek to make London the money capital of Europe, or for all the young people of today? ...

The tragedy is – and it is for me personally, for my party, for our whole people and for my right hon. friend herself, a very real tragedy – that the Prime Minister's perceived attitude towards Europe is running increasingly serious risks for the future of our nation. It risks minimising our influence and maximising our chances of being once again shut out. We have paid heavily in the past for late starts and squandered opportunities in Europe. We dare not let that happen again. If we detach ourselves completely, as a party or a nation, from the middle ground of Europe, the effects will be incalculable and very hard ever to correct.

In my letter of resignation, which I tendered with the utmost sadness and dismay, I said: 'Cabinet Government is all about trying to persuade one another from within'. That was my commitment to Government by persuasion – persuading colleagues and the nation. I have tried to do that as Foreign Secretary and since, but I realise now that the task has become futile: trying to stretch the meaning of words beyond what was credible, and trying to pretend that there was a common policy when every step forward risked being subverted by some casual comment or impulsive answer.

The conflict of loyalty, of loyalty to my right hon. friend the Prime Minister – and, after all, in two decades together that instinct of loyalty is still very real – and of loyalty to what I perceive to be the true interests of the nation, has become all too great. I no longer believe it possible to resolve that conflict from within this Government. That is why I have resigned. In doing so, I have done what I believe to be right for my party and my country. The time has come for others to consider their own response to the tragic conflict of loyalties with which I have myself wrestled for perhaps too long.

Sir Geoffrey Howe, *House of Commons Debates*, sixth series, vol. 180, cols 461–5, 13 November 1990.

## 1.16 **The fall of Thatcher**

The feverish atmosphere of the few days between Howe's speech and the resignation of Thatcher, after she failed to secure a sufficient margin over Michael Heseltine in the first ballot of the ensuing leadership contest, is captured by one of her strongest supporters, Alan Clark.

[17 November 1990:] The Lady [Thatcher] herself is away, out of the country. It's absolute madness. There is no Party mileage whatever in being at the Paris summit. It just makes her seem snooty and remote. And who's running the campaign? Who's doing the canvassing? Who's putting the pressure on? I became more and more dejected, decided to telephone Tristan.[7] He attempted to calm me, said that Peter Morrison was in charge of collating the votes, that he was calmly confident. But when pressed Tristan shared my scepticism as to whether this was really the true picture.

[19 November 1990:] The whole house is in ferment. Little groups, conclaves everywhere. Only in the dining room does some convention seem to have grown up (I presume because no one trusts their dining companions) that we don't talk 'shop'. ... But in the corridors it is all furtive whispering and glancing over the shoulders. ...

Most people are interested – not so much in the result, as in know-

7    Tristan Garel-Jones, at this time a Minister of State at the Foreign Office, but Deputy Chief Whip until July 1990; a noted organiser.

ing what the result will be in advance, in order to make their own 'dispositions'. To ingratiate oneself with the new regime – *a* new regime, I should say, because the outcome is by no means certain – even as little as a week before it is installed, looks better than joining the stampede afterwards. The issue, which can be discussed semi-respectably, is who is most likely to deliver victory at the General Election? But it is packaging, conceals a great basket of bitterness, thwarted personal ambition, and vindictive glee. Talk of country, or loyalty, is dismissed as 'histrionics'.

And there is a strange feeling abroad. Even if the Lady wins – and here I am writing 'even if', pull yourself together Clark, say 'even after she's won' – there will be no escaping the fact that at least one hundred and fifty of her parliamentary colleagues will have rejected her leadership. That's a big chunk. ...

And as the savour of a Heseltine victory starts to pervade the crannies and cupboards and committee rooms, so more and more people are 'coming out'. 'Oh, I don't think he'd be so bad, really ...' 'He's got such a wide *appeal*.' ...

The Cabinet play their cards close to the chest, although Mellor, apparently, speaks to Michael twice a day on the telephone. Some, like Kenneth Clarke, want her out so badly that they don't even need to blink. ... Tristan said, 'Of course every member of the Cabinet will vote for the Prime Minister in the first round.' Like hell they will. ...

It can't really be as bad as this can it? I mean there is absolutely no oomph in her campaign whatsoever. Peter is useless, far worse than I thought. ... There isn't a single person working for her who cuts any ice at all. I know it's better to be feared than loved. But these people aren't either. And she's in Paris. ....

Alan Clark, *Diaries*, London, 1993, pp. 349–55.

### 1.17 John Major and the soapbox

In 1992 the Conservative campaign was making little impact until John Major decided to address the crowds in the old-fashioned way, standing in the open on his 'soapbox'. The result is described by two of his closest advisors, the head of his Policy Unit, Sarah Hogg, and his Political Secretary, Jonathan Hill.

40

But what the battlebus team rapidly realised was the effect the experience had had on the Prime Minister himself. He had come out of the crowd positively crackling with electricity. He was a different person. No more Treasury-speak and whirring sub-clauses. Instead, a tough street-fighter who drew his strength from direct contact with a crowd and knew how to speak their language – simple, uncomplicated English spoken straight from the heart. They had found the key that unlocked the real John Major. And, typically, he had had it in his pocket the whole time.

Why did the soapbox work? Certainly not because it offered good sound-bites or was presentationally slick. Rather, because it showed the Prime Minister as he was: a bit homespun maybe, but transparently honest, physically courageous, and prepared to fight for what he believed in. At a time when all the clever talk was that electioneering in Britain was destined to draw on techniques copied from across the Atlantic, the Prime Minister instinctively went back to an older, truer British political tradition. In doing so, he turned conventional wisdom on its head and destroyed the whole premise on which his own campaign had been constructed.

Sarah Hogg and Jonathan Hill, *Too Close to Call: Power and Politics – John Major in No. 10*, London, 1995, pp. 228–9.

## 1.18 **Major forces a showdown: the leadership contest of 1995**

By 1995 the Major government had suffered setbacks and rebellions, and was far behind the 'New' Labour Party of Tony Blair in the opinion polls. Confidence in the Prime Minister's leadership was crumbling, and a challenge when the rules permitted in November looked likely. Instead, Major seized the initiative by suddenly announcing that he had decided to call an immediate leadership contest. Although shaken when John Redwood resigned from the cabinet to stand against him, Major's victory margin was enough to restore his authority and rule out the prospect of any further challenges before the next general election.

Let me just make a brief statement to you. I've been deeply involved in politics since I was 16. I see public service as a duty and if you can serve, I believe you have an obligation to do so. I've now been Prime Minister for nearly five years. In that time we've achieved a great deal, but for the last three years I've been opposed by a small minority in our party. During those three years there have been repeated threats of a leadership election. In each year, they turned out to be phoney threats. Now the same thing is happening again in 1995. I believe this is in no one's interest that this continues right through until November. It undermines the Government and it damages the Conservative Party. I am not prepared to see the party I care for laid out on the rack like this any longer.

To remove this uncertainty I have this afternoon tendered my resignation as leader of the Conservative Party to Sir Marcus Fox, the chairman of the 1922 Committee,[8] and requested him to set the machinery in motion for an election of a successor. I have confirmed to Sir Marcus that I shall be a candidate in that election. If I win, I shall continue as Prime Minister and lead the party into and through the next general election. Should I be defeated, which I do not expect, I shall resign as Prime Minister and offer my successor my full support.

The Conservative Party must make its choice. Every leader is leader only with the support of his party. That is true of me as well. That is why I am no longer prepared to tolerate the present situation. In short, it is time to put up or shut up. I have nothing more to say this afternoon. Thank you very much.

John Major's press statement, 10 Downing Street, 5.00 p.m., 22 June 1995.

### 1.19 The leadership election rules, 1995–97

After Margaret Thatcher's downfall in 1990, the leadership election rules were revised to remove the provision for an automatic annual election. A serving leader could now only be challenged if at least 10 per cent of the Parliamentary Party demanded a ballot in writing; as before, this could only occur at the start of the parliamentary session (normally in November). However, the key elements were unchanged from the

8   The body to which all backbench Conservative MPs belong, and which since 1965 has had the task of conducting leadership elections.

original scheme of 1965: (i) whatever 'consultation' might take place, the decision was taken by the MPs alone; (ii) the ballots were secret; (iii) the requirement of a 15 per cent margin in the first ballot sought to avoid narrow victories and thereby promote consensus and unity; (iv) if no such clear mandate was secured, fresh candidates could enter the lists for the second ballot – as occurred in 1975 and 1990. These rules applied in 1995 and, despite pressure for a share of the votes to be given to the constituency parties, in 1997.

*Timings of Elections and General Responsibilities*
1. If the position of Leader of the Party is vacant, an election shall be held as early as possible.

2. Otherwise there shall be an election in the House of Commons beginning within 28 days of the opening of each new Session of Parliament ... provided that the Chairman of the 1922 Committee is advised in writing by not less than ten per cent. of the members of the Parliamentary party that they believe such an election to be necessary. On receipt of such advice, which must reach him within 14 days of the opening of a new Session or within three months of the start of a new Parliament, and without disclosing the names of any of the signatories, the Chairman shall inform the Leader of the Party that an election is required, and together they shall determine the actual date. Otherwise the Chairman will declare the Leader of the Party has been returned unopposed for a further term.

3. The Chairman of the 1922 Committee will be responsible for the conduct of all ballots and will settle all matters in relation thereto.

*Nominations and List of Candidates*
4. Candidates will be proposed and seconded in writing by Members of the House of Commons in receipt of the Conservative Whip. The Chairman of the 1922 Committee and scrutineers designated by him will be available to receive nominations. ... The names of the proposer and seconder will be published by the scrutineers. Nominations will close by noon on a Thursday five days before the date of the First Ballot.

*Procedure for Consultation*
6. During the period between the close of nominations and the date of the First Ballot it shall be the responsibility of the constituency Association in each constituency which is represented by a Conservative

Member of Parliament to ascertain, in conjunction with the Member, the views of their membership regarding the candidates by the most effective means available.

7. The Chairman of the Association of Conservative Peers and the Chief Whip in the House of Lords will make such arrangements as appropriate to obtain the views of Peers in receipt of the Conservative Whip.

8. The Leader of the Conservative Members of the European Parliament will obtain the views of MEPs in receipt of the Conservative Whip.

9. In order that all sections of the Party shall be consulted, Area Chairmen of the National Union will obtain the opinions of constituency associations, through their chairmen, and report their findings to the Chairman of the National Union and the Chairman of the Executive Committee of the National Union. In Scotland the Area Chairmen will similarly consult and report to the President of the Scottish Conservative and Unionist Association. They will also report to Conservative Members of Parliament within the area of their responsibility the views of constituencies not represented by a Conservative Member of Parliament.

*First Ballot*

12. The First Ballot will be held on the Tuesday immediately following the closing date for nominations. For this ballot the scrutineers will prepare a ballot paper listing the names of the candidates and give a copy for the purpose of balloting to each Member of the House of Commons in receipt of the Conservative Whip.

13. For the First Ballot each voter will indicate one choice from the candidates listed.

14. Where any Member is unavoidably absent from the House on that day for any reason acceptable to the scrutineers, the Chairman of the 1922 Committee shall make appropriate arrangements for the appointment of a proxy.

15. The ballot will be secret and neither the names of those who have voted for a particular candidate nor the names of those who have abstained from voting shall be disclosed by the scrutineers.

16. If, as a result of this ballot, one candidate both (i) receives an overall majority of the votes of those entitled to vote and (ii) receives 15 per cent. more of the votes of those entitled to vote than any other candidate, he will be elected.

17. The scrutineers will announce the number of votes received by each candidate, and if no candidate satisfies these conditions, a second ballot will be held.

*Second Ballot*
18. The Second Ballot will be held on the following Tuesday. Nominations made for the First Ballot will be void. New nominations will be submitted by the Thursday, under the same procedure and with the same arrangements for consultation as described in paragraphs 4–11 for the First Ballot, both for the original candidates if required and for any other candidates.

19. The voting procedure for the Second Ballot will be the same as for the First, save that paragraph 16 shall not apply. If, as a result of this Second Ballot, one candidate receives an overall majority of the votes of those entitled to vote, that candidate will be elected.

*Third Ballot*
20. If no candidate receives an overall majority, any candidate may withdraw his or her name by advising the Chairman of the 1922 Committee to that effect before 6 p.m. the following day. Of those then remaining, the two candidates who received the highest number of votes at the Second Ballot will go forward to a Third Ballot on Thursday.

21. The candidate receiving a majority of votes cast in this ballot will be elected.


'Procedure for the selection of the Leader of the Conservative Party', amended 1991.

# 2

# The Parliamentary Party

The Parliamentary Party is the heart of Conservative politics – quite literally, as it can often be set racing by a panic or crisis. The tenure of the Leader has always depended upon retaining the confidence of the Parliamentary Party, a fact merely confirmed by the leadership election machinery established in 1965. The path to ministerial office lies through the House of Commons, not just in success in debate or committee work but still more through earning the approval of the powerful Whips, who largely determine the appointments to junior posts. Conservative MPs also provide the most responsive link between the rank and file membership and the Party leaders, and are often a swifter and surer channel than the passing up of formal resolutions. For reasons of electoral self-preservation, the Parliamentary Party is also responsive to the media and to the perceived currents of public opinion, whilst sustained adversity may lead to internal disunity and rumblings of dissatisfaction with the leadership.

Since the Second World War there have been changes in the social character of the Parliamentary Party. The element drawn from the aristocracy and traditional upper class has declined, with the wealthiest MPs in the 1990s being self-made businessmen often of modest origins. Conservative MPs have become mainly middle-class and in that sense more meritocratic in origin; in the 1980s it was said that the Parliamentary Party had changed from being one of estate owners to one of estate agents. There has also been an increasing element who have exclusively pursued a political career from university onwards. The atmosphere in the Parliamentary Party has changed from the more leisurely world of the 'knights of the shires' of the 1950s to one of rivalry and ambition.

The extracts in this chapter examine the role and power of the Whips, the path of promotion to ministerial office, the backbench

committee structure and the '1922' Committee, the social composition of the Parliamentary Party, the methods of candidate selection,
and the demands of contesting a seat.

## 2.1 **The role of the Whips**

The work of the Whips was described by Martin Redmayne
(Chief Whip 1959–64) in a radio interview a few weeks after
the 1963 leadership crisis.

Certainly the first function must be the flow of information from the
backbenchers to the leadership – that is either to the Prime Minister
or to other Ministers, depending on what the subject of any particular
comment may be. Discipline really flows from the success with which
the first function is performed. You never get discipline unless the
backbenchers are happy that the Whips are performing the function
of communication properly. ...

I have thirteen Whips plus my deputy, and each of those has, first
of all, what we call an area – a geographical area of the country in
which there are thirty or forty Conservative members. His business is
to keep contact with them, and not merely to keep contact with them
but to know them so well that he may in emergency be able to give a
judgement as to what their opinion will be without even asking them.
Then each Whip is allocated to one or more party committees; he
keeps in touch with the chairman and the officers of those committees, attends their meetings, and reports to me anything of interest –
that is anything that is likely to be the subject of adverse comment –
And every Whip in his ordinary round of the House – and they live in
the House most of the time when it is sitting – has his own contacts
with those who are his friends or those he may dine with, may meet in
the smoking room, and so forth. He is always ready to pick up anything which may be useful to the government – and equally useful to
the backbenchers, because no party can succeed unless it works as
one in matters of opinion. ...

The Chief Whip sits on various government committees. He is
always there to make comment when asked by the chairman of the
committee, maybe the Prime Minister, maybe other Ministers. Or, if
he thinks that Ministers are taking a view which will not be acceptable to the party, then he speaks on his own account. Of course, these

things are not always done in committee; as the information flows into my desk, literally hour by hour throughout the day, I frequently write notes to this Minister or that, to say that the party or this Member, as the case may be, takes this view or that view, and that in my opinion the policy ought to be amended accordingly; and these things are always taken into account. ... That is where half my function comes in, to look for the snags in advance. ...

Discipline is a difficult thing to explain. I hate to give away secrets, but I sometimes feel that my powers of discipline are not nearly strong enough for the occasions that arise. The fact is that discipline only arises from goodwill, and goodwill arises from good understanding between the backbenches and the government. You can be sure that if your discipline appears to be good, then your morale is good and your policy is good. If, on the other hand, at times your discipline appears to fall down, the fault – and I am not trying to excuse the Whips or myself in this matter – lies much more with the sort of undercurrents that impair morale than with any active discipline that can be exerted by the Chief Whip.

'The Commons in action', *Listener*, 19 and 26 December 1963.

## 2.2 **Whips and rebels**

This account of the bitter struggle over the Maastricht Treaty in 1992–93 by a leading rebel, Teresa Gorman, puts the Whips at the centre of a web of suspicion, intrigue and coercion.

They are like school prefects. Their role is not to try to change our opinion, but to convince us that the Government's policy is more important than our principles. They must get to know their charges. They see that you toe the party line and they give you a wigging if you miss a vote or, heaven forbid, vote against the Government or abstain. You are expected to tell your Whip in advance if you intend to commit this sin. All sorts of pressure is applied. Failure to inform the Whip brings a sharp note in the post next day, demanding an explanation. On a three-line whip, even the dying are brought in to vote. ...

The Whips have a way of hovering about or sitting near enough to overhear conversations. ... The Whips are as secretive as the Masons. What goes on behind that oak door is never revealed, unless they want it to be, of course. They go in for news management on a scale that would do credit to MI5, the CIA and the KGB combined. ...

There were two debates going on that day: one in the chamber under parliamentary rules of courtesy and decorum and another in the corridors, tea rooms and terraces where four-letter words, bribery and bitter insults were being traded between the Whips and the rebels. Every trick in the book, from threatening to expose who knows what scandal to intimating they could kiss goodbye to a knighthood, had been used by the Whips to bring people into line and they were still snarling and snapping at our heels while the debate was in progress.

Teresa Gorman, *The Bastards: Dirty Tricks and the Challenge to Europe*, London, 1993, pp. 55, 104–6, 127.

## 2.3 The qualities for success

The crucial role of the Whips in determining promotion and the characteristics needed for a successful career were described by the backbench MP Julian Critchley.

There is, of course, a straightforward answer to the question 'how best to get on in the Tory Party?' One needs brains, application, cheerfulness and luck; but I think it is fair to say that there have been those who have made the Party's Frontbench who have not been conspicuous for their intelligence, diligence or conviviality. Success, in politics as elsewhere, demands more than just merit. ...

Tories must be clubbable. It was Harold Macmillan's view that only two rooms in the Palace of Westminster were worth visiting, the chamber and the smoking room. Some days after my election in 1959, I sat in the smoking-room reading a book. Charles Hill[1] approached me. 'Young man', he intoned, 'it does not do to appear clever. Advancement in this man's Party is based firmly on alcoholic stupidity.' I have never opened a book since.

A Tory must be both convivial and partisan. He should direct his fire at the enemy. ... Conservatives are inclined to give more weight to character than to cleverness. Competence is preferred to brilliance, diligence to flair and predictability to inspiration. ... In the search for

1  Conservative MP 1950–63, and cabinet minister 1957–62.

its leaders the Tories have often sought comfort rather than clarity, and have on occasion found neither. ...

The ambitious Tory must speak regularly in the House. He must not be discouraged if not called, or by the fact that few listen, and fewer still read *Hansard*. The Whips notice: they are obliged to do so. He should take an active part on the committee stages of Bills. The Whips are paid to listen and report back and it is upon their good opinion that the aspirant for office will depend. The Party leader chooses the cabinet, the members of whom, in the Tory Party at least, have little say in the choice of their juniors. Cabinet ministers can exclude but their patronage, while important, is limited. The bulk of the posts in a Conservative government will be allocated by the Chief Whip after consultations in the Whip's Office. He has to take into account the need to balance the wings of the Party coalition and the exigencies of geography (Welsh Tories have a much better than average chance of promotion, those with seats in the South-East the worst).

Julian Critchley, 'How to get on in the Tory Party', *Political Quarterly*, 49, 1978, pp. 467–73.

## 2.4 Climbing the ladder

The ladder of promotion ascended from parliamentary private secretary or junior whip through several gradations of junior minister (culminating in Minister of State), and then to the cabinet. The years spent in the junior posts often combined a heavy but tedious workload with rivalry and insecurity. During the Thatcher era there was a considerable turnover, and the period before each annual reshuffle was marked by tension and rumour; the atmosphere is caught by Alan Clark, at this point a Minister of State at the Department of Trade and Industry.

[18 July 1988:] The three-quarters of July syndrome. Everything stale and fetid. I walked through the Members' lobby this afternoon, then to the library and down Speaker's corridor. People – many of whom I hardly knew – scuttled and bustled self-importantly. ... That fat creep Bruce Anderson [a journalist on the *Sunday Telegraph*] again wrote about the reshuffle and *again* left me out ... I suppose there is an off-chance of an upheaval if Walters[2] comes back, Lawson goes completely pouty and things fall apart. But in fact the next major reshuffle 'to take us into the Nineties' (ugh) is scheduled for 1989.

[17 January 1989:] What have I got to show for this? Nothing. Shuffled papers about. ... All that has happened is that I am nine hours older. I've had it. The Lady [Thatcher] no longer knows my name. David [Young, the Secretary of State] pinches all the good 'initiatives' and I'm left with nothing. Who am I? Other Ministers of State are high-profile. Waldegrave, Patten (both),[3] Mellor (although everyone loathes him), Portillo. ... All that has happened is that I have become obscure and passé. I should have realised that my enemies, who are numerous (why?) will be able, and will do their best, to exploit either condition equally effectively.

Alan Clark, *Diaries*, London, 1993, pp. 220, 239.

## 2.5 A Tory alphabet

Julian Critchley, whose irreverent wit had earned him nearly thirty years on the backbenches, offered the following sketches in an 'A to Z' guide to the Conservative Party in 1993.

H is for Humbug, the necessary lubricant of public life without which anyone you care to name could not have got to where he or she is today. ...

J is for junior office. The magic moment when the Chief Whip, Richard Ryder, suggests you are ready for a car of your own, a red box and a black driver, triple consolations for a life of obscurity being patronised by leaky Wykehamists in a drab office in Marsham Street. ...

K is for the end of the road. The reward for a life of silent service. It is given to Tories of a certain age to help them please their wives. In other walks of life a K[nighthood] is a deserved recognition of distinction; this is not always the case among politicians. ...

2    Alan Walters, former economic adviser to Thatcher; his return was to provoke Lawson's resignation in October 1989.
3    Chris Patten (a cabinet minister in 1989–92) and John Patten (Education Secretary 1992–94); they are not related.

R is for Resentment, which is the fuel of politics. See Thatcher, Heath, Tebbit, Spicer, Baker, Edward Leigh and almost anyone else you care to mention.

S is for Sound which is still the highest form of Whips' praise. A 'sound' Tory went to Eton, had his money in Lloyd's, was loyal to the leader of the party and is much married. He was an officer of the '22, dealt only with Knight, Frank & Rutley, drove a British motor car and did not keep a diary. Increasingly hard to find. ...

V is for Village Hall, the venue of a thousand ill-attended meetings; gatherings of the faithful and their Labrador dogs, upon whose devoted efforts the Tory Party once relied for sustenance and support. Village halls are hard to find, freezing cold and have acoustics that would have defied the young Ian Paisley. A speaker must observe the golden rule: subject is of no importance; sit down the moment he hears the rattle of teacups.

W is for the Whips. The Tory Whips are recruited from the most promising. In return for the promise of promotion (see J), they are obliged to take vows of poverty, chastity and obedience. ... their task to act as sultan's guard to the leader of our great party. Loyal as hound dogs, their response to the news of the sudden death of a much-loved colleague is 'most unhelpful'.

Julian Critchley, 'The wise child's guide to the Tory Party', *Observer*, 15 August 1993.

## 2.6 The backbench committees

The Conservative Party's structure of backbench 'subject' committees has been in existence since 1924. There are normally twelve to fourteen committees, each of which covers a major government department or policy area. They are open to all Conservative MPs, and can be a useful channel of communication to ministers and the leadership in a crisis. The following comments were made by several Conservative MPs at a series of private dinners in 1972.

If you want an open debate which is really important and influences Cabinet, then you go to one of the party committees – Foreign Affairs, Home, or whatever – and that's where people really let fly and that's what matters. ...

... there you are, you want to say something, you think it's important, so you go up to the committee, and you're bound really to be called because people only talk for about two minutes. For those who are energetic this is the most suitable forum. ...

There's no need to be mysterious about this. A whip is allocated to every committee. He sits there taking notes. If that committee is clearly going in a particular direction or a row is brewing, a report is in the hands of the Chief Whip within five minutes of the end of that committee. And I've sat on several committees in recent months where I'm perfectly clear the Chief Whip has been got to not in five minutes but in one. And this is where we start changing views, because that whip will go back to the Chief Whip and say, 'We've had a very ugly meeting up here – eighty present – and the views was taken that —'. So there's no mystery: if a committee really blows off steam, it's in Cabinet the next day. ...

Ministers are always anxious to be on excellent terms with the officers of the committee affecting their department. And they will, as far as they can, and this is interesting, seek to take you into their confidence. Now, ministers taking committee participants into their confidence is like ministers taking journalists into their confidence: once the confidences have been exchanged, you are to an extent inhibited. My own feeling is that the officers of a committee need to keep a certain distance: you must not allow ministers to emasculate your performance by letting them tell you too much of what they propose to do. You mustn't feel in any sense that you're part of – an agency of – the Government.

Comments quoted in Anthony King, *British Members of Parliament: A Self-Portrait*, London, 1974, pp. 48–51.


## 2.7 **The 1922 Committee**

Conservative MPs' most famous sounding-board was also founded in the early 1920s: the Conservative Private Members' Committee, popularly known as the '1922 Committee'. Its meetings are supposed to be confidential, and its 'behind the scenes' role has led to exaggerations of its power, though it can be decisive in turning against a minister who is in personal or political difficulty. The following comments come from a book written by the Secretary of the Committee to mark its golden jubilee.

As one astute Member of the Executive Committee has noted: 'The meetings ... only become important when the Party is going through a bad patch. When everything is going well, Ministers or Shadow Ministers can ignore the views of the 1922 Committee with impunity, but if there is trouble a firm reaction from the 1922 can be vital. ... We matter intermittently.'

Obviously, the views of the 1922 Committee are more important when the issues are of medium rank. Even if it wanted to, the 1922 Committee could not reverse a Conservative Government's decision to withdraw from Africa, but it could push a Conservative Government into breaking the BBC's monopoly of television. ... Clearly the 1922 Committee can operate most decisively in those issues where the existence of a Conservative Government is not at risk. ...

As one Member put it, 'When it is working well, the 1922 Committee is the conscience of the Party. If the Government is leading a righteous life, we will not bother it, but a Government or a person who has a continually troublesome conscience will not be much good. On the other hand, a weak conscience is no good to anyone. It is no exaggeration to say that if the 1922 Committee does not have a strong, independent existence of its own, the Party as a whole will suffer.'

As Sir Harry Legge-Bourke noted shortly before ill-health forced him to relinquish the Committee chairmanship on the eve of the Committee's 50th birthday: 'Generally the Executive do not wish to enter into dispute with their Leader. Their object is rather to convey to him matters of great concern to the Party, or to hear from him views and proposals which he would like to test as to their likely effect upon the Party, before final decisions are taken.' The traditional right, therefore, of the Chairman of the 1922 Committee to seek audience with the Leader of the Party is one that it is wise to use sparingly. ... It is only on great issues that these meetings are arranged, and even then much will depend on the relationship of the Chairman and the Chief Whip of the day.

Philip Goodhart (with Ursula Branston), *The 1922: The Story of the Conservative Backbenchers' Parliamentary Committee,* London, 1973, pp. 210–12.

## 2.8 **The Chairman and Executive of the '22**

Considerable influence is wielded by the Chairman and Executive of the 1922 Committee. The latter were customarily drawn from long-serving and steadily unambitious 'knights of the shires', although in recent years elections to the Executive have become a focal point of factional strife. The longest-serving Chairman was Edward du Cann, from 1972 to 1984.

At the beginning of each Parliamentary year the Conservative MPs elect five Officers of the 1922 Committee, including the Chairman, and an Executive of twelve. Whatever the formal minutes of the Committee's proceedings may say, it is generally agreed that the largely unrecorded work of the Executive members has been the foundation of the Committee's success. They are trusted to convey the opinions of their fellow members directly to the Party's leaders, frankly and plainly.

There was an old scurrilous view, known as Walder's Law in memory of a colleague who died some years ago, that the first two or three Members who spoke at the general meetings of the 1922 Committee were invariably mad or drunk. I have never known the latter situation: I have probably experienced the former. However, the Committee does not suffer fools gladly and is unwilling to listen to interventions that are self-serving or unreasonable. ...

If I ever wanted to see her [Thatcher], I was given an immediate appointment. ... whatever I had to say to her on my colleagues behalf was always listened to with patience and careful attention. She did not invariably agree but she took notes, and mostly the advice I gave – either my own or the recommendations of my colleagues – was accepted and acted upon. ...

For most of the time the work of the Chairman of the 1922 Committee is done in private; passing a word of warning to a Minister, acting as a continuous listening post, giving advice to a colleague with problems, subtly exercising discipline in the general interest. The Chairman's ideal physical characteristics are the same today as they were in 1923 – a long nose to sniff out trouble, the oversized ears of a ready listener, a firm hand to deal with the problematical and a boot to apply to the recalcitrant.

Edward du Cann, *Two Lives*, Malvern, 1995, pp. 193, 210, 217.

## 2.9 The MPs: from estate owners to estate agents

First elected in 1959, long-serving backbencher Julian Critchley observed the changing social tone and composition of the Parliamentary Party over the following thirty-five years.

In October 1959, there was still something of 'Chips' Channon about the Tory party. The great pre-war diarist would have felt at home. Today, the Conservative Party in the House contains the party conference of ten years ago. Cheerful girls in hats who once moved conference motions in favour of corporal and capital punishment on behalf of the Young Conservatives of some Midland town, small-town solicitors, garage owners and estate agents with flat, provincial accents, are now among its members. Essex Men selected by Suffolk Women. As Mrs Thatcher (who was returned for Finchley in the same election) went up in the world, so the party came down.

Thirty-five years ago you could tell a Tory just by looking at him. Call the roll in the 1922 Committee and it was all Knight, Frank and Rutley.[4] A Tory MP was well suited. The party still retained something of its pre-war sleekness; elderly gentlemen in Trumper's haircuts, wearing cream silk shirts and dark suits, Brigade or Old Etonian ties. They were all called Charlie; today, they all seem to be called Norman. In those days, everyone appeared to be related to everyone else. ... Michael Heseltine once said to me that he passed for white (the reference was to Tavistock, the seat that he won in 1966), and we were both first-generation public school and Oxford. ...

Tory MPs in the early sixties were lawyers, company directors, *rentiers* and ex-senior officers living on their pensions or their wives' incomes. A few owned land; many were the sons and grandsons of MPs, in Paul Channon's case inheriting directly his father Chips's old Southend seat. ... If Tory MPs were well suited they were also well shod. Double-barrelled Knights of the Shires doubtless had their shoes hand-made. For four days a week the uniform was a dark jacket and striped trousers (very occasionally a dark blue suit); on Friday, Private Members' Day, when government business was not taken, and in consequence the House was thinly attended, the whips wore weekend tweed suits and brown brogues. Not long after my maiden speech I was standing in the crowded 'No' lobby waiting to vote at ten o'clock

4  A prestigious West End firm, noted for handling the sales of landed estates.

on a three-line whip when I glimpsed Sir Jocelyn Lucas ... He grasped my elbow, hissed 'You're wearin' suede shoes' and promptly vanished. He never spoke to me again.

Julian Critchley, *A Bag of Boiled Sweets*, London, 1994, pp. 64, 71–4.

### 2.10 **The rise of the professional politician**

> From the 1970s onwards there was an increasing tendency for the MPs who secured safe seats at a young age, and so had the best prospects of rising to the top, to have had little or no experience of any other walk of life. The combination of arrogance and narrowness which could result was critically observed by other MPs; in this instance by Emma Nicholson, whose growing alienation led her to resign the Conservative whip and join the Liberal Democrats in December 1995.

A new type of would-be candidate began to appear in Central Office and the Research Department, straight out of university, where they had read some politics-related subject. The more aggressive among them immediately got their heads down and fought unscrupulous battles for political preferment, their first objective being appointment as special adviser to a minister. These were relatively new and highly-paid political posts, funded by the Civil Service but existing outside its rules of impartiality and its other terms and conditions. Now numbering thirty-nine, on salaries of over £70,000, they emerged in order that ministers should be supplied with political input – euphemistically termed 'political balance' – rather than relying on impartial advice and information from civil servants. Their weekly meetings were chaired by the head of the Conservative Research Department. The huge attraction of appointment as a special adviser for the politically ambitious is the chance it offers to get close to the scent of real power early in one's career. ... Once ensconced with a minister, however, the key objective is to find a seat and therefore to court approval by adherence to the fashionable Government line of the day. Equipped with the knowledge which they acquire at their minister's elbow, they can make the right points, having developed that special breed of cunning which accompanies the fierce pursuit of personal ambition at an early age.

57

Candidates who come into the party the old-fashioned way, by taking time out of non-political lives, are at a hopeless disadvantage alongside these professional young turks. Too many special advisers never even have to fight a hopeless seat. ...

Somehow, along the line, Thatcher's parliamentary children misplaced their hearts. The struggle to get in fast and rise swiftly to catch the leader's eye was so acute that the idea of serving the wider public interest never really impinged upon them. So keenly was this change of ethos felt by some older members that, for example, Sir Anthony Grant, a former Vice-Chairman for candidates said ... in March 1996 that he would not recommend anyone he knew these days to go into the House of Commons since they would find their colleagues unacceptable as friends. 'I don't like the look of the next Parliament one little bit', he said, 'I think it is going to be full of party political "full-time" horrors.'

Emma Nicholson, *Secret Society: Inside – and Outside – the Conservative Party*, London, 1996, pp. 99–101.

### 2.11 **The procedure for selecting parliamentary candidates**

Local associations jealously guard their autonomy in candidate selection; outside influence has to be circumspect and may be counter-productive, although regional officials play a significant advisory role. The procedure established by the Maxwell-Fyfe Committee's interim report of 1948 has been refined in detail, but not changed in principle or substance.

These rules enable an Association to make a free choice of candidate from the widest possible field. The Association must not regard the candidate or MP as a delegate or as one who is under some financial obligation. ...

The procedure approved by the National Union which should be followed when a vacancy for a parliamentary candidate occurs, is as follows:

1. The Chairman of the Association should first study the Association Rules which govern the processes of selection and adoption and these Rules should conform with the Rules most recently approved by the National Union.

2. The Chairman of the Association should consult the Regional Director for the Area and enlist his assistance. He should ask the Vice or Deputy Chairman of the Party Organisation, through his Regional Director, for a list of potential candidates. The Regional Director or his deputy should be present at all stages of the selection for advice and technical assistance to ensure that the correct procedures are followed.

3. An early meeting of the Selection Committee should be called to acquaint members with the approved procedure and they should be given this booklet to read.

4. The Vice or Deputy Chairman will notify all those included in the [national] list of approved candidates that the Association is about to take action with a view to selecting a candidate. The Association should ensure that its own members also know, and the closing date for applications should be advised.

5. The Vice or Deputy Chairman will submit to the Chairman of the association through the Regional Director a list of approved candidates who have applied to be considered. This list will be accompanied by biographical details. The Chairman of the Association will ensure that the names of any local or direct applicants, who are not on the approved list, are added before the list is submitted to the Selection Committee.

6. At this stage, or later, it is mutually helpful if the Selection Committee Chairman meets with the Party Vice or Deputy Chairman to discuss the position.

7. The Association's Selection Committee will consider all names upon this list. Members should make notes on each candidate including a brief description in order to identify them later. It should be made clear that members of the Selection Committee must be present at all of the interviews in order to be entitled to vote when decisions are made. No substitutions should be permitted. The Committee should invite 16–20 applicants who are considered suitable, to come to the Constituency for interviews. (The number invited may be smaller or greater depending on the number of applicants). Voting should be by ballot.

8. From those interviewed the Selection Committee should choose not less than three (ideally, four to six) to appear before the Executive Council of the Association. The Executive Council will vote by ballot. At each stage it is recommended that reserves are agreed, to ensure a full choice. If the Committee wishes to include an applicant not on the

approved list, then approval must be obtained from the Standing Advisory Committee on Candidates prior to final selection. *Short lists or any other details of the selection procedure should not be made public.*

9. *At least two candidates must be put before a General Meeting of the Association.* The person approved by the General Meeting of the Association becomes the prospective parliamentary candidate for the Constituency.

*Notes on Procedure for the Selection and Adoption of Conservative Parliamentary Candidates in England, Wales and Northern Ireland*, National Union Standing Advisory Committee on Candidates, 1994.

### 2.12 Getting selected

Vacancies for winnable or safe seats attract many applicants, and the selection process can be a rigorous and daunting one. Selection committees often have an image in mind of the sort of candidate they want, and this tends to be white, male, middle-class, and aged around thirty-five. In 1964–70 Kenneth Baker followed the common path of progressing from being the candidate in a hopeless constituency to adoption for a marginal and, finally, a safe seat.

Conservative selection procedures for parliamentary candidates are elaborate and unpredictable ... Each constituency is different: one will be looking for a good local MP to represent its interests, and another will be looking for a potential Minister. But the actual process of determination is a bit of a lottery. One certain favourite lost because he assured the selection committee in an old and famous Home Counties town that he intended to 'put them on the map', whereas they thought they were not only on it already but right at its centre. Another front runner for a large rural seat in Suffolk was rejected when he admitted that he didn't drive. ...

Wives are expected to accompany husband candidates and to undergo their own visual appraisal by the Women's Committee. This applies to husbands of female candidates too. There was a time when wives were asked to say a few words or answer questions – Elspeth Howe had to do this when Geoffrey was adopted for Reigate, and

Mary [Baker] was asked a question at Acton. But now this has been quite rightly stopped. On the whole, selection committees like to adopt a family man, and some unmarried candidates would sometimes acquire a girlfriend or boyfriend, as decorative or homely as they thought the Committee required, and an engagement might or might not follow the selection. ...

[After adoption for St Marylebone in 1970] I discovered why I had won. It wasn't because I had been more eloquent, more witty or dealt with the questions more convincingly. It was because Mary, rather bored with the two-hour wait, had wandered round the building, found some of the Women's Committee washing up the cups and offered to help. Later the Women's Chairman, Pam Bevington, told us that this was what clinched my selection.

Kenneth Baker, *The Turbulent Years*, London, 1993, pp. 24–5, 33.

### 2.13 **Pressing the flesh**

> Since 1945 the increasing demands of constituency casework and the need to keep in the voters' eyes have added to the pressures on prospective candidates and MPs. For those fighting a marginal seat, the approach of an election leaves little time for sleep or relaxation – as this guide compiled by Conservative MPs to help newly adopted candidates makes clear.

Where do you eat *breakfast*? Why not find a different B & B joint every day you are in the constituency, or a workman's cafe. Call them up and say you are coming. Let the press know you will be there discussing the problems facing the small firms – the small neighbourhood cafe – talking to lorry drivers about their problems. It's all newsworthy. ... The place at which you take *lunch* is as important as the place at which you take breakfast. If it is a pub, it is useless unless everybody in the pub knows you are coming, that you are there and who you are. Get somebody to take you round meeting the revellers and the publicans. Make use of that time by talking about de-regulation of licensing hours, asking what people think, issue a press statement, either before or after. ... Make sure *every evening* you are doing things and not just at Branch functions! Your day should be packed with action. ... Use Sundays to recharge the batteries – drafting speeches, press statements and reviewing the week – tho' don't spurn a lunch-time drink in a pub or club – or church services. ... Remember, there is no point in waxing lyrical about the problems of farmers, the problems of inner cities, the Health Service or the schools, unless you have an audience and that audience should not just be committed Tories at a local Branch, unless you can ensure that what you say is reported in the local newspapers. ...

Have you visited: All the homes for the retired and sheltered housing schemes. ... All schools? If time is short, at least those with sixth forms! ... Playgroups? Get a list from the Town Hall. Youth Clubs? ... Luncheon Clubs, Lions, Rotary, Round Table, Soroptomists, W[omen's] I[nstitute], Old People's Clubs, the Church and professional groups? Pubs? Clubs? ... Have you asked the Mayor's office to let you have a list of civic events important enough for the Mayor to be going? Have you contacted the local Council of Churches? ... Doctors' surgeries are often worth a visit especially group practices. You should be a familiar face at local hospitals, child health clinics, etc. Finally, visiting businesses, both large and small, is important. You can supplement them with local branches of CBI, BIM, Business & Professional Women, local Law Society, and other professional and managerial organisations. ...

Shake hands with *everybody*, slap backs (where appropriate), take hold of arms (be gentle with the elderly – their joints hurt), pat shoulders, pat babies, pat dogs, stroke cats, make funny noises to budgerigars. Pressing the flesh is essential in any politician's armoury.

*T.I.P.S. – Tested Ideas for Political Success: The 1974 / 79 / 83 / 87 Members' Group Approach to Constituency Work and Winning Elections*, 4th edition, edited by Anthony Steen, May 1991.

# 3

# The Party organisation

The Conservative Party organisation evolved in the second half of the nineteenth century, adapting since then to changes in the electoral system and in response to defeats. The organisation outside Parliament is divided into two parallel but separate parts. The first of these is the professional staff in the Central Office, the 'Party machine'; the second is the 'rank and file' in the constituency associations. The latter are affiliated to the National Union – the body which holds the annual Party Conference in the autumn, and other gatherings such as the smaller Central Council meeting in the spring of each year. Both Central Office and the National Union have a regional level, and for most of the post-war period England and Wales were divided into twelve (after 1963, eleven) Provincial Areas; Scotland has its own separate structure.

Conservative Central Office is solely responsible to the Leader, who appoints the Chairman of the Party to administer its affairs. Central Office provides a range of services to the leadership and MPs, but its primary role is to win elections and to support the efforts of the local associations. The latter are the foundation upon which all else is built; they jealousy guard their right to autonomy, especially over matters of finance and candidate selection. At local level, the Party has enjoyed strong support in many areas and has been active in organising social events and raising funds. Constituencies aim to afford the services of a full-time trained agent; the professional expertise of the latter has been one of Party's greatest assets, although the number of agents has declined by more than half since 1959. The effectiveness of the Party organisation rests upon two foundations: a large membership in the constituencies, and financial resources very much greater than those possessed by its opponents. However, any complacent sense of superiority was severely shaken in the 1990s, as the steady decline of the membership since the 1950s reached serious levels at the same time as the central Party finances were heavily in deficit, with an overdraft rumoured to be approaching £20 million. In other respects, organisational developments since the post-war revival under Lord Woolton have been of a minor but continual nature. Throughout the period, the Conservatives have often been the pioneers in political organisation and campaigning techniques, and have made innovative use of new technology.

This chapter begins by exploring the basic structure of the organisation and the roles of the Party Chairman, Central Office and the regional Area Agents. The main body of the chapter focuses upon the constituency associations: how they are organised, the role of the local chairmen, the work of the agents, and the fund-raising, social and political activities of the membership. It concludes with the Party Conference, the heyday and decline of the Young Conservatives, and the national Party funds – an area which has always been shrouded in secrecy, and in recent years has been highly controversial.

## 3.1 **The structure of the Party**

After the 1945 defeat a committee under the chairmanship of Sir David Maxwell-Fyfe was appointed to investigate the Party organisation, and its report has been the foundation on which all later modifications have been built. The essential features of the Party organisation which it described have remained the same since the late 1940s.

### 1. THE PROBLEM BEFORE THE COMMITTEE

In our task of examining the Constitution of the Party as a whole we have recognised the need, not so much for a Constitution which seems tidy to the student of political history or logical in all respects, as for an organisation which is an educative political force and a machine for winning elections. A political organisation must be judged by its efficiency in securing victory for the fundamental principles for which the Party stands. The Conservative and Unionist Party should be so constructed that it remains based on the long-prized independence of Constituency Associations, yet has full scope constantly to develop its administrative efficiency. With these ends in view we surveyed the whole structure of the Party with open minds.

## 2. THE THREE ELEMENTS

In its constitution and organisation three elements go to make up the Conservative Party – (a) the Parliamentary Party in both Houses of Parliament, (b) the Conservative and Unionist Associations for each Constituency, organised in the National Union, and (c) the Conservative and Unionist Central Office.

## 3. CONSTITUENCY ASSOCIATIONS

The basis of the Conservative Party is the Constituency Association. Every Association is an autonomous body. It appoints its own Officers, adopts its own Candidate, selects its own Agent and runs its organisation in its own way.

## 4. SUB-DIVISION AND REPRESENTATION OF CONSTITUENCY ASSOCIATIONS

Essential sub-divisions in each Constituency Association are the Ward or Polling District Branches, each having its own Committee and Officers and each being represented on the Central Executive Committee of the Constituency Association. These Branch Associations are careful to preserve their own identity and this individualism is often a source of healthy rivalry within the Constituencies. Each Constituency Association appoints representatives to the Council of the Provincial Area in which it is situated, to the Central Council of the National Union and to the Party Conference.

*Final Report of the Committee on Party Organisation* [Maxwell-Fyfe Committee], approved by the National Union Executive Committee, 20 May 1949, p. 6.

### 3.2 **Democracy and authority in the Conservative Party**

The way in which the Party organisation actually worked is described in this memorandum by one of the members of the Maxwell-Fyfe Committee.

It is sometimes said that the Conservative Party organisation is thoroughly democratic. And so it is on the deliberative or quasi-legislative side. Thus all Branch, Divisional, and Area officers are elected. Resolutions moved and carried at Divisional meetings find their way ultimately to the Annual Conference and if carried by a majority vote of democratically elected representatives are forwarded to the Leader. It is seldom that the Leader fails to take action upon a resolution carried by the Conference without giving overwhelming reasons for rejection or delay.

But on the executive side the Party machine is a curious mixture of authoritarianism and anarchy. Thus the principal officers ... are not elected but appointed by the Leader. The machine which operates under these officers resembles more a broad and general anarchy than a democracy ... there are no obligations or compulsions of any importance laid upon local Associations, whether Area, Divisional, or Branch. Every division is perfectly at liberty to select its own candidate whether at a general or a by-election. Every division selects and pays its Agent, who may or may not be certificated. Except for the annual affiliation fee of £1.1.0 no division is compelled to make any financial contribution at all to Party Headquarters. Even the Chairman of the Party Organisation can do no more than advise or warn. He cannot interfere in the choice of a candidate. Moreover, the chain of responsibility from the Chairman of a Branch or ward up to the Chairman of the Party Organisation is nebulous and ill-defined ...

On the constituency level, our Conservative but anarchical autonomy works well where the Member of Parliament, the Chairman and the Agent for the division are all experienced, enthusiastic, and able to devote sufficient time to their duties. But, apart from other indications, the results of Lord Woolton's appeal for funds have shown quite clearly that all Divisions are not equally well-organised or equally willing to take up their fair share of the burden of providing a Party Organisation adequate for modern conditions.

Memorandum circulated to Maxwell-Fyfe Committee, by Earl Castle Stewart, 6 July 1948, CPA, CCO/500/1/17.


### 3.3 Woolton and the post-war revival

One of the architects of the post-war recovery was Lord Woolton, the popular and successful Chairman of the Party from 1946 to 1955. Woolton's background was in business and he only joined the Conservative Party after the 1945 defeat; when Churchill appointed him Party Chairman a year later, he was at first dismayed by the structure which he found.

The organization of the Conservative Party was the most topsy-like arrangement that I had ever come across. It had grown up amidst conflicting and – it seemed – almost irreconcilable claims. ... I faced up to the fact that whilst as Chairman of the Party I had received an enthusiastic welcome from the associations, I had, on paper, no control over their activities: they selected their candidates; they selected their agent, and employed him; they arranged their meetings, and were at liberty to make direct approach to any speakers they desired. I depended on their goodwill, which obviously they were anxious to give, in the creation of a headquarters staff that would be so efficient in performance and so approachable in manner, that their influence would overcome their lack of authority; I relied on the Central Office earning the goodwill and the confidence of all these diversified bodies which troubled my business instincts; if we could do that, I knew that we should, in the end, find them coming of their own free will into one common organization. ...

I rejected caution and decided to ask for a fund of one million pounds, thereby demonstrating my faith in the willingness of the Party to make sacrifices in order to convince the electors of the country of the rightness of the Conservative approach. These were shock tactics. ... This bold demand created an infectious and compelling enthusiasm. People went out for this apparently unassailable goal, and the stimulation of this widespread effort among all the grades of society of which the Conservative Party is composed not only produced the million pounds that I had asked for, but it gave the Party a sense of accomplishment. Their hopes revived; they found that people believed in them in spite of the recent electoral defeat; they recruited members and workers.

Lord Woolton, *The Memoirs of the Rt. Hon. the Earl of Woolton*, London, 1959, pp. 331, 333, 336–7.

### 3.4 **The role of the Party Chairman**

Lord Carrington, Chairman of the Party during the difficult second half of the Heath government in 1972–74, later gave this description of the Chairman's role.

When our party is in Opposition the Chairman is a particularly important figure in the Shadow Cabinet. He has a high profile. His formal responsibilities may be the same as when the party is in Government but he is the chief builder of morale, the chief planner for the battle to come; and, of course, it will be an attacking battle, with the enemy – the Government – defending a record and able to be depicted as responsible for every disaster, every shortcoming in national life. In these circumstances every senior figure in the party is vitally interested in the plan of attack and the morale of the troops. The party's organization and health is crucial, and the Chairman has a great deal of support – of criticism too, no doubt, but certainly of support. ...

In Government all is different. The main difference derives, naturally, from the preoccupations of ministers with their Departments. ... Inevitably, therefore, in Government they worry less about the Conservative Party; and about its Chairman, or his counsel. The Prime Minister tries to keep the political dimension before his colleagues, but no Prime Minister finds it easy. But the Conservative Party worries about the Government – that is the other side of the coin. ... All this means that in Government the Conservative Party has a great, indeed a greater, need for communication between the leadership and the body of the party, whilst most leading figures have less time, energy and interest to devote to it. Therein lies much of the Chairman's problem. ...

I have also noticed that when the Government and party are going through a bad patch there is generally a tendency to blame lack of communication and ascribe the lack to individual failure. People say, 'I'm sure the Government's doing the right thing but they simply don't explain it properly. They don't put it across to the country. That's why they're not as popular as they should be. In fact it's why they're damnably unpopular! And it's why our morale's low!' I am sceptical of this. ... the hard truth is that if a Government loses popularity it is not primarily from a failure of public relations but because the Government's policies appear to be failing people in what they feel they have a right to expect. ... The country is reported as being disappointed, the media fasten on a Government which appears to have lost its way, and party morale sags.

The Chairman of the party can't do a great deal, but he can do his best to show a cheerfulness he may not feel, he can try to enthuse those about him, he can work to see that the Government's achievements are described as widely and as convincingly as possible – and that the Opposition's promises and criticisms are deflated; and he can use his position in the Cabinet to keep the reactions and mood of the party faithful well before his colleagues in general and the Prime Minister in particular.

Lord Carrington, *Reflect on Things Past*, London, 1988, pp. 257–9, 261–2.

## 3.5 **The limits of control: local autonomy**

Constituency associations are suspicious of any proposals which might erode their jealously guarded autonomy, however worthy the purpose. Central Office has to proceed carefully, as a senior official reminded Woolton over the attempt to bring in a standard pay scale for local agents.

The independence of the Constituency is a fundamental principle of our organisation. It has its disadvantages from the point of view of pure efficiency, but in the complex structure of our voluntary organisation it is probably the right answer, and the Party derives considerable strength and a sense of responsibility from it. The Party instinctively distrusts too great a degree of power at the centre. The position of the Chairman of the Party is that he can advise but cannot give orders. Nor can the National Union. If you or I tried to issue instructions, we could impose no sanctions to enforce them. Nothing would be easier than to split the Party by making the attempt.

'Agents' and Organisers' salaries', Chief Organisation Officer to Party Chairman, 18 May 1954, CPA, CCO/500/2/1.

## 3.6 **Central Office in the 1990s**

Central Office is a professional, centralised establishment directly responsible to the Party Leader. Whilst it supports the work of the constituency associations, they often regard it with mixed feelings, as the consultation exercise for the review of the organisation authorised by Party Chairman Norman Fowler in May 1992 admitted.

The Conservative Party has kept on winning because it has always been prepared to change, when change is needed. Although we have recently enjoyed unprecedented success at the polls, there is a general recognition in the Party that our organisation must once again change so that we can carry forward our record successfully in the future. ... Many of the ideas offered in the review stressed how the effectiveness of the Party's structure and operations could be increased if the various parts of the Party worked more closely together. The review showed that many members of constituency associations, and indeed some in the elected Party, did not fully understand the structure and functions either of Conservative Central Office, or the National Union,[1] except in respect of specific services provided to them. ...

Central Office has grown without a careful review of its main objectives and priorities and indeed no comprehensive reform of its functions has been carried out since the 1930s. The way that its work is done, and the organisation of the departments within it, have therefore not proceeded in accordance with a clear plan. The Conservative Research Department was integrated into Central Office in 1980, a Communications Department was established in 1989, and the Party Treasurers have worked closely with Central Office, but there has not been an integrated management system. The history of the Party organisation contains much success: but it also leaves an impression of unfinished business. ...

Many of the professional support services that Central Office offers to constituencies were commended. Legal advice, publications, campaigning support, training and computer support were all praised. Despite this welcome for the services provided from the centre, there was also a widespread feeling that Central Office was out of touch with constituencies. Part of the problem was a lack of communication. 'Central Office should make clear what help is available – in layman's language', as one Party member put it. It was also felt that the needs of the wider membership were not always understood. One view was that Central Office provided 'excellent briefings, but literature for members is poor'.

Poor co-ordination within Central Office itself, wasteful administration and considerable duplication of effort (for example in mailings to constituencies) were also mentioned: 'there is no point in raising

1    The representative wing of the Party, to which all constituency associations are affiliated.

70

money which is spent on administration, rather than persuading people to vote Conservative'. ... Resources had to be directed to the right
place. One typical comment was that 'good associations do not need
more help: Central Office should concentrate more on marginals and
weak associations'. The role of Area Offices was poorly understood,
and it was felt by many that they could make a greater contribution to
the Party. ... Decision-making at Central Office should be more open
to scrutiny. ...

MPs were pleased with the support they received from the Conservative Research Department, which was often their principal point
of contact with the Party organisation. Publications were seen as useful, accurate and timely. Election material was 'effective', as were the
day-to-day Parliamentary briefs. Equally the work of the Campaigning Department was seen as professional, and responsive to the needs
of those in the constituencies.

However, Central Office was criticised for being overmanned, with
a lack of financial management. There was an absence of clear lines
of authority, and the management structure was described by one MP
as 'Byzantine'. Another said that Central Office 'uses people very
badly'.

*One Party: Reforming the Conservative Party Organisation*, report of
the Review committee, Conservative Central Office, February 1993.

### 3.7 **The regional level**

On both the voluntary and professional sides of the Party
organisation, the regional level provides an important link
between the constituencies and the centre. England and Wales
were divided into 'Areas' (eleven to twelve in the post-war
era, renamed as 'Regions' and reduced to seven in 1993). Each
of these has its own elected chairman, officers and committees,
and in each there is a small staff of Area Agents. The latter
had duties in the Area, but were directly employed by Central
Office.

Each Area contains its own branch of Conservative Central Office –
often in buildings of extreme dilapidation. ... The staffing of the offices
varies with the size of the Area. Each is headed by the C[entral] O[ffice]

Agent whose powers are considerable but mostly undefined. ... Most C.O. Agents can go a long way to becoming the 'managing director' of the Area by the judicious use of pressure and the funds which an Area has at its disposal. In relation to the rest of the Area staff the C.O. Agent has true management powers (though not, it is important to remember, over the voluntary organisations they service). Most Areas have a single Deputy C.O. Agent, who is virtually always a woman. Her major jobs apart from being No. 2 are: (i) to service the Women's organisation in the Area; and (ii) to organise the Area Speakers Panel. ... All areas but one (Western Area), including Scotland, have a full-time C.P.C.[2] Officer. He is broadly responsible for political education in the Area, but in practice his field is virtually limitless. ... Every Area has a Young Conservative Organiser ... Most Areas have a Public Relations Officer ... All Areas have an Industrial Organiser.[3] ...

The purpose[s] of the Area Organisation ... are:

(a) Advisory – to express the collective views of the Party in the Area.

(b) Executive –

(i) to utilise the financial and other resources of the Area in the best interests of the constituencies.

(ii) to organise on an Area level such activities as will assist the constituencies to improve their organisation.

It is important to note that only in its advisory capacity is the Area expected to act in its own right.

In practice, however, the Area has achieved considerably more dynamic executive functions as a result of the Party's financial structure. Constituency autonomy is the great theoretical pillar of the Conservative Party. Nevertheless constituencies tend to be only truly autonomous to the extent to which they are financially independent, and a very large number of them are in fact dependent in one way or another on outside funds. This is not merely a question of cash grants to hopeless seats. Even constituencies with solid Tory majorities get into financial trouble, and require either loans or guarantees for loans.

The Areas are in fact the units of organisation with the responsibility for such financial matters. All grants to constituencies from Central Party funds are channelled through the Areas, and all Areas have

2   Conservative Political Centre, the education and political discussion wing.
3   Servicing the organisation for Conservative Trade Unionists.

funds at their disposal guaranteed by the Centre. This means that in administering the 'financial resources of the Area in the best interests of the constituencies' it is the Area organisation (in effect the Executive and the C.O. Agent) who decide what those interests are.

The second executive function, 'to assist constituencies to improve their organisation', also conceals a complex situation. There is a continuous cat-and-mouse game between the Area (the Area Executive and the Area Office, implementing decisions taken at National level) and the constituencies as to what constitutes 'improving the organisation'. C.P.C. Officers, Y.C. Organisers and Industrial Organisers spend a vast amount of time persuading constituencies to establish discussion groups, new branches and D.C.T.U.s[4] (now T.U. Committees). The growth of C.P.C. committees over the last two years in the face of apathy or open hostility ('we don't need a lot of long-haired intellectuals') provides an excellent case study of the game. ...

One of the features of the Party organisation that becomes quite clear on close examination is that, on the voluntary side, it is in fact two organisations. There is the chain of representation and communication which runs: branch–constituency–Area–National Executive. And there is the older structure (based on the idea of the Party as a grouping of independent constituency associations) which runs: branch–constituency + city association–Central Council. The second chain is of less importance than the first. On the other hand, it weakens the structure of the Area *vis à vis* both the constituencies and the city associations. The lines of communication and advice are blurred.

'Reforming the Area structure', Central Office internal memorandum, January 1967, CPA, CCO/4/10/4.

## 3.8 Constituency associations: (i) organisation

The vital element in the Conservative organisation is the constituency association. It is this which recruits members, organises fund-raising and provides volunteer workers for local and parliamentary elections. Although membership has steadily declined, the structure of local associations has changed little in the post-war period, and is generally similar to that set out

4    Divisional Council of Trade Unionists.

in the Colyton Committee's report on the Party organisation in 1957.

We consider the essential organs for the democratic control and administration of a constituency association are:

(i) An Executive Council or Committee

(ii) A Finance and General Purposes Committee

(iii) A Women's Advisory Committee

(iv) A Young Conservative Advisory Committee

(v) A Divisional Council of Trade Unionists

Political Education Committees, and where Local Government is fought on Party lines, Local Government Committees, are considered to be highly desirable in every constituency organisation.

(i) *Executive Council or Committee*

Ideally, this should be a consultative body broadly-based to include the representation of all aspects of Conservative activity in the constituency. *Its principal functions* should be:

(a) To provide a 'platform' for the MP or candidate.

(b) To provide a forum for the expression of opinion, and discussion of matters of policy.

(c) To be the launching ground for centrally-organised activities such as membership campaigns, money-raising schemes, mutual aid,[5] election preparations, etc.

(d) To elect the F. & G.P. and Advisory Committees, to delegate to them powers and duties, and to receive reports from these Committees.

(e) To consider suggested alterations of rules before submission to a general meeting of members.

The Membership of the Executive Council or Committee should include the Officers of the Association, and of all constituency advisory committees; representatives of the polling district or ward branches, the Clubs and other Conservative interests.

*Meetings.* In our view the Executive Council or Committee should normally meet twice a year, with provision for the calling of special meetings if the necessity arises. It is undesirable that the Executive should be encouraged to undertake administrative duties,

---

5   Schemes by which strong constituencies send workers to help designated marginal or weak seats.

which are more efficiently performed by the Finance and General Purposes Committee.

(ii) *Finance and General Purposes Committee*
We are of the opinion that this Committee should be responsible for the normal administration of the Association.

*Membership* should include the Officers of the Association, the Chairman, or a Deputy, of the Women's and Young Conservatives Advisory Committees, and of the Divisional Council of Conservative Trade Unionists, together with about twelve members elected by the Executive Committee on a ward basis, in the case of boroughs, or a 'district' basis in the county constituencies. The Committee should have a limited power of co-option.

*Meetings*. The effective control of Association affairs may well demand a monthly meeting of this Committee. ...

(iii) *Advisory Committees*
The term 'advisory' appears to be interpreted in practice as 'executive within its own sphere'. ... We wish to emphasise that there is very wide scope for recruiting to these Committees people with particular aptitude or qualifications, who have no interest in general constituency work, but who might well be persuaded to help with a specific activity for which they have the talent and inclination. This effort to 'spread the load' should be a priority in every constituency. There is evidence that too few, and often unsuitable, people serve on too many committees. ...

'Report of the [Colyton] Committee on the Party organisation', 1957, CPA, CCO/500/2/1.

### 3.9 Constituency associations: (ii) limitations

Since the late 1950s changes in social structure, patterns of work and leisure, and the role of the media have steadily undermined the position of the local associations. Membership has declined from the post-war peak of 2.8 million in 1952 to below 300,000 by 1997. The concerns raised in this trenchant internal memorandum by Party Vice-Chairman Sara Morrison in 1971 have remained the constant themes of the last three decades, but no solutions have been found.

## THE PARTY ORGANISATION IN CONSTITUENCIES

When the structural pattern first developed the chief vehicles for communication were political meetings (which then drew large audiences) and the canvass (electorates were smaller, so was the percentage actually voting). The organisation is still based on these two means of communication and what has really happened is that it has failed to adapt to changes brought about by the mass media and the big increase in the voting electorate. It has also ignored the social revolution and draws its leaders and Party workers almost exclusively from the middle class. It simply is not in touch with the new meritocracy or the younger generation at all.

*What the constituency organisation does*
It runs a branch system dominated by middle class voluntary helpers which partially covers the electorate to collect subscriptions and appeal for support at elections.

It raises sufficient money to pay agent, running expenses of the office and, in most cases, part only of the quota.[6] *Most of the agent's time and energy goes on raising this income.*

Only a nominal amount is spent on publicity and propaganda.

At general elections it canvasses an average of about 65% of the electorate.

It runs a reasonably efficient local government election campaign but the candidates are chosen from its own circle of members and/or their friends.

It runs a polling day organisation to get out pledged supporters with reasonable success.

It maintains a reasonably good contact with the local press.

It collects postal votes better than our opponents, though not as good as it could be.

*What the constituency organisation doesn't do*
It does not spread the 'charmed circle' of local leaders outside its own middle class elite.

It is not in touch with the new meritocracy or the younger generation and is quite unable to talk or write in language which either understands – it just doesn't communicate with them at all.

It ignores population changes as far as it possibly can. New hous-

6    A payment by each constituency to central Party funds, calculated according to the Conservative vote.

ing estates are usually left alone by the existing branch and have to be tackled as a separate job.

It plays virtually no part in publicity and propaganda except for a very small literature distribution and letter writing to the local press.

It does very little to make the candidate known outside the 'charmed circle' – in fact it often hinders by demanding his constant attendance at association and branch functions at which he only meets confirmed supporters. Occasionally it will help him by providing small teams of canvassers to go round with him between elections.

It fails to brief effectively its officers and canvassers on the Conservative case. Few see the literature and only a tiny percentage attend briefing meetings or conferences.

'The Conservative Party – communication', memorandum by Morrison, 15 November 1971, CPA, CCO/20/7/13.

### 3.10 **The constituency chairman**

The constituency association chairman (the term used, although since the 1960s the proportion of women has greatly increased) is the most important figure at local level. In this pamphlet an experienced local and regional chairman offers some practical advice.

A wise old Agent once said to me, 'If you try to be liked by everyone you will end up being liked by no-one.' He stressed that the only true yardstick for a Chairman was whether you were able to command respect, both as a person and for the job you were doing. Remember, a simple rule to apply is: a Chairman may on occasions delegate his *authority* but his *responsibility* – NEVER. The Buck definitely stops here. ...

YOUR AGENT. He/she has been professionally trained and is responsible for the organisation in the constituency; he acts as secretary to the Association and plays a major role in all elections ... He will be of invaluable assistance to you as Chairman and the relationship between you and your Agent must be one of the *utmost faith in each other*. You must both 'stand back to back and deal with all comers'. Remember – Chairmen come and go but Agents as a profession stay on forever. Most Agents have seen them all – good, bad and indifferent. Support your Agent when necessary and never put him in a situation where you drop him in it! You will find that this stimulates friendly reciprocation on his part. Wholly independent action on your part will ruin this relationship. ...

WARD OR BRANCH CHAIRMEN. Most Ward Chairmen are a little possessive about their 'patch' and can become rather 'touchy' about any outside interference. It is advisable never to get involved in the affairs of a Ward Committee without the knowledge of the Ward Chairman. If you want to get across a message of any kind to a Ward Committee, explain the facts to the Chairman beforehand – win him over if necessary. A Ward Chairman who does not feel 'consulted' can hinder your objective in a courteously obstructive manner. ...

COUNCILLORS. It is quite ludicrous the extent to which some of our [local government] Councillors imagine, upon election, that they have been raised to a higher place from which they can look down upon the lesser mortals in their Association. Too often Conservative policy is ignored and the Party treated merely as a vehicle for ensuring their re-election at regular and dependable intervals. ...

RESOLUTIONS. Those passed by Wards or Branches should always be submitted to your Executive Council. Resolutions passed by your association would normally be sent to your Area Office. The Area Executive Committee considers these and may forward them with comments to the Secretary of the National Union. However, do exercise discretion in the passing of Resolutions. It is easy enough for Associations to pass these. The trouble with Resolutions, however, is that you have to do something with them! Any Association which constantly passes Resolutions for onward transmission is in danger of debasing the coinage of its credibility in this respect. When you feel it is really necessary, do so, but ensure it is carefully worded, never intemperate, so that you as Chairman of your Association could speak in support of it at Area level with conviction and without embarrassment.

YOUR MP ... In general terms I have found that having worked to elect a Member, he or she should be left to get on with the job. A Member may decide, from time to time, to tell the Chairman why he has taken a particular stance, and it is essential that there is a two-way channel of communication between them so that the Chairman

78

can discuss political feelings in the constituency with the Member. ...
A Member of Parliament or Candidate is, of course, part of the Association, but should always be kept apart and regarded as something special.

Sir Ian McLeod, *Chairman at Large*, Conservative Central Office, c.1989.

### 3.11 **The local constituency agent**

The burden of organisational work at local level is carried by the full-time professional agent. Although the number of these has fallen by more than half, from 506 in 1959 to 230 in 1994, the Conservatives have always remained far stronger than their rivals. This review by the Chief Organisation Officer at Central Office dates from the early 1960s, but provides a good picture of the post-war period as a whole.

Broadly speaking, there are three sources of recruitment:

(i) Young Conservatives, or office clerks in constituencies, who are attracted by the life and enter into it young. This is the best source.

(ii) Failures in other walks of life. It should be noted that these gentlemen by no means always turn out badly.

(iii) Retired persons from the Services and the Civil Service. These are few ... Nor indeed are they by any means the most desirable recruits whatever may be thought about their abilities, since the vast majority of them wish to live and work in 'Bournemouth'. In this connection, it should be emphasised that it is most undesirable to train agents for any particular part of England. It has been our custom always to demand mobility as a condition precedent of entering the profession. ...

There are really three avenues of promotion in the agents' profession. The first is from a poorly paying constituency to a well paying constituency. Secondly from an ordinary constituency to a City agency (which may be the best paid positions in the party) and thirdly to the Central Office staff. ...

The standard of agents is a very difficult thing to comment on. The agent's job is a peculiar one. It demands not only long hours and a devotion to the job, but some peculiar quality which the best of men and women may not possess. He or she must be prepared to reconcile

79

the irreconcilables, to conduct the business of their association in accordance with the sensible principles which they have been taught and with the advice that they receive, very often reconciling this, at the same time, with the personality and sometimes uninformed opinions of the chairman and committees under whom they serve. It is a job which requires a great deal of tact and moreover it demands a great deal of energy, having in mind that there is nobody really to kick the agent. ... It demands, therefore, a very conscientious man with a flair for public relations and a capacity for getting on with all sorts of people. ...

The Conservative Party is a large body which has many checks and balances, until it is very difficult to know where the true power lies at any particular moment. What is true of the whole is true of the part. Some agents who by nature have a strong will, clear sight and the necessary qualities of leadership, obtain a large measure of control over their association so that, in fact, the chairman, however eminent in other walks of life, is content to leave the conduct of everyday affairs to the agent. Some agents do not attain this standard and are unwilling to take any step without authority to do so. Others in the lowest grade become mere office boys and minute writers and are ineffective efficiently to perform their real job.

The ideal, of course, as always, lies between these extremes, and the agent who is a good agent is a man who knows his mind, is willing to advise his chairman, if necessary in strong terms, but who in the end is a servant of the association. It is as well to remember that he is subject to a further pressure which will, we hope, always be exerted for the best. It is the pressure which is put upon him by his 'Brigadier', the Central Office [Area] Agent, who himself is in the unique position of receiving orders without being able to give them. The constituency, being autonomous and the agent being the servant of the constituency, the Central Office Agent, however good the cause, in the end cannot superimpose his will on the constituency or its agent and can only advise, and his influence will depend on his own personality. The wise agent is the one who listens to the Central Office Agent's advice, applies it in the correct way to his own circumstances in his own constituency, and persuades his constituency officers to accept it if he thinks it wise. In practice, though this may in theory seem an extremely loose system, it works well. It depends, of course, very largely on the personality of the constituency agent and the Central Office Agent, but on the whole we have little to complain about.

'Some notes on the Agents of the Conservative Party', memorandum by Bagnall, 7 December 1962, CPA, CCO/500/2/4.

### 3.12 **The work of an agent**

The work of an agent is described by Nancy Matthews, who worked for the Party for more than forty years from the late 1940s in the difficult territory of South Yorkshire.

Early in January annual accounts must be completed, petty cash and post books balanced and closed, and annual reports written. ... An agent is also the Secretary of the Association ... It was part of an agent's job to advise on good replacements for retiring officers within his own constituency and to ensure that, should more than one nomination be received, a secret ballot was conducted fairly. Annual General Meetings were the events of the year ...

It was important for an agent to maintain a good relationship with the media at all times, feeding them with information slanted at an original angle to make the stories more print-worthy. ...

The new Executive Committee would meet and prepare plans for the ensuing year. The agent was responsible for sending out notices convening these meetings, taking minutes and putting decisions made into effect. ... plans [were] set in motion for very necessary money-raising events during the following twelve months. It was advisable to form special Sub-Committees to deal with these otherwise far too much time could be wasted thrashing out who would provide the milk, tea or sugar, make scones for a coffee morning, or give the raffle prizes at a cocktail party. The politically motivated, whilst willing to admit the necessity for raising cash, might gradually drift away. How to combine both aspects of the work was a continual problem which the agent, who was primarily responsible, found hard to solve. All types of events were organised in all sizes and shapes of houses willingly offered on Tory behalf: dinners, coffee mornings, wine and cheese parties, home-made slide shows, cocktail parties and ploughman's lunches. ... Other efforts would be held in hired halls – continental evenings, jumble sales, bazaars or dances, and it was part of my job to motivate people to organise such events. ...

Undoubtedly being a Conservative agent should be looked upon as a vocation, not just a job at any price. Like a doctor or a parson he or

she should be prepared to be called upon at any time, politely to receive telephone messages at home late at night, happily to make sudden visits to solve constituents' problems, or tactfully to placate
indignant visitors to the office who come complaining about aspects
of Conservative policy just as the agent hoped to escape for a quick
sandwich!

Nancy Matthews, *Trek onto Tomorrow*, Rotherham, 1980, pp. 207–19.

### 3.13 **Raising the money**

Constituency associations are responsible for raising their own
funds. Since the Maxwell-Fyfe reforms of 1948–49, contributions from the candidate or MP have been restricted to a very
small amount. Associations are also expected to provide the
candidate's expenses in parliamentary elections and to pay a
'quota' contribution to national Party funds, though many
fail to pay all – or, increasingly, any – of the latter.

WHY MONEY IS NEEDED – AND HOW MUCH
An association's first responsibility is to see that all its known supporters are properly registered and able to vote if they are eligible.
Much detailed work goes into this. ... Changes in the organisation of
local government have increased both the extent to which the political parties are involved in contesting these elections and the cost that
falls upon them. Presenting the Party's approach to local issues and
supporting candidates with sound organisation and modern election
techniques may cost a constituency association as much as £1,000 a
year – in some circumstances more.

Adopting a parliamentary candidate, helping him to explain the
Party's policy and putting its case to the public is the association's
primary task – and propaganda material costs money. The day comes
when the candidate has to fight an election costing the average association £1,500 or more should the legal limit be increased.

A typical constituency association may have to administer 30 to 35
branches, covering an electorate of 60,000 spread over more than
200 square miles. ...

Requirements may be summarised as follows:

*Administration*

| | | |
|---|---|---|
| Agent: salary, state insurance, super-annuation, car and expense allowances | £5,000 | |
| Clerical: wages, state insurance | £1,800 | |
| Party Central Fund (quota) | £1,200 | |
| Rent, rates, heating, lighting, cleaning | £800 | |
| General administrative expenses | £300 | |
| Postages, telephones | £600 | £9,700 |

*Political Activities*

| | | |
|---|---|---|
| Local Elections | £1,000 | |
| Literature, printing, stationery, publicity | £1,500 | £2,500 |
| *Provision: contingencies* | £300 | £12,500 |

Clearly some of the figures shown above – e.g. salaries, quota, rents – will vary according to circumstances and locality but, whatever may be the total amount required, raising it is wholly the responsibility of the association. *No provision is made for the expenses of Parliamentary elections because a well-organised association will raise the cost by means of a special election appeal. ...*

HOW THE MONEY IS RAISED

There are four main sources:

Membership subscriptions and contributions

bazaars, fetes, social activities

small lotteries, draws and sweepstakes

special appeals (parliamentary elections, etc.)

The strength of a constituency association stems from its membership. ... It is not enough to have only subscribers; a strong body of men and women helpers from all walks of life, sustained by the support of many others participating in its affairs, is the only sure foundation for a financially and politically successful association. This is primarily a branch commitment since subscribers direct to the centre will probably not exceed one-fifth of the total membership and they are automatically also members of the branches where they reside. There should be no minimum or maximum subscription but regard must be had to the cost of 'servicing' each membership ...

*Bazaars, fetes, social activities.* While these events can be run primarily to raise money, they also keep the association in the public eye and often provide a platform for the Member of Parliament or Party front bench speakers. They are valuable, too, in keeping Party workers together, exercising them between elections, and holding the interest of supporters less inclined to take part in more serious day-to-day political activities. ... Sweepstakes and lotteries should not be regarded as a main source of income but they can be used from time to time ...

*Special Appeals.* Appeals for 'Fighting Funds' are a major source of income, especially when made at the time of a general election or by-election ... Otherwise, special appeals, e.g. for funds for the acquisition of property or equipment, should be resorted to only sparingly; it is better to build up a regular and sufficient income backed by adequate, though not excessive, reserves.

*Constituency Finance: Guide for Association and Branch Officers*, Organisation Series pamphlet, Conservative Central Office, 1977 edition.

### 3.14 The reality in the constituencies

The professionalism of Central Office, better financial resources and a large mass membership made the Conservative organisation the envy of its opponents. In reality, many constituencies struggled to make ends meet, and the 'well-oiled machine' looked very different from the inside.

The Conservative Party claims to be the only truly modern party, the party *par excellence* of competitive enterprise, of business, of initiative. We say this; we believe it; but no-one would imagine it who walked into almost any of our constituency headquarters from one end of the country to the other. Let us admit it: we have tolerated, we have been ready to accept without question, a level of functioning for our party organisation which no management of a business enterprise would tolerate for an instant. Yet we all know that the future of enterprise itself in this country is bound up with the cause which for the outside observer in many constituencies is represented by a couple of dowdy rooms and an ill-paid Agent. The paradox is laughable. ... Whilst the value of money has fallen, constituency budgets have remained at approximately constant levels for years, sometimes for decades. ... How can a party with its paint peeling off persuade people that it is selling them a prosperous future?

Wolverhampton South-West Conservative Association, AGM, 18 December 1964, speech by Enoch Powell MP, CPA, CCO/4/9/46.

## 3.15 **The role of women**

Although there has been an increasing proportion of women association chairmen in recent years, the common pattern at constituency level was that whilst women provided most of the membership and did most of the fund-raising, the key positions and most important decisions remained in the hands of the men. As an experienced Central Office woman organiser warned in this article in the local agents' monthly journal, the resulting sense of 'separate spheres' was a source of friction and diminished effectiveness.

The part women play in the constituencies varies enormously, being largely determined by the structure of their organisation, local tradition and geography. At one end of the scale is the small group of women meeting to play whist and, at election times, to address envelopes. At the other end stands the vast, well organised women's association, largely independent, raising its own funds and employing its own organiser. Whatever size or structure it is important that women should accept their full share of responsibility for the affairs of the constituency associations. Sometimes a tendency creeps in for them to be treated as a separate body, functioning independently, which can be called upon by the constituency association as a special rescue at times of financial or administrative stress. Some of us may be familiar with a traditional ceremony at some annual meetings – the constituency Chairman thanks the women for their rescue efforts 'I do not know where we should be without the ladies.' Heads nod vigorously and the thanks are graciously, perhaps a trifle condescendingly, accepted. The Chairman thinks privately that he has done his stuff, but the ladies' thoughts run on different lines. They are almost certainly thinking how inefficient 'the men' (they mean the association) are.

This attitude is unfortunate. Not only is it incorrect but it may have a braking effect on future effort. 'Why should we do any more, it's time "the men" did something'. The women members are as much a part of the constituency association as the men or Young Conservatives. ...

There is so much potential energy and ability here, that it is a great pity if the women's organisation is allowed to devote its time entirely to social and money-raising activities, with possibly a little desultory collecting from members. They will not give of their best unless there is a correct balance between the three main fields of Conservative party organisation – membership, politics and money-raising.

Membership is the foundation on which all our organisation rests. It is a direct measure of the success and efficiency of the organisation unit. If a branch reports falling membership and a dearth of voluntary helpers, we should see the red light. It is easy to convince ourselves that nothing more can be done and to blame outside factors, lack of leisure, married women going out to work, etc. How many branches really cover their areas, apart from the annual collection of existing subscriptions and a partial canvass at the local elections? ...

For a long time it was believed that women were fundamentally uninterested in politics. However true it may have been when women first entered political organisation, it is certainly not so today. Better education and television have combined to make women, particularly the younger ones, comparatively well informed politically. They are less inclined to enjoy being a captive audience, listening to words of wisdom expounded from the platform of a draughty hall. Brains trusts and forums, any type of meeting in which the audience takes an active part, are more popular. So are discussion groups ...

Money raising is traditionally a field in which women excel. They are experienced and good at it. The chief dangers here are that too much energy is expended on repetitive efforts which bring in diminishing profits and a tendency to rely on the support of a comparatively small circle of people, who are constantly 'milked' for gifts and donations. Here again, we should encourage flexibility and a willingness to experiment; the planning of different types of functions to appeal to different sections of the community, giving old favourites a new look and above all the widening of the support and interest.

Joan Varley, 'No "Lady Bountifuls": the way to an efficient Women's Organisation', *Conservative Agents' Journal*, January 1966.

### 3.16 A sociable party

The atmosphere of a typical local event, more social than political, is described by a journalist who visited a wide range of Conservative gatherings around the country in 1990. A particular feature is the ageing of the membership: by the early 1990s the average age had reached sixty-two.

86

The annual lunch of the West Dorset Conservative Women's Constituency Committee ... Bustling everywhere, briskly solicitous, smart but homely, supremely confident, the younger ones (the under-70s) run an event that, were it not a voluntary fund-raising affair, would require a substantial catering staff and up to a dozen waiters. Most of the 140 guests have parked behind Beaminster Public Hall, just off the High Street of this elegant small town, on a chilly November day. A herd of blue rinses converges on the hall ... As they hand in their tickets, or pay their five pounds, there is much clutching of elbows both in friendship and physical support, and enquiries about one another's health. Purses are retrieved for the purchase of raffle tickets. The amiable jostle spreads into the body of the hall. ... the ladies themselves look dowdy. The prevailing dress style is sensible, not fashionable (village halls can be draughty). Tweed is the favoured material, and there are only occasional splashes of Tory blue amid a forest of green and brown. ... There is precious little talk of politics. Apart from concern over those whose sons or grandsons are at risk in the Gulf, the conversation is much the same as it would be at a meeting of the Women's Institute. Indeed, many of those present belong to that body also, and forget from time to time under whose auspices they are meeting.

The elegant Dame Janet [Fookes MP] then says her bit ... She fields two gentle questions, both of which come from men, although they are outnumbered about 20 to one. No female hand is raised. ... Then comes the raffle, drawn by Dame Janet. No very exciting prizes – bottles of wine, baskets of fruit, a wall-clock – but 10 of them, all donated. As each winner claims her prize, there is a moment of shyness, then smiles and applause. Finally there are words of thanks to everyone involved ... Then speakers, prize-winners and cooks melt back into the warm embrace of the company, and everyone is ready to go home, strengthened by this ritual.

Come the reckoning a few days later, and it is clear the lunch has been a great success. Net profit will be something over £700. The raffle made £147, the bar made £86, and the rest came from the sale of tickets. The most expensive item was the lamb for the stew, which cost £90; hire of the hall was a mere £43.

The Beaminster CWCC lunch was a major fund-raising effort, one which had taken weeks of preparation. The general run of coffee mornings, whist drives, raffles, fetes and lunches that keep the party ticking over throughout the year are more humdrum affairs, but they have much of the same busy, friendly, informal and almost entirely non-political atmosphere. Informal, but always dignified. They raise money which helps towards every association's quota – the sum the local party is expected to forward to Central Office every year. They fulfil other functions, too. They bring people together, and reward the helpers who work for the party not only at election time, but at certain times every year, putting newsletters in envelopes, collecting subscriptions, making phone calls and running errands. They also reassure everyone that the old order changeth as little as possible.

R. Morris, *Tories: From Village Hall to Westminster*, Edinburgh, 1991, pp. 42–5.

### 3.17 **Helping the marginals**

The Conservative Party's superior local network enables it to tackle the problem of being strongest where it needs it least – in the safe seats, where majorities are not counted but weighed. These associations have the largest memberships and the most money, and attract the best agents by offering well-paid and secure employment. In order to bring these resources to bear in the marginals, where elections are won or lost, a sophisticated system of 'mutual aid' has been developed.

The first priority of the Party organisation must be to win elections both parliamentary and local. Obviously it is good sense to concentrate helpers in the polling districts and constituencies which are marginal, in order to hold them if they are already represented by a Conservative or to win them if they are held by an opponent. This means asking voluntary helpers to leave their home district and work in another, either in their own constituency or a neighbouring one. ...

At parliamentary elections more elaborate organisation is needed since the mutual aid volunteers may have to come considerable distances to work in a constituency about which they may know very little. They will be working on unfamiliar ground and probably know none of the local helpers personally. Each constituency has its own election methods and the details can vary greatly which is confusing for workers. ... A good deal of planning is necessary since large numbers of people have to be directed from safe or well-organised constituencies to the marginal ones. This is the responsibility of the Central Office Agent for the area in which the constituencies are situated. He should call a meeting of the constituencies involved at which the help required and the help available can be ascertained and planned. ...

Mutual aid should be started well before an election is expected and the closer the volunteers can be identified with the work in the marginal constituency the more effective will be their help during the actual campaign. If possible a social function should be arranged at which helpers from both constituencies can meet and get to know each other. Where the visitors are prepared to take a wider interest, they can be encouraged to help with the constituency's general organisation of social and money-raising functions, such as fetes, bring and buy sales, etc. They can, if it is practicable, be invited to take over the organisation of a district in which no branch exists.

*The Voluntary Helper and the Party Organisation*, Organisation Series pamphlet, Conservative Central Office, 1975 edition.

### 3.18 **Television and social change**

By the early 1960s it was apparent that affluence, education, wider leisure opportunities and changing social attitudes would require new methods of political campaigning.

There have been important changes in national life. Many of them – not least the higher standard of education in the electorate – must affect certain aspects of Party work and policy. Not enough has been done in the Party organisation to meet these changes. ... We must attract increasing numbers of young people to our ranks if we are to remain in office. ...

Television, for all the criticism levelled against it, does succeed in 'opening windows': awakening the yearning for more knowledge in a million questioning minds. Never let us forget this growing demand for more and higher education, and having acknowledged the wonderful progress made in this field already, let us not overlook the increasing effect this has on the electorate's reaction to old-style political pronouncements. Herein lies the underlying reason for the popular demand for 'straight-talking'. Don't let us delude ourselves. 'They' understand far more than 'they' used to in the old days – and by this we mean the broad mass of voters now exposed to the mind-opening challenge of TV interviews and commentaries.

'Report of the National Advisory Committee on Publicity and Speakers', June 1962, CPA, CCO/120/4/2.

### 3.19 Using new technology

The Conservative Party has been notable for its resilience and adaptability. The effects of social change have often been met by new methods of propaganda and fund-raising, such as targeted direct mail and telephone canvassing. Another innovation during the 1980s and 1990s was the increasing use of computers at constituency level organisation, although this brought both advantages and disadvantages.

There are now as many computer systems installed in Association offices as there are agents, perhaps this is the time to reflect on the changes that have happened and are likely to happen in the future. Even to the casual observer it is evident that not only has there been a revolution in computer technology in the past few years, there also have been major changes in the role of the agent and changes in the work of the volunteers. ...

For most associations without computers the work of collecting membership subscriptions, preparing newsletters and organising election campaigns is usually shared between the office and the branches. With the introduction of computers the trend has been to centralise this work. As a result the branches become less involved, and the 'grass roots' effort withers whilst the agents become data processing managers.

Evidence of this change is perhaps that although most Associations have seen an increase in membership subscriptions since computerisation, many have also experienced a decrease in membership numbers. This fall-off in numbers could be due to the fact that branches have, in the past, been 'optimistic' in their assessment of numbers. More likely is that once subs are being collected by direct mail the branch volunteer is all too ready to give up visiting members and encouraging the more reluctant ones to part with their cash. ...

The Party organisation

It is becoming apparent that to make the best use of the electoral roll more detailed and personal information needs to be collected so that groups of voters may be effectively targeted. The current approach to targeting voters is to direct-mail a standard letter. ... By collecting detailed information at grass roots the potential to target groups of constituents is greatly enhanced.

Roger Pyne, 'The future of computing in Conservative associations', *Conservative Agents' Journal*, Autumn 1990.

## 3.20 The Party Conference

This perhaps idealised account of the Annual Conference was provided by an unnamed Central Office official in the mid-1950s.

... each constituency is entitled to send seven representatives. Of these, two must be women, two members of the Young Conservative organization and one a trade unionist. A conference packed with local big-wigs is not desired, and is impossible under this provision. The MPs, candidates and Tory peers present form a relatively small minority. The majority of these rank-and-file Conservatives are people of modest income. ... No representative is tied to any action. In no sense is he a delegate bound to vote according to instructions. Such a principle, Conservatives think, would render impossible the freedom of criticism, constructive or otherwise, essential to a true democracy. Arising from the same principle, constituencies are free to submit any resolutions which they wish to bring before the Conference. ...

A preliminary notice is sent to each Constituency Association in May, formally announcing the next October's Conference, detailing the entitlement to representation and asking for names and addresses. Associations are also informed at that time that all notices of motion for the agenda must be in by mid-August. After that the General Purposes Committee proceeds to examine and arrange – but never to alter – the hundreds of motions received and to draw up its 100-page agenda.

Two months later the Tory Conference will be over. Four thousand Conservatives will have met, in and out of the Conference halls, debated and exchanged ideas and dispersed. They will have harangued their leaders far more than their leaders will have harangued them. They will have told their leaders and each other what Conservatives throughout Britain are thinking and wanting. That – however idealistic it may seem – is the aim of the Conference. That – however hard to believe – is what really happens.

'Conservatives in Conference', *Parliamentary Affairs*, 8, 1954–55, pp. 385–7.

### 3.21 **The prime of the Young Conservatives**

From the late 1940s to the early 1960s, the Young Conservatives were claimed to be the largest political youth movement in the democratic world. However, the mainly middle-class membership was attracted for social rather than for political reasons.

I remember a bevy of girls called Pam, Pat, Paula and Sue with whom I would play tennis in Gladstone Park in the long summer of 1949. They wore short shorts with turn-ups, dinky white shoes and Aertex shirts; they knew nothing of Captain Macmillan, Oliver Stanley or Ernest Marples, and cared less. They believed in having a jolly good time: Saturday night hops at the tennis club, parties where one drank Merrydown cider, seaside political conferences in dusty Eastbourne hotels, and the vital importance of virginity. ...

The Young Conservatives used to consist, 40 or more years ago, of ten thousand blokes, many of whom, it is true, desperately wanted a political career, for had not 'Fred' Woolton, the Chairman of the Party, by changing the rules, let down ladders of political opportunity into the tennis-playing suburbs? ... The gallant ten thousand were complemented by a hundred thousand girls of marriageable age, who, in the years before the pill, could persuade their ever-watchful Mums that the Young Conservatives were thoroughly respectable, recruiting 'the nicer kind of young man'. ...

It is plain to see what has happened in the past 50 years. Girls who wanted to have a good time have today no need to spend it canvassing drab streets in wet weather, marking up the 'doubtfuls' with freezing fingers by the light of a failing torch, longing for the whole ordeal to be over, when the party could adjourn to the saloon bar of a respectable public house for a glass of Babycham, followed by a long walk across a deserted Hampstead, or wherever, and fumbling and unsatisfactory goodnights. The sexual revolution has done for the Young Conservatives. ...

It is a lifetime ago since 5,000 London Young Conservatives marched through Hammersmith (the men's uniform were grey flannel bags and Harris tweed jackets) in order to 'Get Fell In' (the Tory candidate's name was Anthony Fell) at a by-election. ... we were a very unthreatening procession, our real purpose being to dance the night away at the Hammersmith Palais, which had been taken over lock, stock and barrel by Conservative Central Office. Anthony Eden took us into his confidence, and we quickstepped with the trim secretaries of North London YC branches, tangoed with armour-plated girls with plunging necklines, made sure of the girl of our choice, and then took the last Tube back in safety to leafy, silent suburbs.

Julian Critchley, 'Young, gifted and blue', *Daily Mail*, 23 August 1994.

### 3.22 The problems of the Young Conservatives

By 1963 Young Conservative membership had fallen by 50 per cent from its peak in the late 1940s of around 160,000. The decline has steadily continued, dwindling to 27,500 by 1978 and to under 10,000 by the mid-1990s. The movement's Central Office organiser sketched its strengths and weaknesses at a time when the fall was beginning to cause alarm.

What's wrong with the movement:
(a) Too small a membership
(b) Too middle class in membership
(c) Makes too little impact on Youth – young voters in particular
(d) At present inclined to be predominantly the 21–25 age group
(e) Not passing to Seniors [i.e., members not moving on to the main Association on reaching the upper age limit]
(f) Not attracting Young Marrieds
(g) Too many committees

What's right with the movement:
(a) Good training ground for future Political Leaders, MPs and

Agents

    (b) Supply of troops for election campaigns ...

    (c) Policy Group Scheme, working well, informing Members, keeping interest of older YCs but failed to get back older type

R. Durant, National Organising Secretary, Young Conservatives, evidence to Selwyn Lloyd Inquiry, 25 April 1963, CPA, CCO/120/4/16.

### 3.23 The national Party funds

The 'quota' contributions from the constituencies provide only a small fraction of the money needed to finance Central Office and the increasingly costly media campaigns before each election. Most of this money comes directly from large firms or wealthy businessmen, through the Party Treasurers and their separate organisation, the Conservative Board of Finance. Their work and the sources and amount of the central funds have always been shrouded in secrecy, but some light is shed on the process by Lord McAlpine, the longest-serving post-war Party Treasurer (1975–90).

... in the Director of the Treasurers' Department, General Sir Brian Wyldbore-Smith, I found an ally. Brian Wyldbore-Smith is a man of considerable class and great ability and when it comes to getting money out of people, there are few to match him. He led a troop of exemplary men who worked, at that time, for salaries that were derisory.
...

    The Treasurers had rules that any donation from an individual was a matter kept confidential between the donor and the Treasurers. This was the rule long before I arrived at Central Office and I sincerely hope that rule will always be kept. A citizen in Britain is entitled to privacy as to which political party they support at the ballot box, so why should they declare which political party they support financially? As for the people who give away other people's money, such as directors of companies who make donations to political parties from shareholders' funds, the law says quite clearly that such a donation must be declared in the accounts of the company concerned. The onus for deciding whether a donation is political or not lies with the directors of the company who give the donation. It is not the responsibility of the Treasurers of the Conservative Party, or any other political party, to decide whether a donation should be declared. ... Those who demanded certain assurances from the Party for their cash were unacceptable. There is only one valid reason for giving money to a political party and that is to help the party of your preference be elected so that you, along with the rest of the nation, can enjoy the supposedly beneficial results of that party's government.

In recent years there has been much talk of rich foreigners supporting the Conservative Party. It is true that foreigners, some richer than others, do. In my day they mostly owned companies in Britain....

I had only one rule: the Party needed money to encourage people to vote Conservative at elections. If the money I took was in any way likely to lose the Party votes and so put winning the election in jeopardy, then far better send that money away. ...

In 1983, I bought 3,000 copies of the Labour Manifesto. ... I merely tagged the relevant pages and sent the documents to potential donors and money rolled into the Conservative coffers.

Alistair McAlpine, *Once a Jolly Bagman*, London, 1997, pp. 204–5, 251–5.


### 3.24 **The financial crisis of the early 1990s**

> The Party's central finances were already in deficit before the combination of economic recession and the heavy expenditure during the 'long campaign' of 1990–92 sent the overdraft soaring. A review of the organisation was set in motion after the 1992 victory by new Party Chairman, Norman Fowler, and cuts and greater centralisation followed. However, the bulk of the deficit was wiped out in 1994–96 by the more traditional method of securing large donations from sympathetic wealthy businessmen.

The Party's present severe financial position has arisen over a number of years. Fund-raising has achieved considerable success; the annual accounts of the Party have shown that over £50 million was raised in the four years up to 31st March 1992. This is a considerable tribute to the efforts of the Party treasurers and their staff. Yet, this increased level of income was exceeded substantially by rising expenditure.

During the 1989 European elections and the 1990 Local Government elections, through to the 1992 campaign, the Party organisation was maintained at a high level of political activity and election preparedness. A long campaign leading up to the 1992 elections and the cost of communications kept the expenditure of Central Office above even the increased level of income. Added to this, there were substantial exceptional items of spending in 1989 and 1990, including the expansion and refurbishment of the Smith Square offices, and computerisation. As a result, the Party experienced an annual deficit of about £5 million in each of the last three financial years, leading to a cumulative deficit of £17 million at the end of March 1992.

The overall deficit is expected to rise during the current year from £17 million to around £19 million at the end of March 1993. It must be reduced from that level as fast as possible.

The first objective must be to reduce current expenditure to within our income. In April 1992, the running costs of the Party organisation, excluding all costs arising from the General Election, were equivalent to £12 million a year. By April 1993, these costs will have been brought down to £7 million a year which includes higher interest costs. ... spending is to be reduced to its lowest level in real terms since 1979.

As compared to levels early in 1992, staffing will be reduced by more than a third. The surveys of the Party showed widespread recognition of the need to improve our financial position, and of the consequent need for the demands placed on Central Office to be reduced accordingly. ...

It is essential to the future health of the Party that the accumulated deficit should be tackled. The Party's objective is to eliminate the deficit by 1996. This will be a considerable challenge, both for the Party's fund-raising efforts and for the control of expenditure.

*One Party: Reforming the Conservative Party Organisation*, report of the Review committee, Conservative Central Office, February 1993.

# 4

# Home affairs: governments, policies and elections

The documents in this chapter focus upon the most important themes and events in domestic affairs. They begin with an examination of the way in which Conservative policies are developed and then presented to the electorate in the manifesto. After this, the extracts proceed in chronological order from Churchill's infamous 'Gestapo' speech in the 1945 election campaign to the general election of 1997. The documents deal with those aspects of social and economic policy which were either the centre of attention at the time or which have a lasting significance in the history of the Conservative Party. These include the reappraisal of policy after 1945; the idea of a 'property-owning democracy'; the development of a post-war consensus; the end of austerity and rise of affluence in the 1950s; the problems of the social services, industrial policy and inflation in the difficult period from the early 1960s to the mid-1970s; and the platforms adopted by the Thatcher and Major governments from 1979 to 1997.

The chapter is concerned not only with the making of policy but also with its impact upon the Conservative Party and its electoral fortunes. Extracts deal with the pledge on housing before the 1951 victory; the Treasury resignations of 1958; the causes of the victories of 1959 and 1970 and the defeat of 1964; the problems of the Heath government; the crisis over the budget of 1981; the Westland affair of 1986; and the 1992 election. It is difficult to draw a line between problems of domestic policy and the leadership crises which may be their result, and for that reason the documents in Chapter 1 should be interwoven with those printed below.

## 4.1 The making of Conservative policy

The process by which Conservative policies are developed is described by Andrew Lansley, Director of the Conservative Research Department (CRD) from 1989 to 1995.

Conservative Party policy is the policy of the Leader of the Party. When the Party is in Government, that means the Party's policy is synonymous with that of the Government. When the Party has been in Opposition, policy has likewise been the result of collective decision-making within the Shadow Cabinet. Studies into policy-making inside the Conservative Party do not, therefore, need to focus in detail on the formal structures inside the Party, but instead should seek to identify the relationship between Party bodies and the Ministerial inner core, where influences are weighed and decisions are made. ...

Over-estimates of CRD's role in the origination of policy persist. This is because it fulfils a wide-ranging function as handmaiden to the policy-making process and as provider of policy material. ... CRD is the only body which has access to each 'circle' or layer of policy-making, as individual desk officers liaise with Ministers and their Special (or Political) Advisers in Departments, they attend Party backbench committees, liaise with external think-tanks, service the work of the Conservative Political Centre, which co-ordinates policy discussion within the voluntary side of the Party, and act as advisers to the Party Chairman who is a participant in the collective decision-making of the Cabinet.

This places the CRD in an excellent position to observe and influence policy-making, and to ensure that the concerns of different parts of the Party are accurately understood in the places where decisions are made. It does not, however, mean that CRD is itself a policy-making body. Nor are we equipped to fill that role whilst the Party is in Government. Those key responsibilities rest with Ministers, with the Prime Minister's Policy Unit at 10 Downing Street, and with Special Advisers in Departments. The strengths of our role are in the provision of policy briefing, in support for policy-based campaigning, in opinion research, and in ... criticising opposition policies.

Conservative Party policy-making was colourfully described by 'Rab' Butler as an 'octopus', reaching out to draw into the process many bodies and groups who are able to contribute. That remains true today. ... the role the various bodies play in policy-making may be [divided] between those bodies which *originate* policy; those which *shape* or *guide* policy; and those which *decide* policy.

In Government, Ministers through their departments are much the most significant source of policy proposals; Departments respond to many external stimuli in offering up policy options to Ministers and responding to events. Officials have also excelled in the process of applying a policy, e.g. privatisation, to new and more complex circumstances. But it remains true that the *origination of policy* objectives and themes rests on the shoulders of Ministers and external bodies. The Conservative Party has always encouraged policy discussion in groups and think-tanks as an alternative to seeing a struggle for control of policy break out within the formal Party structures. So, for instance, our process for determining the content of motions for debate at Party Conference is not an effort to determine policy, but to select a motion wide enough to permit contributions to debate from all parts of the Party, whilst being in line with Party policy.

Debate in the Conference proper is about offering views, facts and differing perspectives, while astute observers listen to the tone, mood and the enthusiasm of response. Meanwhile, the Conservative Party fringe has about 120 meetings – much the largest fringe of any party conference – at which policy issues are vigorously debated, including both the presentation of interest group agenda, as well as wider-ranging policy speeches, competing for the ear of the Party as a whole. ...

So far as *shaping policy* is concerned, the parliamentary party, and the voluntary party, are clearly the bodies with the greatest potential to guide and shape policy. The mechanisms for this within Parliament – both formal, like the 1922 Committee and backbench committees, and informal, like Whips' soundings, are well attested, and proven day-by-day. Those inside the voluntary party – the National Union – are less well observed and less well known. ...

*Decisions* lie essentially within the realm of Ministers collectively either at full Cabinet or in the various Cabinet Committees. In the run-up to the general election, promising ideas from policy groups are tested through the process of collective discussion. ... As we move towards an election, so the needs of campaigning, the need to focus on future policy, the need to emphasise policy differences between the parties, and the need to synthesise and simplify the presentation of policy, all offer the Party machine an increased influence over the content and presentation of policy. This is delivered principally by the involvement of the Party Chairman and senior colleagues, in advising on the final content of the Manifesto, identifying those proposals which support a coherent and effective political presentation, and discarding those elements which are inconsistent with that. ...

Policy-making inside the Conservative Party orientates around the Manifesto. It is necessary that it is a Party-led process in its early and its closing stages even if, in the middle, ideas are tested against practical criteria in Government.

In conclusion, therefore, how might one summarise the Conservative policy-making process? Policy is the prerogative of the Party leader. He uses the Policy Unit, and the Cabinet Committee system (or Shadow Cabinet), to manage the process of detailed policy-making. The Leader's power of patronage and control enables him to test policy in any of three areas – through the Party organisation for its electoral and campaigning impact; in particular, through the National Union/CPC for its impact within the Party, and through the Whips for the view within Parliament. The Leader's office – through the Policy Unit, and via the CRD – maintains contact with a wide range of policy institutes, academics and others. Cabinet Ministers and their Advisers keep up a network of contacts. This is intended to tap into original work outside the realms of Government Departments, other public bodies and related interest groups. The Party Conference acts as a sounding-board for policy ideas and influences and [acts] as a guide to priorities. Individuals in the Party, up to and including Cabinet Ministers, use Party-related bodies to influence the agenda. The National Union and the Parliamentary Party exert more or less direct influence on how policy is taken forward, in particular to test policy proposals against a general sense of Conservative priorities and for their electoral impact. Moving towards an election, the Leader initiates more systematic consultation over the future directions of Party policy, which is increasingly co-ordinated by the Leader and senior colleagues directly, to fashion an election platform, in consultation with the Party Organisation.

'Policy-making in the Conservative Party', text of lecture by Andrew Lansley, 23 May 1995, Conservative Research Department, 1995.

## 4.2 **The manifesto: (i) finding a theme**

The elements needed in a manifesto were analysed by Sir Michael Fraser, Director of the Conservative Research Department 1951–64 and Deputy Party Chairman 1964–75.

Every Manifesto, whether prepared in Government or in Opposition, has certain necessary requirements.

(a)*A central theme*. This may be set out in the title, as in the case of 'A Better Tomorrow' (1970) or 'United for Peace and Progress' (1955), but even when not in the title it must exist and be clearly seen to exist in the text.

(b)*Several major proposals*. For example, in 1970, we had the tax package, industrial relations reform, Europe, social service reorganisation and the new style of Government.

(c)*A number of more minor proposals*. These may often be quite limited in scope, and may apply only to small sections of the community – for example, pensions for the over 80s, freedom for local authorities to sell council houses to sitting tenants who wish to buy them.

(d)*Knocking copy*. This has normally been given more importance and substance when the Manifesto has been written in Opposition, as it is then a matter of criticising the current Labour Government's record. When writing in Government, it is more a matter of undermining the current Labour Opposition's credibility as an alternative government, both in terms of their previous record in office and their current proposals.

(e)*The record*. When in Government, the record, though it may be only relatively briefly deployed in the Manifesto, is nevertheless the essential rock on which all else is built. Without a good, or at least defensible, record new proposals from a governing party have little credibility and will cut little ice. It was Labour's execrable record in office and their desire to gloss over this which made it impossible for them to deploy a new policy in 1970, even if they had one.

Of these requirements, (d) and (e) merely need writing, assuming appropriate ammunition is available. The theme (a) may become clear at any time, but often just grows out of the other work as it is being done, and in relation to the political 'mood' of the time.

'Future policy', memorandum by Fraser, 19 January 1972, CPA, ACP/3/(72)74.

### 4.3 The manifesto: (ii) drafting

The Conservative manifesto is shaped by a group of senior cabinet ministers, chosen and overseen by the Party Leader. They are assisted by Party officials and Research Department briefs. The process is not always easy: Iain Macleod, then

Minister of Health, recalls the frustrations of drafting the manifesto for the 1955 general election.

... the Manifesto was much criticised for prolixity and lack of precision. I doubt whether its critics ever had to write one. This is an educative and humbling process. It is, in the Conservative Party at least, the result of a prolonged and uncomfortable pregnancy. The eventual product reflects not only political aspirations but the interests, hesitations, and even foibles of a composite authorship. In earlier days individual contributions were sewn together into a patchwork quilt. In 1929, for example, you can see without any special knowledge exactly where Neville Chamberlain left off and Winston Churchill began. By 1955, however, editorship had been entrusted to party officials and had become a sort of art – the unique and exasperating art of presenting the major themes of contemporary politics whilst several dozen voices obtrude several dozen variations of 'We must say something about white fish'.

Iain Macleod, 'Election perspective', *Punch*, 30 September 1964.

### 4.4 Churchill's 'Gestapo' speech, 1945

Many Conservatives assumed that victory in the 1945 general election was assured by Churchill's wartime popularity. However, the doubts which many people had regarding his suitability as peacetime Premier were reinforced by Churchill's tone during the campaign, in particular the lurid attack upon the Labour Party in the first of his election radio broadcasts.

My friends, I must tell you that a Socialist policy is abhorrent to the British ideas of freedom. Although it is now put forward in the main by people who have a good grounding in the Liberalism and Radicalism of the early part of this century, there can be no doubt that Socialism is inseparably interwoven with Totalitarianism and the abject worship of the State. It is not alone that property, in all its forms, is struck at, but that liberty, in all its forms, is challenged by the fundamental conceptions of Socialism.

Look how even today they hunger for controls of every kind, as if these were delectable foods instead of wartime inflictions and monstrosities. There is to be one State to which all are to be obedient in every act of their lives. This State is to be the arch-employer, the arch-planner, the arch-administrator and ruler, and the arch-caucus-boss.

How is an ordinary citizen or subject of the King to stand up against this formidable machine, which, once it is in power, will prescribe for every one of them where they are to work; what they are to work at; where they may go and what they may say; what views they are to hold and within what limits they may express them; where their wives are to go to queue up for the State ration; and what education their children are to receive to mould their views of human liberty and conduct in the future?

A Socialist State once thoroughly completed in all its details and its aspects – and that is what I am speaking of – could not afford to suffer opposition. ... But I will go farther. I declare to you, from the bottom of my heart, that no Socialist system can be established without a political police. Many of those who are advocating Socialism or voting Socialist today will be horrified at this idea. That is because they are short-sighted, that is because they do not see where their theories are leading them.

No Socialist Government conducting the entire life and industry of the country could afford to allow free, sharp, or violently worded expressions of public discontent. They would have to fall back on some form of Gestapo, no doubt very humanely directed in the first instance. And this would nip opinion in the bud; it would stop criticism as it reared its head, and it would gather all the power to the supreme party and the party leaders, rising like stately pinnacles above their vast bureaucracies of Civil Servants, no longer servants and no longer civil.

Winston Churchill, BBC radio broadcast, 4 June 1945.

## 4.5 A 'property-owning democracy'

The aim of encouraging a 'property-owning democracy', as an attractive counter to the appeal of Socialism, became a fundamental part of the Conservative programme in the post-war era and has remained an evergreen slogan ever since. It was placed in the forefront as early as 1946 by Anthony Eden, the second figure in the party after Churchill; Eden played a

103

key part in shaping a moderate and attractive Conservative appeal after 1945.

The objective of Socialism is State ownership of all the means of production, distribution and exchange. Our objective is a nationwide property-owning democracy. These objectives are fundamentally opposed. Whereas the Socialist purpose is the concentration of ownership in the hands of the State, ours is the distribution of ownership over the widest practicable number of individuals. Both parties believe in a form of capitalism; but, whereas our opponents believe in State capitalism, we believe in the widest measure of individual capitalism. I believe this to be a fundamental principle of political philosophy. Man should be the master of his environment and not its slave. That is what freedom means. It is precisely in the conception of ownership that man achieves mastery over his environment. Upon the institution of property depends the fulfilment of individual personality and the maintenance of individual liberty. In a Socialist State, where ownership is the monopoly of the government, where everyone must rely on the State for his job, his roof, his livelihood, individual responsibility and individual liberty must die. And so it is that we of the Conservative Party must maintain that the ownership of property is not a crime or a sin, but a reward, a right and a responsibility that must be shared as equitably as possible among all our citizens. ...

How is this wider distribution of ownership to be achieved? There is one way in which it certainly cannot be achieved, and that is by mere redistribution of existing income. ... The fundamental condition for achieving a wider distribution of ownership is surely a great increase in the production of wealth in the country and in particular in the productivity of industry. The saving by an individual that leads to ownership can be achieved only where there is a sufficient margin of income over the requirements of day-to-day consumption. Recent developments in scientific methods of production and in the technique of industrial organisation hold out possibilities of a very substantial increase in the rate of growth of our national income. But this will be achieved only by a united national effort. It does no service to this country to dwell as Socialists do, on the antagonisms between capital and labour, between individual enterprise and the function of Government. Rather we should concentrate on the essential unity of purpose between them that does exist and the harmony of occupation that can be achieved.

Sir Anthony Eden, speech to the Annual Conference, 3 October 1946.

### 4.6 *The Industrial Charter*

The most important of the policy documents produced after
the 1945 defeat was *The Industrial Charter*, published in May
1947. The work of the Industrial Policy Committee, chaired
by R. A. Butler, it was endorsed by Churchill despite his reservations.

Man cannot live by economics alone. Human nature will give of its
best only when inspired by a sense of confidence and hope. We base
all our plans on a belief in the unlimited power of the human personality to meet and to overcome difficulties and to rise above them. We
are completely opposed to the imposition of a rigid strait-jacket of
doctrinaire political theory, either upon the individual regardless of
his individuality or upon the nation regardless of the economic facts
of the moment. Our abiding objective is to free industry from unnecessary controls and restrictions. We wish to substitute for the present
paralysis, in which we are experiencing the worst of all worlds, a
system of free enterprise, which is on terms with authority, and which
reconciles the need for central direction with the encouragement of
individual effort. We point to a way of life designed to free private
endeavour from the taunt of selfishness or self-interest and public
control from the reproach of meddlesome interference. ...

The desire for increased rewards, whether it be expressed in terms
of the profit motive or higher wages, animates the great bulk of man-
kind. We hold that there should be healthy rewards for work done.
We shall propose methods to curb monopolies and unfair privileges.
We are determined to restore by all reasonable means that great stimulus to personal endeavour – fair incentive. A restoration of freedom
and incentives would not mean, as has been falsely held, an end to
security in our social and industrial system. Justice demands that the
aim of national policy should be to provide a basic standard of living
and security of outlook for all our people. This can be achieved in a
variety of ways. Our national system of social services, which we have
helped to create, has recently been enlarged to cover better provision
for pensioners in their old age, for the sick through the universal health
service, for the unemployed, for widows and for parents of large fami-

105

lies. But something more than provision for exceptional circumstances is necessary. ... We describe how each individual must be given the chance to rise above the level of security and to win special rewards. Justice is frustrated by exact equality of reward to all, but it is found where there is equality of opportunity and incentive to win a variety of rewards.

*The Industrial Charter*, Conservative and Unionist Central Office, May 1947.

### 4.7 **The pledge to build 300,000 houses**

The acceptance of Labour's welfare reforms helped the Conservatives to recover eighty-eight seats in February 1950, reducing Labour's overall majority to six. Labour's record on house building was vulnerable, and at the 1950 Annual Conference the Conservative leaders accepted pressure from the floor to commit the Party to a target of building 300,000 new homes a year – a pledge which many believed helped to secure a narrow Conservative majority in October 1951.

I have been impressed and encouraged by what I was told of the gust of passion which swept through our body yesterday about the shameful failure of the Socialist housing policy. ... You have demanded that the target that we should put in our programme should be 300,000 a year. I accept it as our first priority in time of peace. ... it seems to me that houses and homes come even before the reform of the health system, etc. Houses and homes come before health, because overcrowding and slum dwellings are fatal to the family life and breed more illnesses than the doctors can cure. It may well be that hard times lie before us, and that the opportunities for making a better Britain, which these foolish Ministers have squandered for party purposes, will not be opened to those who take their places when the nation records its final verdict. ... However our fortunes may go and from whatever angle the pressures of life may come, the Tory Party puts homes for the people in the very forefront of all schemes for our development.

Winston Churchill, speech to the Annual Conference, 14 October 1950.

## 4.8 **The virtues of home ownership**

Social stability and electoral success for the Conservative Party became identified with the expansion of home ownership, the virtues of which were identified in this internal Party memorandum of 1952.

The advantages of home ownership to the individual all flow from the possession of an asset. This can be made a source of income if required by sub-letting and it is a sheet-anchor in times of financial stress. A fuller life is possible in one's own house than in rented rooms. A sense of responsibility is engendered. If the house is purchased in early or middle life it can be paid for during the purchaser's period of highest earning capacity and when in old age his earning capacity declines, he has the asset of a house to relieve him. To the State, there is the advantage that the owner-occupier houses himself at his own expense and not at that of the State. From the property point of view, while there are a few cases of owner-occupiers not being able to afford the cost of repairs, the general rule is that owner-occupied houses are more conscientiously and economically maintained than rented houses.

'Home ownership', memorandum, 1952, CPA, ACP/3/(52)19.

## 4.9 **The end of austerity**

The 1951–55 Conservative government was able to remove the wartime rationing and controls which Labour had maintained and even increased in 1945–51, thereby making a telling contrast with the 'austerity' now identified with Socialism.

Britain's economic strength was built, and must be rebuilt, in an atmosphere of freedom. Socialists multiplied controls in a wholly vain attempt to curb inflation and bring down prices. Their policy bred shortages and queues, rationing and power-cuts, restriction and red-tape, black markets, spivs and snoopers. Conservatives have used sound monetary and fiscal policy to remove inflationary pressure at its source. This has helped the Government to abolish an increasing

107

number of controls, and that in turn has freed our industry and commerce to provide more and better goods. Freedom and abundance – that is our policy. ...

Our nation of shop-keepers can now open any food-shop without a licence; can light their shops as gaily as they wish; can open later in the winter months to serve their customers. Controls on the use of many materials, controls on the distribution of iron and steel, controls on the manufacture of a long list of machines and electrical goods, controls on the motorist's petrol, controls on the housewife's cups and saucers – all have gone. Price controls on every one of the goods for which the Board of Trade used to be responsible have been scrapped; sometimes prices have fallen, on average they have kept fairly steady.

It is the Government's policy to restore freedom of choice for the housewife by increasing food supplies. To-day there is more food available in the shops and infinitely more variety. Fifteen per cent. more meat and bacon were eaten in 1952 than in 1951, and this year has been the best since the war. There are good supplies of unrationed canned meat, gammon and shoulder bacon, and a greater quantity and variety of sausages. In September for the first time since the war, real white bread will be on sale; the national loaf remains for those who prefer to buy it. Sweets and chocolates, tea and eggs have all been taken off the ration. The rationing of sugar will also end this year. Our Conservative goal is to do away with all rationing and to wind up the administration of the Ministry of Food.

Draft of pamphlet 'Onward in freedom', 17 June 1953, CPA, ACP/3/(53)25.

## 4.10 **The politics of consensus**

The domestic policies of the Churchill, Eden and Macmillan governments suggested the existence of a 'consensus'. This avoided the appearance of confrontation and was based upon the acceptance of an element of nationalisation, the use of Keynesian methods of economic intervention, the aim of full employment and the maintenance of the 'welfare state'. The following extract is from Churchill's speech in the debate on the address in 1953.

... after the fearful exertions, sacrifices and exhaustions of two world wars, the element of calm, patient study and a sense of structure by both sides may render lasting service to our whole people and increase and consolidate their influence for good and for peace throughout the quivering, convulsive and bewildering world.

More especially is this true of a period in which the two-party system is dominant and about fourteen million vote Tory and about another fourteen million Socialist. ... It is not really possible to assume that one of these fourteen million masses of voters possesses all the virtues and the wisdom and the other lot are dupes and fools, or even knaves and crooks. Ordinary people in the country mix about with each other in friendly, neighbourly relations, and they know it is nonsense for party politicians to draw such harsh contrasts between them. ...

I am not suggesting that our goal is a coalition; that, I think, would be carrying good will too far. ... I am pleading for time, calm, industry and vigilance, and also time to let things grow and prove themselves by experience. It may sometimes be necessary for Governments to undo each other's work, but this should be an exception and not the rule. We are, of course, opposed, for instance, to nationalisation of industry and, to a lesser extent, to the nationalisation of services. We abhor the fallacy, for such it is, of nationalisation for nationalisation's sake. But where we are preserving it, as in the coal-mines, the railways, air traffic, gas and electricity, we have done and are doing our utmost to make a success of it, even though this may somewhat mar the symmetry of party recrimination. It is only where we believed that a measure of nationalisation was a real hindrance to our island life that we have reversed the policy, although we are generally opposed to the principle.

Winston Churchill, *House of Commons Debates*, fifth series, vol. 520, cols 22–3, 3 November 1953.

### 4.11 **Working with the trade unions**

In their endeavour to avoid any return to the industrial and unemployment problems of the inter-war years, the Conservative governments of 1951–64 sought a better working relationship with the trade unions. The flavour of the times is conveyed by Walter Monckton, who was nicknamed 'the oil-can' for his conciliatory approach as Minister of Labour in 1951–55.

I must, in all honesty, say how impressed I have been, in what I assure you is not the easiest job of my life, by the wisdom, the moderation, and the sense of responsibility of the great bulk of the Trade Union movement and the great bulk of their leaders, certainly of the TUC itself. ... So many leaders of the Trade Union movement have publicly stated all the time we have been in office that the duty of the movement is to work with the Government of the day, even if they do not share its political complexion. It really would be most ungenerous of me if I were not to take this chance of saying how loyally they have done that. Do not let it be thought that it is merely because I am talking about the Trade Union movement that I say this about them in particular. It is true also of the employment and management side. In effect, what I am trying to work with is a great living industrial partnership trying to bring about the prosperity of the country, which cannot be had unless we work together in a partnership of that kind with mutual confidence and goodwill.

Walter Monckton, speech to the Annual Conference, 9 October 1954.

## 4.12 The Thorneycroft resignations, 1958

The Conservatives were beginning to recover ground after the traumas of the Suez crisis when a dispute over economic policy led to the resignation of the Chancellor of the Exchequer, Peter Thorneycroft, and his junior ministers in January 1958. The crisis was contained by quick work on the part of the Party Chairman, Lord Hailsham, whilst Macmillan's calm response enhanced his 'unflappable' image.

When a Chancellor of the Exchequer and his two junior colleagues resign in concert on a question of policy, it is no small thing, and a government as tottering and unpopular as ours was must be considered to be near the end. My own duty, I thought, was absolutely plain. As I had not supported the resignations it would be my duty to minimise their effect with all the speed and all the authority of which I was capable. I met Oliver Poole,[1] and together we concerted a plan. That very night telegrams went forth to every Chairman of every area Conservative organisation and association giving our account of the matter. Our critics were astonished at the speed and manner with which we acted, and the principal critics, including the resigning ministers, were very angry. To my mind they had nothing to be angry about, since, although I had been effective and prompt, I had done nothing dishonourable. I believe my actions steadied the party at a very critical time, at least as much as Harold Macmillan's studied insouciance on his departure at the airport on leaving for his Commonwealth tour, which he would not put off. His judgement was correct, although his reference to the 'little local difficulty' which is how he described the loss of his Chancellor of the Exchequer had more panache than accuracy. ...

After the Thorneycroft resignations things, as I have said, became worse for a time ... The first local elections in May 1958 were almost as bad as they could be. But the borough elections which followed showed modest but significant improvement, and this time there were no more resignations to nullify the result. By autumn we were well ahead, and at the conference in Blackpool I was able to strike a thankful, indeed almost a triumphant, note. By May 1959 there was a strong movement in the party to hold an immediate election.

Lord Hailsham, *The Door Wherein I Went*, London, 1975, pp. 163–4.

### 4.13 **Affluence and the 1959 election victory**

When the general election was held in October 1959, despite some concern over Labour's progress in the early stages of the campaign, the Conservatives were victorious for the third time in succession and increased their majority from 60 to 100.

The fact that a Conservative Government had been in office for eight years rather than three-and-a-half made a swing of the pendulum much more likely, and the cry 'time for a change' more appealing. ... Conservative difficulties between 1956 and 1958 were still recent history. The recovery had been spectacular both in extent and speed, but this

1    Party Chairman 1955–57, and Deputy Chairman 1957–59.

very fact made some people suspicious of the stability of the resulting situation. Conservative self-confidence on a number of issues had been somewhat shaken and clever exploitation of these could have proved damaging. ... On the other hand, the arguments for the status quo were again very strong.

(a) The election, like that of 1955, was fought in a general atmosphere of hope – of peace abroad and rising standards of living at home – and this strongly favoured the continuation of existing policies.

(b) All the economic indicators were good. Production, exports and the gold reserves were rising; the balance of trade was favourable; the price index had been stable for over a year; unemployment was down and falling; the growth of the high-consumption economy since 1955 had been remarkable, and this had a particularly strong influence on the younger people and the new voters.

(c) There was general confidence in the Prime Minister's leadership and, in particular, in his efforts for peace and the breaking of the diplomatic log-jam between East and West.

... As the campaign developed, therefore, the essential out-of-dateness of Labour Party policy became more and more apparent; with nationalisation ever more of a mill-stone, the cries of the class war ever more irrelevant, and the technically effective publications and broadcasts wasted on painting pictures of a depressed and poverty-stricken Britain which the voter found laughably unlike the world which he saw around him. ...

Television, as expected, proved very important, but not in any way to the exclusion of other media. It is obviously more powerful in putting over a Party image, and in generally interesting the electorate in the fact that there is an election going on, than it is in converting people from one Party to another. ...

The slogan, 'Life is better with the Conservatives – Don't let Labour ruin it', and the poster campaign which presented it, were most effective and clearly linked the improvement in the conditions of life with the Conservative Party. ... Finally, the campaign underlined once more the fact that elections are won between elections and not during the campaign.

'Some reflections on the general election campaign, 1959', memorandum by Fraser, 1 December 1959, CPA, ACP/3/(59)76.

## 4.14 **Public opinion and the Party's image in the early 1960s**

The Macmillan government took on a beleaguered appearance in 1961–63, as economic problems became linked with scandals and a change in public attitudes. A paper prepared for the Steering Committee, the group of senior ministers charged with shaping the next manifesto, analysed the changes and the Party's popular image.

The post-1959 honeymoon lasted, mainly because of Labour disunity on defence and nationalisation, till July 1961. After July 1961, public opinion moved against the Conservative Party. According to the evidence of the public opinion polls and of recent by-elections, the average swing to Labour from the 1959 General Election to the present time (December 1963) is around 6 or 7 per cent, i.e. sufficient if it took place at a General Election roughly to reverse the positions of the two parties in the House. ... By June the Gallup Poll was registering the Labour Party 20 percentage points above the Conservatives, the lowest figure for Conservative support since 1946.

... by comparing the age, social class and sex of those who intended to vote Conservative or Labour in 1959 with those intending to vote Conservative or Labour in 1963, it seems that we have lost support more among women than among men, more among the under-forties than among the over-forties and more among the working classes (manual occupations) than among the middle classes (non-manual occupations). ...

From the work already published by the public opinion polling organisations, it would seem that the shift in voting intention may be due as much to generalised impressions about the parties as to the impact of specific policy issues. The rather sketchy work that has been done so far suggests that the Conservative Party is seen today as a united party, supported by business, capable of making the country prosperous but with little concern for ordinary people and with rather unsound domestic policies. The Labour Party, on the other hand, is seen as a forward-looking party, supported by the trade unions, with honest leaders concerned for ordinary people but doubtfully united and rather less sound on foreign policy than the Conservatives – though on the crucial aspect of foreign policy, the ability to work for world peace, the public have for long regarded both parties as much the same. So far as specific policies are concerned, housing stands out as the one in which the comparison between the parties is least favourable to us. Defence and armaments are the field in which the comparison is most favourable to us, but it is a field regarded by most people as far less important.

... The Conservative Party seems to have accentuated its tendency to be seen as remote from the aspirations of ordinary people. But even in 1959 the Labour Party was seen as the party of the ordinary man and the Conservative Party as the party of the elites – in society, in education and in industry. The difference seems to be that in 1959 the electorate voted with and for the elites because they represented the aspirations with which the electorate was then prepared to identify itself. It may be that the elites for which the Conservative Party is now thought to stand seem in some way narrower or more closed than they seemed in 1959.

'Public opinion since 1959', memorandum by Fraser and Douglas, 11 December 1963, CPA, SC/63/14.

### 4.15 Playing for time, 1964

The crisis over the succession to Macmillan in 1963 left the Party shaken and unsettled, whilst Home was unable to match the presentational skills of the recently elected Labour leader, Harold Wilson. However, the Conservatives slowly began to close the gap in 1964, and they saw a chance of victory if the election was postponed until the last possible date of October, as this internal memorandum shows. In the event, Labour won with an overall majority of only four.

The Prime Minister's decision not to hold a General Election until the autumn has averted a certain defeat in June. But the additional time by no means ensures a victory in October. Indeed, unless there are some radical changes it could be that support for the Party will deteriorate even further.

Much of the recent criticism of the Government since 1959 has been that it has lost its sense of direction, and that, therefore, the material progress of the last twelve years has got us nowhere. This 'image' which certainly exists in many quarters cannot be changed by mere philosophical speeches or by a few paragraphs in a Manifesto.

Basically it is what a Government does and how it behaves that matters – whether it gets all the credit it should depends on its public relations. Publicity, however good, can never overcome mistakes of policy or behaviour. All it can do is make the most of what is good.

The following points seem to me to be worth considering.

(1) The management of the economy is the most important electoral factor. The essential thing is to look as if the Government were in effective control. A 'give-away' policy in itself will of course get nowhere, but there is no electoral alternative to a high, secure and improving standard of living.

(2) The apparent dissensions in the Cabinet must stop. Whether they are real or not is important, but it is also important that it is not thought they are there [*sic*]. This is not confined to two or three Ministers but goes right through the Cabinet. Even the way in which the consultations on the date of the General Election took place have helped to add to this impression. It is no good blaming the Whips Office or Back-benchers. The fault lies, and has lain for some time, in the Cabinet itself. Never has it been so easy for journalists and others to find senior ministers who will talk indiscreetly. The seriousness of this must be accepted. The deterioration in the polls in recent weeks is due to this. If it continues it will mean electoral disaster.

(3) One of the most difficult problems facing a Government is its own public relations. When the Party is in Office, the Publicity Department of Central Office can have only a relatively small impact. When Government publicity is being efficiently handled e.g. Morrison, Swinton, Charles Hill, all goes well. There is no doubt that the present arrangement is not working and changes must be made. Time is against us.

(4) I believe we have to draw a careful balance between trying to calm down the political atmosphere and making the most of the time available. We are a long way behind and our only chance of catching up is to go flat out on all fronts until October. We must try to run the Socialists off their feet without boring the electorate. This must be a carefully co-ordinated programme. Some risks must be taken: we have not got much to lose. ...

The Cabinet must appear united; government business must be efficiently conducted; one or two interesting pieces of legislation must be contrived; the Minister responsible for Government public relations must be consulted in advance, so that plans to handle every detail to the Party's advantage can be prepared. Above all, there must be no more legislation which is controversial within the Party.

Memorandum from Lord Poole (Vice-Chairman) to Lord Blakenham (Chairman of the Party), 13 April 1964, CPA, CCO/20/16/3.

## 4.16 Policy-making in opposition, 1964–70

The policy review on which the Party embarked whilst in opposition during 1964–70 was unusually intense and extensive. The thinking behind the exercise, and some of its dangers, are outlined in this discussion paper.

The contrast between Labour promise (more perhaps even than promises) in opposition and Labour performance in office produced a natural reaction against talking about broad objectives. This was reinforced in our case by the knowledge that many of the electorate felt that at the end of the thirteen years we had run out of new ideas. In recent years, therefore, we have tended to seek 'Action not Words',[2] policies not aspirations, and to talk about means not ends.

This philosophy underlay both the unprecedented policy group activity after 1964 and the 1966 manifesto with its 131 action proposals, vigorously presented without any very explicit conceptual themes. ... Action proposals of the 1966 Manifesto type do have a valuable effect on informed opinion in making the Conservative Party more credible as an alternative Government. But all electoral studies show that the electorate does not base its choice of parties on a cool assessment of the probable effects of the proposals and action programmes of the alternative parties. If policies are to have any effect on the voters, they have got to meet fairly stringent conditions:

(a) They have to be *sound* technically. ... Ensuring this – which can be called the intellectual respectability of the party's programme – is the traditional role of the Research Department, including the policy groups. It is the aspect on which we spend most time and resources and about which in our view there is least cause for concern. But by itself it is not enough.

(b) They have to be *relevant* to voters' *ordinary lives*. ...

(c) They must appear *distinctive* as between the parties. This is

2   The title of the 1966 Conservative manifesto.

probably the most difficult characteristic to achieve. The circumstances in which both parties have to operate are common to both. This means that the scope for manoeuvre is limited technically and the areas on which the Government have to operate are very much the same for both parties. ... So long as we confine ourselves to defining the areas of operation, we are bound both to sound very alike. The room for manoeuvre is limited too in other fields. In the social services, we are both limited by the obligation to honour our commitments to past and present contributors. In foreign policy we are both torn between the strain on our resources and the extent of our commitments. The danger is that one merely adopts the stance 'Anything you can do, I can do better than you'. On this the electorate will compare records rather than policies. Comparison of the records must be a continuing element of propaganda but it may not be enough and in any case leaves the party in a backward-looking rather than forward-looking posture.

Yet it remains true that what we would do frequently differs from what the Labour Government would do or does. Here we are on the horns of a dilemma. Detailed statements of how we would do things are not the solution. ... Policy groups by their nature inevitably tend to adopt the technique of looking at the problems facing the country and seeking more or less technical solutions to them. If we merely rely on them and then attempt to weave their various proposals into some sort of continuos narrative, there is a real danger that the result will be an equally heterogeneous collection of ideas and proposals without any clear picture of where we are trying to go.

'Policy formulation and presentation', memorandum by Sewill and Douglas, 23 November 1967, CPA, OG/67/2.


### 4.17 **Selectivity and social policy**

Since 1951 the Conservatives had been cautious in their handling of the Welfare State, but the growing costs forced a reappraisal. The theme of greater selectivity, which had emerged in the late 1950s, was endorsed in the policy review exercise of the 1960s.

The general principle of selectivity was widely accepted by the Party, but what we had to do now was to develop our ideas as to how and where this principle could be applied and this would vary with each of the social services. The subject had to be considered against the background of three general points. First, the Party was clearly committed to maintaining the contributory principle and to ensuring that social service benefits maintained their value. When we were in office, we had gone further and said that they would continue to share in the country's general prosperity and this could be taken to imply that they would rise with general living standards. Even maintaining the real value of benefits imposed quite a high minimum. Second, since 1964 we had said that there should be more for those in real need. Thirdly, we had also said that people ought to pay more for what they got from such services as school meals and council houses. ... On education and the health services ... more could be done in the tax field to help those who were helping themselves ...

Sir Clyde Hewlett was sure that if we concentrated help on those in dire need and distress, this was the right line and we should get electoral support for it. But we would have to be very much clearer where we stood. It was not sufficient to make woolly statements about helping those in need, the Party should stand as the real champions of those genuinely in need and at the same time opposed to further public expenditure except for this purpose.

Mr Maude agreed. In conditions of financial stringency, the social services would serve people worse and worse because there would be an upper limit on expenditure and, so long as the principle of universality was maintained, the available resources would be spread thinner and thinner. We ought to get across to the electorate that the health services were deteriorating because of the load put on them. Already there were cases: for example kidney machines being paid for by private subscription because the health service could not cope.

Advisory Committee on Policy, minutes, 27 July 1967, CPA, ACP(67)83.

### 4.18 **The limits of consensus**

Between 1945 and 1975 Conservative policy was framed within the economic assumptions of the post-war 'consensus'. The 1968 policy review on the nationalised industries provides a good example of this – even though it was chaired by Nicholas Ridley, one of the most influential advocates of rolling back the state in the 1970s and 1980s.

There is widespread feeling that public industry is expensive and inefficient. Most people complain of poor service and of high prices, but many who know are aware of overmanning, inefficiency and bad management. A confidential Central Office poll into public attitudes showed that 80 per cent think the industries have too much bureaucracy and red tape, 60 per cent think they waste public money, and 50 per cent think they provide services badly. There is a welcome for the Party that can show a way to improve their performances. ...

Whatever is done about denationalisation, it is clear that a large public sector of industry will remain. For both political and economic reasons, there is a pressing need to seek new ways of managing it more efficiently. Moreover, in practice, denationalisation will in many cases only be possible when industries have been put on a sounder basis than at present.

The answer is not to try and make the nationalised industries as like private commercial concerns as possible. They are essentially different from each other. By the very fact of public ownership the State possesses a unique position with regard to the public sector which means that it must take major decisions itself and these decisions cannot therefore be left to the forces of the 'market'. The market forces which determine the prices, profits, capital investment, and therefore the sizes of commercial concerns, are meaningless when applied to the State industry, which has the bottomless purse of the Exchequer behind it to make up losses and to provide new capital.

We must seek solutions peculiar to nationalised industries, and not try and dress public concerns up like private ones. ... We conclude that a public industry cannot ever be a truly commercial enterprise. ...

This, then, is the legitimate justification for Government intervention. The Government must find the capital (or allocate the resources, to use the modern jargon). How best should the Government exercise this control? ... Everyone emphasises the need to insulate the industries both from political pressures and from detailed bureaucratic control. We believe it is vital to do this, if good managers are to be attracted. ...

We believe there should be set up a small Holding Company between the Government and the industries. The Holding Company would be in the position of the 'owner' of all the industries. It would appoint the managers of the industries, settle their salaries, and dismiss those who failed. It would co-ordinate their capital programmes. ... The Government would appoint the members of the holding company. Beyond that, it would have to rely upon the Annual Directive to obtain its will.

'Report of the Policy Group on Nationalised Industries', 11 July 1968, CPA, ACP/3/(68)51.

## 4.19 The general election of 1970

The Conservative victory of 1970 was an unexpected triumph, which finally established Heath's authority within the Party.

Sir Michael [Fraser] said that the result of the election campaign was satisfactory, and not only in the obvious sense. There had been the biggest swing from one party to another since 1945; it was the first occasion since 1945 that an entrenched majority for one party had been turned into a satisfactory majority for the other; ... Labour had a poor record, a record of broken promises on which we concentrated. The improved balance of payments had enabled Mr Wilson for a time to rebuild his credibility but this was eggshell thin. Though there had been much criticism of the tactics employed by Mr Wilson, he probably did not have much choice: he could not fight on the record or on new policies which would bring up the record of the past. All he could do was tiptoe over the eggshells and say as little as possible. This succeeded for a time but eventually the eggshells cracked, memories of the record flooded back, and many voters returned to the view that they had held some months before of the competence of the Government.

Advisory Committee on Policy, minutes, 25 November 1970, CPA, ACP(70)109.

## 4.20 The Heath government and the 'U-turns'

Rising inflation, high unemployment and industrial strife led to the 'U-turns' of 1972: interventionist industrial and regional measures, a compulsory prices and incomes policy, and a massive expansion of public expenditure. The dilemma which the Party faced was expressed by the Chairman of the 1922 Committee, Sir Harry Legge-Bourke, in the debate on the Industry Bill.

This is a Socialist Bill by ethic and philosophy. I fear that it is the most grievous piece of legislation introduced by the present government so far. I hugely admire the other legislation which has been introduced by my right hon. friends but this Bill I find obnoxious for many reasons. At least, however, I recognise that there is a streak of enormous compassion running through it. I realise that there are some areas desperately needing the help which the Bill can give. It was only for that reason that I was prepared not to vote against it on Second Reading; it is only for that reason I shall not vote against it on Third Reading. I believe that these thoughts are shared by many of my hon. friends.

Sir Harry Legge-Bourke, *House of Commons Debates*, fifth series, vol. 841, col. 2402, 28 July 1972.

### 4.21 **The outlook for the Heath government, 1973**

In the wake of the most striking 'U-turn' of the Heath government – the statutory control of prices and incomes – the Party's most senior official reviewed the present position and the prospects for the future.

There are a number of areas in which the Government has done, and to a greater or lesser extent has been recognised to have done, well. The most obvious of these is *Europe*, which is rated an achievement even by those who disapprove of it. ... *Taxation* is one of the few unblemished success stories and a clear-cut contrast with the Labour record. ... Appreciation of the Government's record on *social services* presents a more confusing picture. ... So far as the informed minority are concerned, the very real achievements in channelling aid to those in specific need has won considerable respect for the present administration in general and for Sir Keith Joseph in particular. So far as the more general public is concerned, the Party continues to suffer from the traditional weakness of its image in this field ... The most striking success has been in pensions ...

Anxiety about *unemployment* which was a very major source of concern a year ago has diminished not only as the figures have improved but as a general feeling of confidence has been built up that the problem is on the way to solution. ...

Public opinion has also remained calm on three potentially very explosive issues: *Northern Ireland*, where opinion in Britain has remained stable, no doubt partly because it has been kept out of the strictly Party political arena; *immigration*, where the Home Secretary's recent statement to the House has helped to allay some of the fears engendered by the Uganda crisis, and *law and order*.

By far the most salient issues and the most likely to affect the outcome of the next general election are the two related problems of the *cost of living* and the *standard of living*. ... Public reaction to the Government's counter-inflationary measures has so far been not unsatisfactory. About two-thirds of the electorate give support in general terms and about half consider the Government's proposals fair. What is somewhat disturbing is that the trend of opinion has been slowly moving in the wrong direction ...

What is more serious is that a policy which ultimately depends largely on social pressures for its efficacy requires in the long-term the support of a good deal more than half to two-thirds of the people. As a temporary expedient to deal with a critical situation, most people are probably prepared, if reluctantly, to submit their demands to the procrustean judgement of a statutory authority, but few people are in the long-term going to be prepared to leave it to the Government to decide the remuneration appropriate to their work. The prodigious extension of the powers of the state which this would represent would be distasteful to a large section of the middle-class, while that third of the working class on which we depend for success at the polls might well think that if the Government is going to settle their wages they would do better with a Government of their own kind.

We are unlikely to be able to return to free collective bargaining and statutory powers of some sort (if only as a safeguard of last resort) are likely to be required certainly for some years to come and probably until some fundamental change in the techniques of economic management provides a completely new solution to the problem of cost-push inflation.

'The strategic/tactical situation in 1973', memorandum by Fraser, 14 February 1973, CPA, SC/73/17.

## 4.22 Inflation: the scourge of the 1970s

The two issues which dominated politics from the late 1960s to the mid-1980s were the linked problems of trade union power and inflation. Sir Keith Joseph, already moving rapidly in the direction of monetarism and free-market economics, outlined the problem shortly after both factors had brought about the defeat of the Heath government in February 1974.

We all agree that inflation is our most urgent preoccupation. It was our object to abate the size of the borrowing requirement and the rate of growth of the money-supply back from the high levels we thought necessary to reduce unemployment and to stimulate investment. ... But if the country is to return to sound money by gradual steps then consistent policies – involving some unemployment, some bankrupt-cies and very tight control on public spending – will be needed for at least five years. ... Inflation at the present rate let alone worse spells disaster for us as a country, as a society and as a party. It is cruel beyond words for the poor and the thrifty, and it destroys the middle class. Moreover private enterprise, caught between rising costs and controlled prices, will be forced more and more to seek rescue – on Benn's[3] terms.

There will be conflicting views on the right policies. But this is surely true – that government will need for some years to tread, if practicable, a narrow path between hypcrinflation on the one side and intolerable unemployment on the other. ...Against this background the climate for wage claims and for price increases will be altering. I hope that we can find an incomes policy that is selective and involves as few decisions and as little bureaucracy as possible. As we used to say, controls help the militants and reduce efficiency.

'Inflation', memorandum for shadow cabinet, by Sir Keith Joseph, 1 May 1974, CPA, LCC/74/11.

---

3    Tony Benn, Industry Secretary 1974–75, a leading figure on the Labour left.

## 4.23 **The 'wets' and the 1981 budget crisis**

After winning the 1979 election, Thatcher and Howe, her Chancellor of the Exchequer, implemented the monetarist strategy which they had devised in opposition, cutting taxes and public spending. This led to a cabinet crisis over Howe's 1981 budget, but the critics – contemptuously dubbed 'wets' by the Thatcherites – failed to make a stand, as one of them recalls.[4]

It was a moment when several of us in the Cabinet were close to resignation. We were particularly divided over the 1981 budget. By this time the recession was becoming marked and what came to be described as the 'wets' were alarmed at the steep rise in unemployment. We believed that the government should be doing more in the regions. Ian Gilmour, Jim Prior and myself were clearly identified as 'wets', but others like Peter Carrington, Christopher Soames and Willie Whitelaw took a similar viewpoint.

What aggravated our feelings on this occasion was the practice of telling the Cabinet nothing about a Budget before the Tuesday morning it was delivered. ... Jim Prior had picked up an idea of what was in the package. He told Ian Gilmour when they both attended the same official dinner on the Monday evening. Ian phoned me and the three of us had breakfast together and discussed whether we should resign.

At the Cabinet, the Chancellor outlined the tough policies he was going to follow and there was serious criticism. An important proportion felt the Budget was too deflationary with a recession setting in. Ministers accept that they do not always get what they want at Budget Cabinets, but this one was different. ...

Afterwards a number of us discussed again what we should do. We were faced with an impossible dilemma. If we decided we could not accept the Budget and must resign, we had to take into account the damage it would do to Sterling and the economy. ... You had to ask: Is it worth it? If you did it, you knew it was unlikely the government would change the Budget. It would be too late. The statement was at 3.30 p.m. and the Prime Minister was not going to say that because three Cabinet Ministers had resigned she was going to go into full retreat. Margaret would try to get Tory MPs behind the Budget and carry it through, but the government side would be seriously divided.

4    See also the views of another leading 'wet', Francis Pym, document 6.12.

The downside risk for the country was considerable.

Immediately after the Budget Cabinet, in the hallway of No. 10, a number of us chatted for ten minutes. I had a longer conversation with Ian Gilmour, who was a close personal friend, but there was no formal group. You simply knew that a large proportion of the Cabinet was troubled and hardly anyone had expressed enthusiasm for the Budget.

We decided we could not get it changed, and resignation would do more harm to the economy.

Peter Walker, *Staying Power*, London, 1991, pp. 159–60.

### 4.24 Privatisation

The Thatcher governments developed a popular programme of privatisation: returning nationalised industries to the private sector by selling shares in them to the public. The major utilities of telecommunications, gas, electricity and water successfully led the way, giving instant profits to investors and increased efficiency in the long term.

In a market economy there can be no guarantee that there will never be failures. If the market fails to support an enterprise, public sector or private sector, if its goods or services are not wanted by its customers, it ceases to be a wealth creator and its future and its purpose are at risk. But what is clear today is that privatisation has been a success ... the privatisation programme is not driven by some overwhelming imperative to raise cash. It is driven by the pragmatic conclusion ... that nationalisation does not work and free enterprise does. It is driven by a desire to introduce competition where it does not exist and to increase competition where it is weak. It is driven by the belief that businesses exist to serve their customers, and it is driven by a belief that to combine economic power and political power in the same hands constitutes ... a needless and unacceptable risk, not just to economic success but to political freedom too. After that, well, I know that Nigel[5] finds the cash quite useful too.

... the ownership and control of property and capital should be

5   Nigel Lawson, Chancellor of the Exchequer.

widely distributed. The citizen with property is inherently better able to stand up to the state than the citizen who has no property. ...Above all, we see the need to create wealth in order to lift compassion from hollow rhetoric to practical help. Then in the last ten years this party has widened its appeal across the spectrum of classes and income groups, just as Labour has retreated into an ever narrower, bigoted, sectarian redoubt. The Alliance continues, in Roy Jenkins own prophetic words, to play a fuddled fiddle in the muddled middle. It is up to us to unite capital and labour, to give more people a stake in the success of business – not just through wages but through ownership.

Norman Tebbit, Trade and Industry Secretary, speech to the Annual Conference, 11 October 1984.

### 4.25 The Westland crisis, 1986

The most serious crisis of Thatcher's middle years came suddenly when Michael Heseltine, then Defence Secretary, walked out of a cabinet meeting on 9 January 1986 after his efforts to promote a European rescue bid for the Westland helicopter company were thwarted. The involvement of No. 10 in manoeuvres against Heseltine, and in particular the leaking of a confidential letter from the Solicitor-General, put the Prime Minister in a vulnerable position; in the end, the Trade and Industry Secretary, Leon Brittan, took the blame and resigned. However, the issues underlying the drama – Britain's future in Europe, and Thatcher's conduct of cabinet government and treatment of senior ministers – were to lead to her downfall in 1990.

The background is for me clear. So is Government policy on this critical matter. The Government White Paper of 1985 made clear that we were committed to a major drive forward in the co-ordination of the defence industrial base in Europe. ... The longer that we in Britain go on preserving an unco-ordinated, fragmented European industrial base, cowering behind our frustrations every time somebody else wins, or tries harder than we do, or gets up that little bit earlier than we do, the longer our relative decline compared with the United States of America will continue.

Let us come to that small helicopter company in the west of England. ... I had been empowered by my colleagues in the British cabinet to pursue the possibility of a British-European rescue for Westland, but I was given no chance to report back my proposals to the Cabinet Committee which authorised me, or to the full cabinet ... In the absence of any collective judgement, which I continued to ask for as late as 23 December, I continued publicly to answer questions ...

I had no doubt where my duties lay. I had been entrusted by my cabinet colleagues to seek a European deal. I had been entrusted by my European colleagues with the advocacy of their case. I therefore circulated details to my colleagues in cabinet and sought a collective decision. That was denied me. I was told not to raise the matter in cabinet. I refused to be silent. I protested about the cancelled meeting in cabinet on 12 December. The cabinet minutes did not record my protest.

At the next cabinet meeting, on Thursday 19 December, it was stated that we should show no preference. ... the public controversy was to be cooled and there were to be no ministerial public statements. That night, the Secretary of State for Trade and Industry implied that I was holding a pistol to Sikorsky's[6] head. I did not respond to those words. On Sunday he spoke on radio and recorded a broadcast for 'The World This Weekend'. The BBC informed me, and I agreed to respond only if I was convinced that he had broadcast. I heard the broadcast by the Secretary of State and agreed to go ahead. Efforts were made to stop the programme – [Hon. Members: "Oh."] – but I was told that, whatever the Secretary of State for Trade and Industry did, I was not to appear. I could not accept such one-sided treatment. ...

Suffice it to say that the culmination of events came in the cabinet on 9 January. We were supposed to be even-handed, leaving the matter to the shareholders, standing back. ... There were then the selective leaks from the Law Officers' letters, which were used, wrongly, to damage my credibility. ... in cabinet, it was suggested that all answers to questions on Westland should be submitted to the Cabinet Office before release. ... This included answers to questions which already publicly carried my name. I had no confidence, in the light of what had already happened, that such a constraint would be used fairly or without prejudice to the interests of the British-European

6   The American company which had made the original bid for Westland.

offer. ... With great regret, but no doubt, I left the Government.

Michael Heseltine, *House of Commons Debates*, sixth series, vol. 89, cols 1099–107, 15 January 1986.

## 4.26 **The poll tax**

The main domestic reform of Thatcher's third term was the replacement of domestic rates by a broader-based system of financing local government – the Community Charge, more popularly known as the 'poll tax'. Ministerial over-confidence, encouraged by the enthusiastic support for the policy at the 1987 conference, led to a rapid implementation with little cushioning of the higher costs faced by many – and the resulting unpopularity played a large part in Thatcher's downfall.

... we are committed, absolutely committed to abolish domestic rates and introduce the Community Charge. We fought the election on it. And never forget, we won it! People know that rates are unfair. We promised them a fairer system and we shall not disappoint them. ...

The Community Charge actually fulfils our requirements: it is simple, it is fair, and it restores accountability. First, it is simple. There can be no simpler concept than that everyone should pay the same amount for the same standard of council services. The less our council spends the less each one of us will pay. All councils will get a Government grant to help. That too will be simple. It will be paid partly per capita and partly according to need ... Secondly, it is fair. The better off will pay much more for local services, but everyone will pay something. The Community Charge would cover only a quarter of local authority spending; three-quarters will come from the central taxpayer, and the business rate. ... If a system is fair it must not cause hardship for the less well off and I assure this Conference that will not happen. That is why at the lower end of the scale there will be rebates for the less well off of up to 80 per cent and help through the income support system to meet the amount they have to pay.

The third – the vital – element of a system of local government finance is that it must restore accountability to local government. For years we have relied on public spirited councillors of all parties – but mainly Tory – to weigh the need for services with the need for low taxation. But the Labour Party in Local Government has – er – changed. It is now a party whose power is based cynically upon the impoverishment of the ratepayer, whatever the damage to the local economy, in order to bribe minority groups so that they vote for them again. The damage is suffered not only by those who live there. We all pay, through rates and taxes for the extra social security, for the extra police, for the extra grants necessary to restore jobs. It is an affront to all of us to see the social distress in our cities for so much of which Socialist councils are responsible.

The choice we face is a stark one. We must either have more and more central control, or local electors must exert real local control. We vote for local control. Only the Community Charge makes that possible. No other tax can guarantee local democracy. I must emphasise this: it is because we as a Party believe in local democracy that we must have the Community Charge.

Nicholas Ridley, Environment Secretary, speech to the Annual Conference, 6 October 1987.

### 4.27 **Thatcherism triumphant: pride before the fall**[7]

After a third successive victory in 1987, it seemed to many Conservatives that they had achieved a permanent transformation of the entire political landscape. Enjoying the 'Lawson boom' at home and the Thatcher–Reagan 'special relationship' abroad, Thatcherite Britain was basking in international prestige. This spirit of confidence – soon shown to be overconfidence – was trumpeted by Sir Geoffrey Howe in 1988, shortly before it all began to fall to pieces.

The Conservative Party entered office in 1979 determined to halt and reverse this apparently ineluctable process of national decline. Nine years later, we can, I think, say with confidence that, as a party and indeed as a people, we have succeeded in that goal. Today, in 1988, Britain is once again confident in the world. Confident in Europe. Confident in her relations with both Washington and Moscow. Confident that around the world we are moving with, and even ahead of,

---

7  See also Thatcher's conference speech of 1986, document 6.14.

the currents of the times. How has this happened? ...

The British revival starts with economics: the process of economic disintegration has been spectacularly reversed. The last decade, the Conservative Decade, has been a period of British economic revival on a major scale. ... The British disease has become the British cure. The indicators for growth and productivity have moved from low to high. The indicators for inflation and taxation have moved from high to low. And the turn-round has been witnessed in rising living standards on an unprecedented scale. ... Trade union power has been significantly curtailed. The labour market has become more flexible and competitive. Taxes are now amongst the lowest in the industrialised world. The public sector has been liberated through privatisation on a massive scale – half of State enterprise has been sold. Consumer choice has been decisively increased by deregulation and liberalisation in many fields, from buses to telecom, from aviation to State housing. ...

All this we have achieved by recreating the conditions for competition, opportunity and initiative in Britain, and so releasing forces pent up within the national fabric for too long. We have reawakened the spirit of enterprise. ... What is more, around the world, our message that markets really work has become the established orthodoxy of the day. Whether in English or Chinese, in Russian or Japanese, the message is the same. The language of privatisation, of tax cuts, of free collective bargaining, of enterprise zones, of the abolition of price and exchange controls, of financial deregulation – all policies we pioneered – has become the *lingua franca* of the new international economic order. ... Today, in taxation, as in so many other fields, people look to Britain as a model to follow. The world has become a huge market-place for the export of our ideas. And with that has come renewed confidence and credibility for Britain in its dealings with other countries around the globe. ...

The British insistence that the West maintain a united front against the Soviet arms build-up and against Soviet adventurism abroad has been unswerving. ... At the same time the British recognition that Mr Gorbachev was a new brand of Soviet leader with whom the West could do serious business is now widely accepted. ... The 'firm, eloquent voice' of Margaret Thatcher – as President Reagan put it in the Guildhall – has been heard approvingly in both Washington and Moscow. It has been a vital force in improving the East–West dialogue and helping in the process of superpower detente. Just as it has been crucial to the revival of self-confidence in Britain as a whole, and our growing authority in world affairs.

Sir Geoffrey Howe, address to CPC Summer School, Cambridge, 2 July 1988, *The Conservative Revival of Britain*, Conservative Political Centre, October 1988.

### 4.28 'Basildon man' and the 1992 victory

It was symbolic that John Major's unexpected victory in 1992[8] should be heralded by the early result from the Essex marginal of Basildon. The vital element in Conservative success was the retention of the votes of the skilled working class – the 'C2' social category, for whom the popular stereotype was 'Essex man'. Afterwards, the successful Conservative MP for Basildon reflected on the priorities and aspirations of this group, to whom Thatcherism had made a potent appeal during the 1980s.

The key to success for the Tories, achieved by Margaret Thatcher, was to release ordinary people from the shackles of socialism. People from working-class backgrounds – like me – had been told by the Labour Party that socialism was the hope for the future. But people wanted the truth. We were all sick and tired of left-wing clichés backed up by the power of the trade unions. People were interested in independence, a sense of real community, and the chance to take responsibility for their lives and the lives of their families.

Housing was a central issue. ... When the Conservatives introduced the policy of families being able to buy their own homes from the local Council, it was as if a breath of fresh invigorating air had swept into a stuffy room. Here at last was the common sense approach for which people had been waiting. People were enthusiastic. The very appearance of the housing estates changed as people became proud home-owners. Smart new front doors, beautiful wood-finished windows, attractive gates and hedges, all began to make their appearance. This was tangible evidence of a fundamental rejection of socialism, literally at street level. Attitudes changed too. People liked

8    See also document 1.17.

the independence and security that comes from owning your own patch of Britain. ...

The working-class Conservative vote has always included a large measure of support for us as the Party of the ordinary family against the criminal. This has never been more important than it is today. ...

Basildon people are not 'anti-Europe' – on the contrary, they are more widely travelled, and more familiar with different European resorts, food, and so on than previous generations of their families could ever have dreamed. They have, however, a robust and grateful understanding of British independence and the British parliamentary system, both of which they wish to retain. They will not support a party which does not support this approach. ...

The whole idea of Essex man and his political beliefs has become a sort of cliché or joke in the 90s – but like all good jokes it rests on a solid reality. ... The Conservative Party can articulate, to a very satisfying degree, the hopes and plans of working-class people who believe in independence, patriotism, common sense and common loyalties. We really do believe that ours is a land of 'Hope and Glory', and we want to share this understanding with the next generation with confidence. ... Conservatives ought to be glad to tell the Essex story of how socialism was defeated and people were given a chance to enjoy home ownership, revitalised schools, Trust hospitals, and a new vision of enterprise and initiative. ... A free enterprise culture, centred on a moral base enriched by a spiritual heritage cherished for centuries – that's a realistic way of life. It is one we can offer as the next century approaches.

David Amess, *The Basildon Experience*, Basildon, 1992.

## 4.29 'Back to basics'

1992–93 was a stressful period: disunity over the Maastricht treaty, the exit from the Exchange Rate Mechanism (ERM) on 'Black Wednesday' in September 1992, the introduction of VAT on domestic gas and electricity, the absence of economic recovery and record by-election defeats. Major sought to recover the initiative in his conference speech with a new slogan, 'back to basics'. However, this became entangled with other ministers' criticisms of single mothers, and then with the exposure by the press of the extra-marital affairs of a succesion of junior ministers and backbench MPs.

I want to share some thoughts with you and see if they strike a chord with your own experience. I think that many people, particularly those of you who are older, see things around you in the streets and on your television screens which are profoundly disturbing. We live in a world that sometimes seems to be changing too fast for comfort. Old certainties crumbling. Traditional values falling away. People are bewildered. Week after week, month after month, they see attacks on the very pillars of our society – the Church, the law, even the Monarchy, as if 41 years of dedicated service was not enough. And people ask, 'Where's it going? Why has it happened?' And above all, 'How can we stop it?'

Let me tell you what I believe. For two generations, too many people have been belittling the things that made this country. We've allowed things to happen that we should never have tolerated. We have listened too often and too long to people whose ideas are light years away from common sense. ...

Do you know, the truth is, much as things have changed on the surface, underneath we're still the same people. The old values – neighbourliness, decency, courtesy – they're still alive, they're still the best of Britain. They haven't changed, and yet somehow people feel embarrassed by them. Madam President, we shouldn't be. It is time to return to those old core values, time to get back to basics, to self-discipline and respect for the law, to consideration for others, to accepting responsibility for yourself and your family and not shuffling off on other people and the state. ...

In many parts of the country, crime figures have risen remorselessly. Crimes once confined to the cities have spread out into rural areas, bringing alarm where alarm was never before. We have tried persuasion. Madam President, it hasn't worked. ... If someone belongs in prison, then that is where they should be and that's why we're building more prisons. Better the guilty behind bars than the innocent penned in at home. Let me tell you how I see things. We need tougher rules on bail and no bail for the worst offenders. An end to the right to silence, as Michael Howard[9] announced earlier this week. ... Here too it's back to basics. For some, punishment seems to be a dirty word.

9   The Home Secretary.

133

Well, you'll find it in my dictionary and I strongly suspect that it's in yours. ...

We stand for self-reliance, for decency and for respect for others, for wages that stay in the pay packet and don't drain away in tax. We stand for money that keeps its value, for a country united around those old, common-sense British values that should never have been pushed aside.

The message from this conference is clear and simple: we must get back to basics. We want our children to be taught the best, our public services to give the best, our British industry to be the best and the Conservative Party will lead the country back to those basics right across the board. Sound money, free trade, traditional teaching, re-spect for the family and respect for the law. And, above all, we will lead a new campaign to defeat the cancer that is crime.

John Major, speech to the Annual Conference, 8 October 1993.

## 4.30 'Clear blue water'

As the next election approached, Conservatives were uncertain how to respond to the popularity and centrism of Tony Blair's 'New' Labour Party. The right wished to put 'clear blue water' between the parties, believing that the 'conviction politics' of a vigorous Thatcherite agenda would be both populist and distinctive.

I believe politics is about conviction as well as the pursuit of power. The politician's task is not simply to achieve office. He must persuade the electorate that his views are distinct from those of his opponent. He must have the courage to plant his standard firmly on the battle-field of ideas. That is why we Conservatives have a historic duty be-fore the next election to declare time and again the differences between ourselves and Labour. We should not underestimate the scale of the task; nor should we be daunted by it. ...

Labour will seek to confuse the electorate. It will try to exploit the sense of national renewal that accompanies economic recovery. It will try to steal the fruits of Conservative policy. We must not allow that to happen. We must say loud and clear that Labour is quite different from the Conservative Party. We must point with a strong hand to the clear blue water that divides us from them. ...

When Labour politicians speak of enterprise, they do so nervously without knowledge or conviction, as though they were speaking a foreign language. For let us not forget what Labour's instincts have always been: against profit, success and achievement. In favour of levelling down, the wrong sort of equality. Theirs is the politics of envy, enforced by ever more State intervention and paid for by creeping taxation. ...

We must never let people forget where Conservatism begins – with the individual. The bedrock of our philosophy is the quest for self-reliance and the crusade to lift the horizons of each and every citizen. We must remind voters why we seek to liberate the talents of the individual and to reduce their dependency on the State. Not simply because we oppose high public spending – though we do – but because the essence of community is the active individual. No economy can be dynamic, no community stable without a body of citizens who feel they have control over their lives and destinies; who willingly take responsibility for their own behaviour and the welfare of those closest to them. ...

I want to see a Britain where people are encouraged to rise by their own efforts, to accept personal responsibility and to recognise their duties. Where their successes produce prosperity and their values form the foundations of community. Fifteen years after the Conservative Party came to power, between us and the party that has sat on the Opposition benches all that time, there stretches still clear blue water.

Michael Portillo, speech to Conservative Way Forward fringe meeting, Annual Conference, 12 October 1994.

### 4.31 The 1997 defeat: (i) Major, Europe and unity

Apart from a flurry of scandals at the start concerning several Conservative MPs and candidates, the long general election campaign of 1997 aroused little public interest. In mid-campaign it seemed briefly as if the adoption of a more Eurosceptic tone might erode Labour's massive lead in the opinion polls, but just at this point Conservative disunity over the European single currency issue resurfaced. Not only many candidates but now also some junior ministers were dissenting from the cabinet's compromise 'wait and see' policy, either in speeches or in their election addresses. With the whole carefully constructed façade of party unity wobbling like a jelly, the Prime Minister's frustration boiled over. In a remarkable performance which stands out as a defining moment not only of the campaign but of his whole period as Leader, Major used the next daily press conference as the platform for an unheralded and intensely personal defence of his position, in a final attempt to gloss over the rifts and restore his authority. The speech and the lengthy answers to the questions which followed were delivered in his own inimitable style, at once both prosaic and passionate.

Everyone who has been out there in the country in this campaign knows where the heart and gut of this election lies on the doorstep. The question that re-emerges whichever part of the country you're in, apart from the other important questions, the one that is now beginning to bounce forward everywhere is the question of whether we are going into a Federal European Union or not going into a Federal European Union. ... Now let me turn to the issue that has excited so many of you so often, and it keeps bobbing up in this particular campaign and that is the question of a single currency. I don't believe in the time I've been in politics or indeed the time anybody in this room has been reporting it, that we have had an issue of such magnitude, such importance to our present and our future in this country that has been so woefully misunderstood collectively, in terms of all its implications, both for this country and for the way in which the decision is taken. There is no doubt in my mind that this is the single most important decision that any government has been asked to make for generations. ...

People have characterised my policy as wait and see on Europe. I have to say to you with a great friendliness if I may, that is an utter mis-statement of what my policy is and always has been. My policy has been on an issue like this, of such importance that we have never seen its like, in the political lifetime of anybody alive today, the policy has always been that we would negotiate until we knew what was involved and then we would decide having negotiated the very best deal for the United Kingdom. ... Now I am often urged the advantages of taking a particular position on Europe at this stage. I'm often told it would be a great advantage if I would rule the whole thing out or rule the whole thing in – it would be splendidly decisive, they say. So splendidly decisive that you would send a British Prime Minister naked into that conference chamber with nothing to negotiate and nothing with which to wring the best deal for the United Kingdom out of our partners in those negotiations. ...

[in answering questions from the media:] No option has been closed: I've made it perfectly clear the option's open. If the option had been closed, I would be doing exactly what I said we mustn't do in the interests of the United Kingdom, by closing off the option. The option is open and I don't know what people may have got by ringing up the private offices of this Minister or that Minister; all I can say is, whomsoever they spoke to in the private office isn't sitting round my Cabinet table and if they said what they apparently said to you, they sure as hell are never going to be sitting round my cabinet table. ...

These people[10] have expressed what their instincts are; I've said many people have expressed what their instincts are. They don't know any more than anybody else does at the moment precisely what the outcome of the negotiations will be. To take an earlier Minister who was worried; when one actually examined what that Minister was principally worried about, they were principally worried about the fact that it would be the tax and spend policies that would be surrendered to Brussels. I worry about that; when I was asked the other day I said, 'Yes, I agree with that Minister, I have no intention of having our tax policies determined in Brussels or our spending policies determined in Brussels.' There is a dividing line; in any decision to be made there is a balance of advantages and disadvantages. Some things weigh so strongly in the balance for the advantage that you'd say yes to whatever it may be, others so strongly to the disadvantage that you'd say no. Any suggestion on tax policies or spending policies going to Brussels is so heavily weighted against my instincts, never mind any other Minister's instincts, so heavily weighted against my instincts, so heavily weighted against the sovereignty of the House of Commons, which is more important than any of us – short-term, long-term, individual or party – that the answer to that is no. And if that's what my colleagues are out there saying, even if they may have expressed it inadequately, inelegantly and unhelpfully, if that is what they are saying, I agree with them upon that, I agree with them upon that. What I am saying is that they don't know what I'm going to negotiate – nobody does, nobody does. And what I'm saying to my colleagues, my

10 The dissenting junior ministers, Horam and Paice.

Ministers and you in the press ... What I'm saying is no-one in this room doubts these are the most important negotiations we've had; whether you agree with me, disagree with me, like me or loathe me, don't bind my hands when I am negotiating on behalf of the British nation.

John Major, morning press conference, Conservative Central Office, 16 April 1997.

### 4.32 **The 1997 defeat: (ii) the view from a marginal seat**

The causes of the shattering defeat of May 1997 lie not in the campaign but in the events of the previous four and a half years. The Major government had been struggling from one crisis to another ever since the humiliating exit from the Exchange Rate Mechanism in September 1992. This had been followed by a painfully slow climb out of recession, the breach of a manifesto pledge in extending VAT to domestic fuel, the BSE 'mad cow' crisis, and recurring public strife within the Parliamentary Party over Europe. On top of this was 'sleaze', the generic label for the sexual and financial scandals which embroiled a succession of MPs and ministers. Despite all this, and the dire record in by-elections and in local and European elections, few politicians or pundits expected that the huge Labour lead in the opinion polls would remain solid during the campaign and translate into actual votes in the polling booths on the day. The atmosphere of the final weeks of the Major government are caught in the diary kept by Phillip Oppenheim, a junior Treasury minister who was defending the vulnerable Midlands marginal of Amber Valley.

[4 February:] Smoking Room[11] with Eric Forth, Michael Brown and others after a day on finance bill committee. Everyone's downbeat. I reflect on how buzzy such a New Right group would have been a few years ago. ... Talk turns to an early election. Word is that the Wirral by-election campaign is horrific.

[5 February:] There's a nervous, edgy air. The heart seems to have gone out of C[entral] O[ffice] and No. 10's media efforts.

---

11 Of the House of Commons.

[4 March:] David Evans,[12] voice of the common man, or his perception of the genre, has been taped addressing sixth-formers in derogatory tones about 'black bastards'. The PM disowns him. The damp smell of crumbling masonry is in the air.

[21 March:] I go to my favourite pub, the New Inn. ... A few weeks ago people were coming up wishing me luck, saying they thought it would be close. Now they're cooler. I have a feeling we're going to get stuffed.

[14 April:] We do a run-down terrace. There's none of the bitterness of 1992 when memories of the poll tax were still fresh, we were in deep recession and the pit closures were round the corner. Instead, just an uneasy boredom which is almost harder to handle.

[7 April:] The sun is out and I'm feeling back on the programme. Some pressure on Labour and, best of all, Mawhinney[13] is being kept off the media.

[27 April:] I fear the natural reaction to defeat will be to 'put clear blue water' between us and Blair. Of course, it will be difficult to oppose a government which has adopted most of our own policies. But there's real danger in diving off your own patch of land just because someone else is muscling on to it. Initially bracing though the clear blue water might be, you may not find any other firm land. The risk is that we become an unelectable rump. I'm often said to be a head-banging free-marketeer, but too many at the top and on the Right have cosy, safe seats and aren't used to arguing the toss with instinctively unsympathetic people on draughty council house doorsteps.

[1 May:] As the polls close, I hope that I might just shade it; but the BBC exit poll makes me realise this is a fantasy. I prepare myself for the count, feeling like a kamikaze pilot going to his doom.

Phillip Oppenheim, 'Diary of an underdog', *Sunday Times*, 4 May 1997.


### 4.33 The 1997 defeat: (iii) explaining the landslide

The scale of their defeat left the Conservatives stunned, and Major's immediate announcement of his resignation focused

---

12  Conservative MP for Welwyn Hatfield, a self-made millionaire and football club owner, on the Eurosceptic right wing.
13  Conservative Party Chairman.

attention on the leadership contest rather than an inquest into the disaster. Several months later Michael Portillo (who had been unable to stand for the leadership after losing his seat in the Commons) gave a frank analysis in a speech to a packed fringe meeting at the 1997 Annual Conference.

Let us begin by recognising the scale of our defeat and of our problem. Perhaps as one who went in an instant from being in the Cabinet to being a member of the general public, I am qualified to offer an opinion. I do not accept the view that the Conservatives lost the election of 1997 because we abandoned one-nation Toryism or split the nation. We did not. ... The causes of our defeat were different. I would like to identify what I believe to have been the four principal factors.

First, the Party became associated increasingly with the most disagreeable messages and thoughts. Much of that linkage was unjustified, but since it is what people thought – what people still think – it must be appreciated as a deeply-felt distaste, rather than momentary irritation. We cannot dismiss it as mere false perception. Tories were linked to harshness: thought to be uncaring about unemployment, poverty, poor housing, disability and single parenthood; and considered indifferent to the moral arguments over landmines and arms sales. We were thought to favour greed and the unqualified pursuit of the free market, with a 'devil take the hindmost' attitude.

Second, we abandoned almost completely the qualities of loyalty and the bonds of party without which party effectively ceases to exist. Some of this was ideological. Passions about the future of our country rightly fired people up, but wrongly led them to attack and despise their colleagues. Part of it was egotistical. There were MPs anxious to oblige whenever the media came looking for dissent, seizing the opportunity to be famous for fifteen minutes. ... We must re-discover the old instincts that led Tories to support one another and to rally round. Loyalty was never a secret weapon: it was because it was so visible in *public*, and reinforced in private, that it was so effective. The impact of disunity upon us is clear to see. The Party must in the very near future learn again to display the camaraderie and common purpose that are fundamental to a party's prospects. ...

Third, we were thought to be arrogant and out of touch. Much of it may have been no more than personal mannerisms that grated on the public after years in office. Some of it was insensitivity – using the language of economics and high finance when people's jobs and self-esteem were at stake. And when people looked at the composition of our party, they thought it too elderly, or too vulgar, or too out of touch in vocabulary and perceptions, or in some other way, unfamiliar and unrepresentative.

Fourth, there was sleaze. I did not believe all that Conservatives were accused of. Even today, I do not think that wrongdoing was any more prevalent in our party than in others, and I expect the rotten boroughs of the Labour Party to prove as much in coming months. But it was certainly bad enough. Sleaze disgraced us in the eyes of the public. Their perception was of corruption and unfitness for public service. Such distasteful perceptions can endure and do us damage for a long time.

We should face these issues head on and deal with them. The last years profoundly disappointed our supporters and disgusted many others. Those of us who were in the parliamentary party, and those of us who were in the Government, bear a particular responsibility.

Michael Portillo, speech to Centre for Policy Studies fringe meeting, Annual Conference, 9 October 1997.

# 5

# External affairs: from Empire to Europe

Britain's position in the world changed profoundly during the second half of the twentieth century. At the end of the Second World War Britain was still a great power, one of the victorious wartime 'big three', possessing a world-wide empire; by the 1990s Britain had become a European offshore island with a troubled and ambivalent relationship with her continental partners. The transition from Empire to Europe took place in three stages. The first was the period from 1945 to the Suez crisis in 1956, during which Britain sought to perpetuate a global role and develop the Empire, even after the independence of India in 1948. The second and transitional period of 1957–73 saw a rapid process of decolonisation and withdrawal, culminating in the abandonment of 'east of Suez' under economic pressure in 1968. This was paralleled by an increasing determination to join the European Community, from the first application of Macmillan in 1960 to entry under Heath. The final period was that of Community membership from 1973 onwards, although Britain's possession of nuclear weapons, a 'special' relationship with the United States, and a global export trade meant that there still remained a wider involvement in world affairs.

The documents in this chapter trace the reactions of the Conservative Party to this process: the hopes for world influence and imperial modernisation after 1945, the recognition of change in the late 1950s and 1960s, and the issue of Europe from Heath to Major. The Conservative Party has always placed great importance upon external affairs, but it has also generally been pragmatic and adaptable. Only at a few points have issues in external affairs – the Empire, defence and foreign policy – led to tensions within the Party or to public controversy. These are also reflected in the extracts: the Suez crisis of 1956, the long-running sore of Rhodesia from 1965 to 1979, immigration (a domestic consequence of the imperial role) in the 1960s and early 1970s, and the question of Europe. The latter caused divisions at several points: the initial application under Macmillan and the eventual entry under Heath were both supported rather reluctantly by the rank and file and most MPs due to the lack of alternatives and from loyalty to the leadership, whilst a minority of MPs were actively hostile. However, the most serious rifts on Europe came in the later Thatcher and the Major years, with the Conservative right becoming preoccupied by the erosion of Parliament's sovereignty and antagonistic to the federalist agenda for closer political unity. By 1997, these tensions had produced five years of faction and rebellion in the House of Commons, and had become focused upon the symbolic issue of whether or not Britain would join in the plans for a single European currency at the end of the decade.

### 5.1 **Britain's world role: the 'three circles'**

Churchill believed that Britain's unique position as the link between three groups – the Empire and Commonwealth, the 'special relationship' with the United States (described here as 'the English-speaking world'), and western Europe – would enable her to maintain a leading role in the world. This outlook and ambition remained the basis of Conservative attitudes, even after entry into Europe in the 1970s.

As I look out upon the future of our country in the changing scene of human destiny I feel the existence of three great circles among the free nations and democracies. I almost wish I had a blackboard, I would make a picture for you. I don't suppose it would get hung in the Royal Academy, but it would illustrate the point I am anxious for you to hold in your minds. The first circle for us is naturally the British Commonwealth and Empire, with all that that comprises. Then there is also the English-speaking world in which we, Canada, and the other British Dominions play so important a part. And finally there is United Europe. These three majestic circles are co-existent and if they are linked together there is no force or combination which could overthrow them or ever challenge them. Now if you think of the three inter-linked circles you will see that we are the only country which has a great part in every one of them. We stand, in fact, at the very

143

point of junction, and here in this island at the centre of the seaways and perhaps of the airways also we have the opportunity of joining them all together. If we rise to the occasion, in the years that are to come it may be found that once again we hold the key to opening a safe and happy future for humanity, and will gain for ourselves gratitude and fame.

Winston Churchill, speech to the Annual Conference, 9 October 1948.

## 5.2 **From Empire to Commonwealth**

Pride in the Empire and belief in its importance was central to the Conservative outlook. The Party's first major post-war policy statement was concerned to show that it would seek to work with rather than against the process of greater self-government: the aim was not to end the Empire, but to preserve it by adapting to changing circumstances.

The Conservative Party regards the British Empire and Commonwealth of Nations as the supreme achievement of the British people. Throughout its vast area reign three of the four freedoms: freedom from fear, freedom of expression, and freedom of conscience. A great and unique brotherhood has been built up which has been tried in the white hot fire of two great wars, and has stood the test. It is the most successful experiment in international relations which the world has ever known. We believe that if the British Empire were to break up Britain would become a third-class power, unable to feed or defend herself. The same fate would quite certainly befall every other country of this great family of nations, one by one, and thus would crumble to ruin the world's greatest bulwark of liberty and democracy. This is our hour of destiny. If the countries of the Empire and Commonwealth have the vision to make the most of their opportunities, years of prosperity and peace lie before the British quarter of the world. ...

The Conservative Party recognizes that the British Empire now as ever can only survive through a process of constant evolution, and aims at advancing the political progress of our peoples in accordance with the best interests of each community and of the Commonwealth as a whole. ...

The Conservative Party recognizes that the Empire and Common-

144

wealth are entering upon a period of fresh political experiment. No one can, at present, forecast how the difficult questions involving constitutional and international law will be resolved. We are, however, determined to play our part in ensuring that the experiment does not fail from any want of sympathy and goodwill on our part, however great may be the stresses which recent changes impose upon us all. Everything will depend upon the reality of the sense of common purpose existing between its various members and upon their willingness to accept mutual responsibilities towards each other. ...

The Conservative Party, in pursuing its policy of Imperial unity, will take care to safeguard the good name of Britain as an essential element in fortifying the strength of the Empire, and as a condition of its moral leadership in dangerous times. ...

The Conservative Party will do everything that lies within its power to improve the standards of living throughout the Colonial Empire. ...

The Conservative Party reaffirms that self-government within the British empire and Commonwealth is an aim to be achieved as soon as Colonial peoples are ready for it. It is impossible to state in black and white the precise moment at which a country is ready to govern itself, but the Party considers that two conditions should be laid down which should be fulfilled before full self-government is achieved:

(1) That the country is economically sound and that social services have reached a reasonable standard of efficiency.

(2) That power can be transferred to the people as a whole and not to a small and unrepresentative political, racial or religious oligarchy.

We believe that we should try to develop evolutionary forms of self-government, but should not slavishly follow what may be called the 'Westminster model'.

*Imperial Policy: A Statement of Conservative Policy for the British Empire and Commonwealth*, Conservative and Unionist Central Office, June 1949.

### 5.3 Leadership by example

As the former colonies moved towards autonomy and independence in the second half of the 1950s, Conservatives sought to establish a role for Britain based upon moral leadership and paternalist guidance.

We must destroy the myth that Britain is old and decrepit and has nothing more to contribute. Instead, we must seek to establish in the minds of people everywhere that what we have cast away is simply the old idea of our inalienable right to carry the white man's burden. Our purpose now – and it is one which can raise our fame to even greater heights – is to work towards a position in which, with our centuries of political, technical and economic progress and achievement, we can help those who will go with us to reach a standard of civilisation and living comparable to our own. To use a fresh metaphor: we must convince the world that we have exchanged the role of headmaster for that of committee chairman.

As a corollary of these aims, we must reassess our function as a colonial power and consider how we can apply the techniques evolved by experts in social and economic matters to contrive that the means for the full expression of the human personality are given to all the peoples of our Colonial territories. We must ensure that our philosophy and approach to colonial questions are clearly explained to the governments and peoples of the outside world not merely in terms of facts, but in those of ideas and concepts. By all our actions in international relations and international councils we must demonstrate our maturity and sense of responsibility.

Conservative Commonwealth Council, *Colonial Rule: Enemies and Obligations*, Conservative Political Centre, 1955.

## 5.4 **The Suez crisis**

The Suez crisis caused severe strains in the Parliamentary Conservative Party. The left were unhappy over the invasion whilst the right were angered when it was abandoned; most MPs supported Eden, but were left bewildered by the turn of events. The issues and atmosphere are recalled by Anthony Nutting, who resigned as Minister of State at the Foreign Office when the invasion began.

To say the least, it was an extraordinary situation. For, in truth, we had achieved none of the objectives, whether pretended or real, with which we had set out upon this sorry adventure. We had not separated the combatants [Israel and Egypt]; they had separated themselves. We had not protected the Canal; it was blocked. We had not safeguarded British lives and property, but had subjected them to the gravest hazards. Nor had we achieved our real aim of seizing control of the Canal. Least of all had we toppled Nasser from his throne. In fact, we had fallen between every stool ...

Small wonder that the House of Commons and the country was baffled and confused ... And as the confusion spread, cracks began to show in the monolithic unity of the Conservative Party. Edward Boyle had resigned four days after my own letter of resignation was published; and men like Nigel Nicolson, Jakey Astor, Alec Spearman, Lionel Heald, Robert Boothby and Frank Medlicott were confessing themselves in open revolt against the Government, whilst members of the Suez Group,[1] such as Julian Amery, were up in arms because we had agreed to a cease-fire before the operations were completed. It took all the efforts of the Government Whips, together with fervent appeals for unity from Rab Butler and Harold Macmillan, to prevent the Party from being split from top to bottom. Still, thanks to these efforts and to that inherent sense of self-preservation which holds the Conservative Party together in moments of crisis, the Government were able to command a considerable majority whenever the House divided on the Suez issue.

Anthony Nutting, *No End of a Lesson*, London, 1967, pp. 145, 149.

### 5.5 **Problems in Africa**

In 1960 Macmillan spoke of the 'wind of change' sweeping through Africa, but in many areas political and economic development was complicated by the wide gulf in status and education between the white settler minority and the native majority.

We firmly believe that all Commonwealth territories have the ultimate right of internal self-government, or of sovereign status within the Commonwealth, dependent upon their size, economic viability and other related factors. ... However, it is important to recognise that the criteria will be more complex in multi-racial societies because

1   MPs who had previously opposed the evacuation of the Suez base in 1954.

of the need to ensure justice for minorities.

In multi-racial territories, but not in predominantly uni-racial territories, the watchword of political progress must be Cecil Rhodes' dictum: 'Equal rights for all civilised men'. The grant of universal suffrage to the peoples of multi-racial territories where the preponderant numbers of the majority race are, on the most sympathetic assessment, very backward, can only lead to the swamping of the numerically inferior but politically educated minorities, to the detriment of all sections of the community alike. The more advanced partner or partners, who have hitherto contributed most to such economic prosperity as the territory enjoys, have the right to demand that their high living, educational and cultural standards, which are the result of their own achievements, should be maintained in the process of securing the advance of the more backward, but numerically preponderant, partner. The need is therefore energetically to promote the educational and economic advance of the latter, and at the same time to ensure that minorities do not abuse their temporarily privileged position by arresting or retarding the development of a real political partnership.

This argues a continuing role of the highest importance and difficulty for the United Kingdom, especially in Africa. She must undertake the thankless task of holding the ring in the interests of the respective racial partners. The heritage of the African majority must be held in trust, the political franchise schemes to be devised in a manner just to all, and real educational opportunity increasingly provided for the more backward, until the Africans have not only acquired the ability to look after their own real interests in an advanced society but, more important, have reached an understanding of the meaning of partnership and respect for the rights of minorities. Such a United Kingdom role, open to the constant criticism and misrepresentation of extreme elements of both sides, demands time, understanding and immense patience. It follows that to discharge her responsibility, the United Kingdom must not only be united and single-minded about her objective, but equipped with the necessary means and facilities, financial and defensive, to reach it. That objective will have been attained when racial consciousness is no longer the dominant feature of local politics.

'Report of Policy Committee on Commonwealth and Colonies', 4 May 1959, CPA, ACP/3/(59)73.

## 5.6 **Rhodesia**

These problems surfaced most acutely in Rhodesia, and led to its Unilateral Declaration of Independence in 1965. Although this illegal step was condemned, many Conservatives felt strongly the links of 'kith and kin' with the white settler population and Rhodesia was an emotive issue at Party Conferences until the settlement of 1979. The views of the right found a forum in the Monday Club, and their most prominent advocate in the 1960s was Lord Salisbury, a former Party Leader in the Lords whose dissent over colonial policy had led to his resignation from Macmillan's cabinet in 1957.

... I believe that this present crisis over Rhodesia raises most fundamental issues for the Conservative Party. It raises, indeed, the whole issue of what our Party stands for, whether it stands for anything at all before this country and the world.

I was brought up, as I am sure many others of you here were brought up, to believe that one of the great principles of the Tory Party was to spread the British ideas of liberty and justice among the more primitive peoples of the world and educate them up to formal self-government in accordance with those ideas. But of late it must seem at any rate to a good many of us that there has been a sad change. There has been a confusion in the minds of our leaders, and this I would say applies to all parties alike, between liberty and independence, which are in fact very different things, as recent events in the Congo and elsewhere have shown. There has been a tendency to throw the reins over the horse's head, to get rid of our responsibilities at whatever cost to our kinsmen who are still trying with courage and devotion to carry out our traditional policy in the remote parts of the world.

That was bad enough, but now it seems to me, over this question of Rhodesia, there has come a moment when we are being faced with the final degradation. For we are now being asked by the present Labour Government, not only to abandon our friends and kinsfolk, but in certain circumstances to tell them peremptorily to hand over at a very early date their fate and the fate of their wives and families to the tender mercies of men who they must know, as others here must know, are as yet totally unfitted to conduct any free form of government at all. ...

There are, I am sure, many people in this hall like myself who

149

know Rhodesia and the Rhodesians well. ... They are ordinary, decent people, very much like us, with our background and our traditions, trying to lead the Africans forward and train them in the ways of civilisation. These are the people we are asked by our political opponents to bludgeon and blackmail into submission.

... we owe a great deal to these white Rhodesians. They have brought to their country peace and justice where there were formerly war, pestilence and famine. They have brought increasing prosperity to countless thousands of Africans. ... They have always been the loyalest of the loyal. They have fought for us in our agony during two world wars. I hope, therefore, that this great meeting will say, with no uncertain voice, that we will not have any lot or part now, in this their hour of trial, in turning on them and stabbing them to the heart.

Lord Salisbury, debate on Rhodesia, Annual Conference, 15 October 1965.

### 5.7 **The purpose of entering Europe**

Although Macmillan's attempt to join the 'Common Market' (the European Economic Community) failed in 1963, the Party's commitment to securing entry was reaffirmed in opposition in 1965 and became a central plank in the manifestos of 1966 and 1970.

1. The pace of economic and technological development has opened up a rapidly widening gap between the 'super-powers' and the rest. Faced with continental-sized economies in the U.S.A. and Soviet Union, we cannot hope to expand living standards in Britain unless our own economy is secured on a wider basis.

2. The six Common Market countries intend to advance from economic integration to a form of political union on which they are not yet agreed. Such a union would not only be capable of providing a European market approaching that of the U.S.A., but would also be in a position to exercise an influence on world affairs of the same order. The Group believes not only that Britain has much to gain from becoming a partner in this union, but that the highest interests of Britain and Europe alike demand that we should not be left out.

3. Such a Europe should remain a close ally and partner of the United States, but not be dependent on it. It follows from this that

economic and political independence must also extend to greater military independence for Europe, both conventional and nuclear.

4. Enlarged by the inclusion of Britain, a united Western Europe could be a magnet attracting all other European states, not excluding those of Central and Eastern Europe.

5. A united Europe would provide Commonwealth countries with wider trading opportunities, more capital investment, and increased political and defence support.

6. The Policy Group considers that United Kingdom membership of an expanded European Economic Community is in the best interests of Britain, Europe and the Commonwealth alike. It recommends the inclusion in the next Conservative Manifesto of a statement to this effect. It believes that the British people would support action to implement this policy and that the need for it is urgent. ...

The matter is urgent. If Europe continues to cling to doctrinal purity, to shrink from the dilution inseparable from expansion, she will find that the limits to what she can achieve fall far below the high hopes with which she set out, and that the influence of the EEC will gradually decline, while political unity remains for ever just around the corner.

If Britain continues to cling to an outdated concept of nationalism, to insist upon the unrealistic conditions put forward by the Socialists, or to imagine that European unity can be achieved by piecemeal co-operation, if she shirks the imaginative leap, then we will find that the choices open to us are dramatically narrowed and that our chances of playing an effective role on the world stage have suddenly vanished.

'Report of the Policy Group on Foreign Affairs', 6 August 1965, CPA, ACP/3/(65)20.

## 5.8  The end of the world role

The commitment to Europe was linked to a reluctant acceptance that Britain could no longer maintain a world role, in the phrase of the time, 'east of Suez'.

The cost of Britain's commitments 'East of Suez' is not less than about £365 million a year, and probably more if consequentials could be included. More significant is the extent to which they dominate Britain's military thinking and preparations. In their absence our sea, air and land forces would be constructed on very different lines, and more resources and energy could be devoted to the advanced technological aspects of modern war. The possibility that other European powers would be willing to share the burden of our commitments 'East of Suez' is, unhappily, remote. ...

After the War, the danger to the free world was the threat of Russian expansion. NATO was conceived to meet this, and it succeeded. The threat of Communist expansion now emanates from Peking rather than Moscow. What is the answer to it in the long term? There are basically two alternative policies. One is to maintain a military presence on the continent of South-East Asia itself. The other is to endeavour to organise a counterweight, in the form of a group of independent and more or less neutralist countries, whose integrity would be guaranteed by Western military presence on the outer fringes of the region, for instance in the Philippines and Australasia.

We believe the latter course is infinitely preferable politically, since the military presence inherent in the former is likely to prove a red rag to nationalist movements in the different countries, aided and abetted by local Communist parties. ... In either case the military strength will have to be overwhelmingly American, and British participation could hardly be important either in physical or military terms ...

As a government, our policy would therefore consist of these elements:

(a) To show that where British forces are engaged in pursuance of a specific obligation, this will be honoured.

(b) To seek to work with the United States towards the kind of equilibrium in South-East Asia described above.

(c) To be ready to take opportunities, as and when they present themselves, to withdraw with the minimum 'loss of face', from such positions as are not absolutely indispensable to (a) and (b).

As an opposition, our criticism of the government should be on lines which leave it open to us to follow the above policy in office, but to make no commitments on timing or detail.

'East of Suez', memorandum for the Leader's Consultative Committee [shadow cabinet], by Christopher Soames and Enoch Powell, 25 October 1965, CPA, LCC/65/51.

## 5.9 **Powell and immigration**

Enoch Powell's sensational speech of 1968 caused his swift dismissal by Heath from the shadow cabinet. However, immigration was an acute concern of the Conservative grass-roots throughout the 1960s and 1970s, and 'Powellism' remained a significant force until he left the Party over Ulster in 1974.

It almost passes belief that at this moment twenty or thirty additional immigrant children are arriving from overseas in Wolverhampton[2] alone every week – and that means fifteen or twenty additional families of a decade or two hence. Those whom the gods wish to destroy, they first make mad. We must be mad, literally mad, as a nation to be permitting the annual inflow of some 50,000 dependants, who are for the most part the material of the future growth of the immigrant-descended population. It is like watching a nation busily engaged in heaping up its own funeral pyre. ... In these circumstances nothing will suffice but that the total inflow for settlement should be reduced at once to negligible proportions, and that the necessary legislative and administrative measures be taken without delay. ...

The discrimination and the deprivation, the sense of alarm and of resentment, lies not with the immigrant population but with those among whom they have come and are still coming. This is why to enact legislation of the kind before Parliament at this moment is to risk throwing a match on to gunpowder.[3] ... The sense of being a persecuted minority which is growing among ordinary English people in the areas of the country which are affected is something that those without direct experience can hardly imagine. ... As I look ahead, I am filled with foreboding. Like the Roman, I seem to see 'the River Tiber foaming with much blood'.

Enoch Powell, speech at the AGM of West Midlands Area Conservative Political Centre, 20 April 1968, in R. Collings (ed.), *Reflections of a Statesman: The Writings and Speeches of Enoch Powell*, London, 1991, pp. 374–9.

2   Powell was MP for Wolverhampton South-West.
3   The Race Relations Act of 1968, which extended the Act of 1965.

## 5.10 **Party opinion and entry into Europe under Heath, 1971**

Since the late 1940s the party leadership have taken the pulse of rank and file opinion through the Conservative Political Centre's 'three-way contact' programme, which sends questions on a topic of the moment to the discussion groups in the local associations and reports on their responses. The consultative exercise on entry into the Common Market, taken after the terms were negotiated but before the crucial Commons vote, stimulated 'a tremendous response'.

*Are you in favour of British Entry into the European Community on the conditions negotiated by the Government?*
The answer to this question was overwhelmingly 'Yes'. Most of the reports actually gave voting figures within the groups and from this it has been possible to make a fairly accurate head count ... [491 groups voted Yes, 23 groups voted No, and 55 groups were divided or abstained; within the groups, 4,775 persons voted Yes, 730 voted No, and 847 abstained.]

In several reports it was shown that with the additional information available in the Contact Brief and from listening to other members of their groups, a number of people who had previously been against the Common Market had changed their minds. Other reports also showed that although members of their groups were still in principle against the Common Market, once the decision had been taken they would back the Conservative Government. Quite a number of people within the groups said that they would be reluctant to see Britain taking this step but they added that they could see no possible alternative and therefore were in favour, if not for their own sakes, for the sake of their children.

The two most important reasons given for were the future of Britain's economy and her place in the world. ... In order for Britain's economy to survive the groups said it was essential to find a rich new market. The only possible one was Europe. ... Many groups had been worried by Britain's decline in the power structure of the world and felt that although the present Government had done a great deal to reverse this trend, it was important for the country to be allied to Europe, thus once more having a voice in world affairs. ...

A large number of groups thought that Britain's position within the Community could be an important one, balancing the powers of

France and Germany. It would also ensure that there would be no more European wars. Several groups thought that the Community would gain by having the benefit of Britain's long history of democracy and diplomacy. ...

There were many reasons given against joining the Community. Loss of Sovereignty was the most quoted although there appeared to be some confusion as to what would actually be lost, and many groups who mentioned this thought that any power lost would be minimal and compensated by our increased say in the affairs of Europe. Some thought that as we would have the power of veto nothing much would change. ... Quite a few of the groups who were against thought that the estimated cost of entry was too high, that there was no telling whether it would not be even higher and that the whole project was based on speculation, especially the assumed benefits. ...

There were doubts expressed about whether the Community as a whole could work in the long run as there were too many widely differing countries involved. Other doubts were that the public had not been told all the facts and that in Europe the rich were getting richer while the poor became poorer. Despite all the depressing pictures painted by those against entry, the general feeling was one of hope and conviction that the Government was doing the right thing. Many groups thought that if we did not take this chance, we might not be offered another one or that the cost of entry would be far higher.

'The Common Market', CPC Political Contact Programme, discussion paper 42, September–October 1971, CPA, CCO/4/10/81.

### 5.11 Thatcher and Europe: 'I just want my money back'

Thatcher's relations with the other member states in the European Community were difficult throughout her governments. The tone was set at the start, in the abrasive way in which she tackled the question of adjusting Britain's heavy financial obligations. Ian Gilmour was then a member of the cabinet as Lord Privy Seal, acting as deputy to the Foreign Secretary, Lord Carrington.

If the EEC's financial arrangements were ill-suited for Britain's needs, the row over them was perfectly adapted to the temperament and opinions of the incoming Conservative prime minister, who looked forward to the prospect with relish. Margaret Thatcher had never been an enthusiastic European. Except for denouncing the referendum as a device for dictators, she had played a minor part in the referendum campaign in the mid-seventies. She regarded the Community's chief use as a back-up to NATO in the struggle against Communism. Leading a crusade against public spending at home, she could conceive no less desirable item of expenditure than payments to foreigners. A crusade against our partners in the EEC over our budget contributions was thus an ideal complement to her monetarist crusade.

Mrs Thatcher's strength – and weakness – as a controversialist was that she could rarely see that her adversaries often had an arguable case. ...At the Dublin summit, however, the Prime Minister lived down to all Peter Carrington's worst fears. After giving a shrill exposition of the British case – 'I am not asking for anybody else's money, I just want my money back' – at the first afternoon session of the Council, she again harangued her colleagues for almost the whole of a working dinner which took some four hours. Schmidt feigned sleep, Giscard sat back contentedly watching her weaken her own position, and the others became increasingly unconvinced of the validity of the British case. ...

[In May 1980 Carrington and Gilmour returned from negotiating a reduction of two-thirds, but found Thatcher vigorously opposed:] To my mind there was only one explanation for the Prime Minister's attitude. Her objection was to the fact of the agreement, not to its terms. That was not because we had succeeded where she had failed. It was because, to her, the grievance was more valuable than its removal. Not for the last time during her term of office, foreign policy was a tool of party or personal politics. However badly things were going in Britain, Mrs Thatcher could at least win some kudos and popularity as the defender of the British people against the foreigner. Hence a running row with our European partners was the next best thing to a war; it would divert public attention from the disasters at home. Her attitude was of course inflaming British antagonism to the Community, but that did not worry her at all; it probably pleased her.

Ian Gilmour, *Dancing with Dogma*, London, 1992, pp. 233–5, 240.

External affairs: from Empire to Europe

## 5.12 **A special relationship**

Apart from Heath, every Conservative leader since Churchill
has attached the greatest importance to the 'special relationship' with the United States. The 'Atlantic alliance', given form
by NATO, and co-operation over atomic weapons were the
cornerstone of British defence planning during the Cold War.
In the 1980s the bond was further strengthened by the political affinity and mutual admiration between Margaret Thatcher
and Ronald Reagan, US President 1980–88.

The election of Ronald Reagan as President of the United States in
November 1980 was as much of a watershed in American affairs as
my own election victory in May 1979 was in those of the United Kingdom, and, of course, a greater one in world politics. As the years went
by, the British example steadily influenced other countries in different
continents, particularly in economic policy. But Ronald Reagan's election was of immediate and fundamental importance, because it demonstrated that the United States, the greatest force for liberty that the
world has known, was about to reassert a self-confident leadership in
world affairs. I never had any doubt of the importance of this change
and from the first I regarded it as my duty to do everything I could to
reinforce and further President Reagan's bold strategy to win the Cold
War which the West had been slowly but surely losing.

... Above all, I knew that I was talking to someone who instinctively felt and thought as I did; not just about policies but about a
philosophy of government, a view of human nature, all the high ideals
and values which lie – or ought to lie – beneath any politician's ambition to lead his country. ...At this point, however, the policies of military, economic and technological competition with the Soviet Union
were only beginning to be put in place; and President Reagan still had
to face a largely sceptical audience at home and particularly among
his allies, including most of my colleagues in the Government. I was
perhaps his principal cheerleader in NATO.

So I was soon delighted to learn that the new President wished me
to be the first foreign head of government to visit the United States
after he took office.

Margaret Thatcher, *The Downing Street Years*, London, 1993, pp. 156–8.

## 5.13 Thatcher and Europe: the Bruges speech

*Thatcher's vigorous and controversial address to the College of Europe in 1988 was seen as the seminal statement of Conservative reservations about the future development of the European Community – so much so that the body formed to support these opinions chose as its name the Bruges Group.*

My first guiding principle is this: willing and active co-operation between independent sovereign States is the best way to build a successful European Community. To try to suppress nationhood and concentrate power at the centre of a European conglomerate would be highly damaging and would jeopardise the objectives we seek to achieve. ... I am the first to say that on many great issues the countries of Europe should try to speak with a single voice. I want to see us work more closely on the things we can do better together than alone. Europe is stronger when we do so, whether it be in trade, in defence, or in our relations with the rest of the world. But working more closely together does *not* require power to be centralised in Brussels or decisions to be taken by an appointed bureaucracy. ... We have not successfully rolled back the frontiers of the State in Britain only to see them reimposed at a European level, with a European super-State exercising a new dominance from Brussels. Certainly we want to see Europe more united and with a greater sense of common purpose. But it must be in a way which preserves the different traditions, parliamentary powers and sense of national pride in one's own country; for these have been the source of Europe's vitality through the centuries. ...

My second guiding principle is this: Community policies must tackle present problems in a *practical* way. ... My third guiding principle is the need for Community policies which encourage enterprise. If Europe is to flourish and create the jobs of the future, enterprise is the key. ... And that means action to *free* markets, action to *widen* choice, action to *reduce* Government intervention. ... My fourth guiding principle is that Europe should not be protectionist. The expansion of the world economy requires us to continue the process of removing barriers to trade ... My last guiding principle concerns the most fundamental issue, the European countries' role in defence. Europe must continue to maintain a sure defence through NATO. There can be no question of relaxing our efforts even though it means taking difficult decisions and meeting heavy costs. It is to NATO that we owe the peace that has been maintained over forty years. ...

Let us have a Europe which plays its full part in the wider world, which looks outward not inward, and which preserves that Atlantic Community – that Europe on both sides of the Atlantic – which is our noblest inheritance and our greatest strength.

Margaret Thatcher, speech to the College of Europe, Bruges, 20 September 1988, in A. B. Cooke (ed.), *Margaret Thatcher: The Revival of Britain*, London, 1989, pp. 256–66.

### 5.14 The politics of defence

The Conservative Party has always benefited from its identification with patriotism and a strong defence policy. The 1995 conference address of Defence Secretary Michael Portillo, on the Eurosceptic right and considered by many at the time to be Major's most likely successor, both wrapped the party in the flag and touched on deeper domestic and European issues.

At a time when our national institutions are under attack, our armed forces have maintained the respect of the British public. Perhaps they have done so because their traditions and ethos have changed so little. They have kept political correctness at bay. Their values – discipline, respect, honour – have triumphed over time. Values shared by the Conservative Party. Values cherished by the British people. ...

Britain maintains her own independent nuclear deterrent. Trident has put to sea in the giant submarines built at Barrow-in-Furness. While risks remain to our security, Britain should never give up that ultimate guarantee of our nation's freedom. A Conservative government never will. Our special forces have been in action more often than will ever be told. Around the world three letters send a chill down the spine of the enemy: SAS. And those letters spell out one clear message: don't mess with Britain. ...

We are a significant nuclear power. We are one of the five permanent members of the security council of the UN. We command respect as the world's oldest parliamentary democracy. Twice this century we have risked everything to restore freedom to Europe. Today our armed forces retain a global reach. For all those reasons, our voice is heard in the highest counsels of the world. The objective of British foreign policy is to promote Britain's national interest. ...

The Atlantic Alliance is the rock of our defence policy. ... It would be absurd, as some of our partners are urging, to try to merge our defence co-operation into the European Community. Brussels. You knew I'd mention it. ... We will not allow Brussels to control our defence policy. With a Conservative Government Britain will not join a single European Army. ... Britain will not be told when to fight and when not to fight. ... Britain is blessed with very brave soldiers, sailors and airmen willing to give their lives. For Britain. Not for Brussels. ...

Let us teach our children the history of this remarkable country. I don't mean the wishy-washy sociological flimflam that passes for history in many of our schools today. I don't mean the politically correct, debunking, anti-patriotic nonsense of modern textbooks. I mean the real history of heroes and bravery, of good versus evil, of freedom against tyranny. Of Nelson, Wellington and Churchill. The history that created a sovereign nation. The defence that protected our parliamentary democracy when every country in continental Europe fell to the dictators. The defence that will sustain that sovereignty yet.

We are not ashamed to celebrate Britain's military prowess. On the land. At sea. Or in the skies. To remind the world that this great nation will not be put upon. We are Conservatives. We will speak of pride, of honour, of valour in battle and yes, of glory. The SAS have a famous motto: Who dares, wins. We dare. We will win.

Michael Portillo, Defence Secretary, speech to the Annual Conference, 11 October 1995.

## 5.15 Doubts about Europe, 1996

Conservative disunity over Europe became even more serious during 1995–97.[4] Whilst the disunity amongst MPs attracted the media spotlight, the attitudes and concerns of the rank and file were revealed by the consultation exercise initiated by John Major in 1995.

The vast majority of constituencies favour continued British membership of the European Union. British membership is seen as essential in order to maintain Britain's trading position and influence. This should

4   See also document 4.31 on the European issue during the 1997 election campaign.

not, however, mean that Britain should give up its sovereignty, or that it should accept everything coming from the European Commission. There is common agreement that any move toward a 'United States of Europe' should be resisted fiercely and a clear view that no more powers should be transferred to Brussels. ...

The single currency was a topic of serious debate in the constituencies. The majority of participants were sceptical about the benefits of the single currency and were reluctant to see Britain join up. Some recorded 'virtually unanimous opposition to joining a single currency under any circumstances' (Torridge and West Devon) whilst others argued that 'only when we know what is proposed need we decide' (Portsmouth South). Many constituencies doubted that a single currency would ever come about.

There is some support for the suggestion that 'a parallel currency might contain practical benefits' (Tunbridge Wells). Other comments included the argument that a single currency would 'aid business' (Roxburgh & Berwickshire) and a warning of 'dangers if we opt out of the single European currency' (Bristol NW).

There were differing views on the issue of a referendum. 'There are no conceivable circumstances under which this country should join a single currency – therefore a referendum should never be considered' (Weston-Super-Mare). 'If any British government proposes to join a single currency there must be a referendum, whatever the circumstances are' (Newbury CPC[5]). Other constituencies believed that referendums undermine the British system of parliamentary sovereignty; whilst others reported 'growing acceptance for the need for a referendum on matters concerning constitutional change' (Charnwood). ...

There is great concern about the role of the European Court of Justice and its overruling of decisions by British courts. Many constituencies raised their concerns about the supremacy of European Community law over domestic legislation. This is seen to be deeply worrying, as it has fundamentally changed the flexible, unwritten nature of our constitution, a constitution which has served us well for hundreds of years. There is also some disquiet about the European Court of Human Rights.

*Our Nation's Future: Listening to the Conservative Party*, Conservative Central Office, 1996.

5   Conservative Political Centre, i.e. local political education committee.

# 6

# Conservatism, the state and society

The Conservative Party likes to think of itself as having no ideology, and that it approaches problems simply from common sense. This attitude has three aspects: first, that a 'conservative' party naturally tends to be comfortable working within the assumptions already existing in society; second, that such a self-image identifies the Party with the outlook of the ordinary 'man in the street' – it is democratic, populist, and deliberately anti-intellectual; and finally that it gives the advantage of flexibility and pragmatism – nothing is fixed in advance. Certainly, the Conservative Party has been able to shed both leaders and policies when either seemed to threaten its prospects of getting or keeping office, and to do so with comparatively little trauma or regret.

However, it is a mistake to regard the Conservative Party as driven only by a desire for power, or acting only on the basis of pragmatism and expediency. There is a clear relationship between the different approaches and tools which may be used – the details of policy and legislation – and their underlying foundation of principles. British Conservatism is not so much a doctrine or theory, as a way of looking at the world. It is founded upon scepticism about human nature and distrust of grand designs or of too great a reliance upon reason and man-made institutions. Given the challenge of Socialism, the principal theme of the post-war era has been the role of the state and its relation with the freedom of the individual – in economic choice as well as liberty of expression. The counter-weight of widespread ownership of property has been a Conservative theme throughout the period. However, the influence of economic planning and corporatism in the 'consensus' era from 1945 to the early 1970s has given way to the emphasis upon the free market which emerged in the 1970s and

162

triumphed in the 1980s. The nature of society has been another theme throughout, and this has come more to the fore in recent years as the economic argument seems to have been won.

The extracts in this chapter are taken partly from speeches and partly from books and pamphlets. Many of the latter have appeared under the aegis of the Conservative Political Centre, which was founded by R. A. Butler after the 1945 defeat to foster education and discussion within the Party. There have been more analyses of Conservatism than might be expected, and it is striking that nearly all of them have been written not by academics or journalists but by those actively engaged in parliamentary politics. Whilst discussion can be found in every period, the greatest degree of reappraisal has followed from the combination of electoral defeat and the discredit of past policies, in particular during the post-war decade of 1945–55 and the 1970s. Even so, there has been no transformation of British Conservatism since 1945; the essence remains timeless and unchanging, a point underlined by the very last extract of all.

## 6.1 **The basis of society**

This account of the relationship of individuals and society was provided in the late 1940s by T. E. Utley, for many years a leading Conservative journalist and intellectual.

Individuals are not in fact isolated from each other. They exist and always have existed in society. They belong to societies not because their primitive ancestors at some point resolved to form a community but because they are so constituted as to make it impossible for them to survive outside society. Their thought, inseparable from the language in which it is expressed, is largely a social product. They receive from society more than they give to it, and what they give and what they receive are not easily distinguished. They are born with obligations arising out of society and with needs which can only be satisfied within it. Individual wills, unchecked by society, are a succession of self-contradictory desires which can be made consistent with each other only by the discipline of social relations. Society is natural. Government does not create it, it sustains it; and in proportion as a society is old and has entered deep into the consciousness of its members the aid of government is not needed to keep it together. It is young societies, created by politicians, which have to live in political strait-jackets.

Human nature is violent and predatory and can be held in check only by three forces, the Grace of God, the fear of the gallows, and the pressure of a social tradition, subtly and unconsciously operating as a brake on human instinct, and imparted in childhood. Of these three forces the politician can only direct the last two, and within certain limits he can choose which of them he is going to employ. He can break down societies, uproot their traditions and scatter their members, and then rebuild them, not by the force of convention but by the regime of the policeman and the hangman; or he can build upon existing communities, nurturing their traditions, fencing them round with protective barriers and leaving them free within large limits in the knowledge that their excesses will be checked by the power of tradition. The tragedy of twentieth century enlightenment in politics is its instinctive preference for the former method. Socialism is destroying the community to install the State.

T. E. Utley, *Essays in Conservatism*, Conservative Political Centre, 1949.


## 6.2 The limits of politics

Given their view of human nature, Conservatives distrust grand programmes as naïve and unworkable, and they regard the politics as being more limited and less important. An eloquent statement of this view comes from the influential discussion of Conservatism written by Quintin Hogg (later Lord Hailsham) in the wake of the 1945 defeat.[1]

The Conservative does not believe that the power of politics to put things right in this world is unlimited. This is partly because there are inherent limitations on what may be achieved by political means, but partly because man is an imperfect creature with a streak of evil as well as good in his inmost nature. By bitter experience Conservatives know that there are almost no limits to the misery or degradation to which bad governments may sink and depress their victims. But whilst others extol the virtues of the particular brand of Utopia they propose

1 See also *The Industrial Charter* of 1947, document 4.6.

to create, the Conservative disbelieves them all, and, despite all temptations, offers in their place no Utopia at all but something quite modestly better than the present. He may, and should, have a programme. He certainly has, as will be shown, a policy. But of catchwords, slogans, visions, ideal states of society, classless societies, new orders, of all the tinsel and finery with which modern political charlatans charm their jewels from the modern political savage, the Conservative has nothing to offer. He would rather die than sell such trash, and consequently it is said wrongly by those who have something of this sort on their trays that he has no policy, and still more wrongly by those who value success above honour that he ought to find one. But if he is to be true to the light that is in him, the Conservative must maintain that the stuff of all such visions political is either illusion (in which case they are to be pitied) or chicanery (in which case they are to be condemned).

Quintin Hogg, *The Case for Conservatism*, Harmondsworth, 1947, pp. 11–12.


### 6.3 **Churchill's Conservatism**

The definition of Conservative principles given by Winston Churchill in 1946 reflected his Tory romanticism and Britain's role as a world power, as well as the more recent themes of anti-Socialism.

But if you say to me, 'What account are we to give of the policy of the Conservative Party? What are we to say of our theme and our cause and the faith that is in us?' That is a question to which an answer can always be given. Our main objectives are – To uphold the Christian religion and resist all attacks upon it. To defend our Monarchical and Parliamentary Constitution. To provide adequate security against external aggression and safety for our sea-borne trade. To uphold law and order and impartial justice administered by courts free from interference or pressure on the part of the Executive. To regain a sound finance by a strict supervision of national income and expenditure. To develop and defend our Empire trade without which Great Britain would perish. To promote all measures to improve the health and social conditions of the people. To support as a general rule, free

165

enterprise and initiative against State trading and nationalisation of industries.

Winston Churchill, speech to theAnnual Conference, 5 October 1946.

## 6.4 **National unity**

Conservatives have always given priority to the unity of the nation as a whole, particularly in contrast to the Socialist theme of conflict between classes.

Conservatism is impregnated with a belief in the essential unity of the nation. It does not believe that it is possible in the long run for one section of the community to be benefited at the expense of another. It believes that just as no human toe is helped by the mutilation of the same body's little finger, so all sections and classes in our community are all members of one another. It believes in the organic unity of the nation. There is no section of the community for which it 'does not care two hoots'. It believes that it is much more important to increase the absolute size of the slice of the national cake which each individual receives than to secure a mathematically exact division of an ever diminishing cake. It believes that sectional antagonisms do general harm. It recalls that our periods of national unity have been periods of national greatness, and that our periods of internal strife have been periods of national impoverishment and humiliation.

John Boyd-Carpenter, *The Conservative Case*, London, 1950.

## 6.5 **The ladder and the queue**

In a radio broadcast during the 1951 election campaign, Churchill used this metaphor to illustrate the essential difference between Conservatism and Socialism.

The difference between our outlook and the Socialist outlook on life is the difference between the ladder and the queue. We are for the ladder. Let all try their best to climb. They are for the queue. Let each

166

wait in his place till his turn comes. But, we ask, 'What happens if anyone slips out of his place in the queue?' 'Ah!' say the Socialists, 'Our officials – and we have plenty of them – come and put him back in it, or perhaps put him lower down to teach the others'. And then they come back at us and say 'we have told you what happens if anyone slips out of the queue, but what is your answer to what happens if anyone slips off the ladder?' Our reply is 'we shall have a good net and the finest social ambulance service in the world'. This is of course only a snapshot of a large controversy.

Winston Churchill, BBC radio broadcast, 8 October 1951.

## 6.6 Property, choice and responsibility

The social and moral superiority of a property-owning democracy[2] is argued in this pamphlet by David Eccles, a rising MP who later served as a cabinet minister in the Macmillan era.

I wonder if the Labour Party realise that the whole of the Social Security system is a substitute for some of the advantages which a reasonable slice of property would bring? The imitation is flattering, but it falls far short of the genuine article. ... The man of some property is free to choose the school for his child, the doctor for his wife, the place to take his family for a holiday. He commands a very different kind of opportunity, and one so infinitely more varied and creative that Conservatives put at the centre of their policy a determination to bring this resourceful freedom within the reach of every hard-working man and woman.

This is the first reason why we shall work for the property-owning democracy. We know that it is a better form of social security. But besides giving a man elbow room to live a full life, property also buttresses his character in a way that State benefits or pensions cannot do. Conservatives are convinced that this second aspect of ownership is of great importance. We have always judged a nation by the men she breeds, and we have constantly in mind that men and women have to struggle all their lives to be good and that their success or

2 See also Eden's use of this phrase in his 1946 conference speech, document 4.5.

167

failure is influenced by the institutions under which they live. Ownership of property is an institution which far more often than not has a creative and beneficial effect upon character. ...

The Communists and most Socialists place the power of the State ahead of the character of the citizen. They cannot tolerate a body of independent and self-reliant men and women able and willing to criticise the mistakes of the central planning authority. They support nationalisation for reasons of political power; we shall govern without this clumsy bludgeon. Obviously in the property-owning democracy we shall only be able to guide industry by consent ... The wider is the distribution of property the more citizens there will be who are in a position to thumb their noses at would-be dictators. On this point Conservatives and Liberals should be able to agree: private ownership is an indispensable insurance against totalitarianism of any sort.

Private property is then a good thing because it fortifies and enlarges the personality and bars the way to tyrants, and Conservatives, looking at human nature in the round and having faith in what they see, desire that as many men and women as possible should enjoy the opportunity to show that they can be trusted to use possessions responsibly.

David Eccles, *About Property-Owning Democracy*, Conservative Political Centre, 1949.

### 6.7 **Elevating the many**

R. A. Butler, a leading figure from 1945 to 1964, voices the perennial theme of achieving equality through providing opportunities rather than imposing restrictions, of 'levelling up' rather than 'levelling-down'.

We have moved into a new period. There are our Tory 'neo-Fabians' who say that *Change is our ally*. There are others who prefer to stress that 'the general and perpetual voice of men', the common judgement of centuries, cannot be lightly dismissed but must be treated with reverence and respect. The classical role of Conservatism has always been to find the right mean between its dynamic and its stabilising aspects.

When there was an excess of *laissez-faire* we leaned towards the authority of the State; now that there is an excess of bureaucracy we are leaning towards individual enterprise and personal liberty. We should continue to lean, but without losing our balance.

Society is a partnership, and so underlying all our differences there should be a fundamental unity – the very antithesis of the 'class war' – bringing together what Disraeli called the Two Nations into a single social entity. The Tory record and contribution to social unity and welfare are unrivalled; and the present administration has sought faithfully to maintain this honourable tradition, particularly by our housing programme, by increases in insurance benefits, and by legislation to improve working conditions, for example in the mines.

But if Disraeli provided us with inspiration, he was no less prescient in warning us of the pitfalls. He cautioned us, for example, that posterity was not a pack-horse always ready to be loaded with fresh burdens. He cautioned us no less strongly that we should seek to secure greater equality, not by levelling the few, but by elevating the many. ... We are confronted now with the Socialist concept of the social services as a levelling instrument, a means of securing that everyone shall have just the same average uniform standard of life. Wherever we meet it, we can see how self-defeating this concept must be.

... it is our policy to give real help to the weak. It is no part of our policy to repress the initiative and independence of the strong. Indeed, unless we allow men and women to rise as far as they may, and so allow our society to be served by what I describe as *the richness of developed differences*, we shall not have the means to earn our national living, let alone to afford a Welfare State.

R. A. Butler, in *Tradition and Change: Nine Oxford Lectures*, Conservative Political Centre, 1954.

### 6.8 **Growth and intervention: a 1960s perspective**

Keynesian ideas of government intervention had become the economic orthodoxy by the 1960s but Conservatives remained doubtful, as shown in this pamphlet by Sir Edward Boyle, the leading figure on the liberal wing of the Party.

If we want to preserve full employment, to curb inflation and to safeguard our balance of payments, then the Government must ensure a balance, by means of monetary and budgetary policy, between the total of our available economic resources and the claims made upon them. Furthermore, quite apart from the restraints imposed by our balance of payments and by the need to defend sterling, we shall never secure growth and efficiency if we allow the economy to become over-heated. ...

I think the really difficult questions about economic intervention arise when one goes on from the objective of controlling the overall level of demand to consider how far the government should intervene to influence the whole future development of our economy. ...

It seems to me clearly right, and in full accordance with our own Conservative Party philosophy, that the Government should deliberately make it their business to encourage faster growth, for a number of reasons. First, as our policy document says, 'The Conservative Party is not afraid of the consequences of prosperity' ... And secondly, we have also said that we believe in people leading 'a new and more worthwhile style of life'. In other words our pursuit of economic growth has a social purpose as well as an individual purpose. ... Then thirdly, we believe in the encouragement of economic growth because we know that Britain's future is bound up with the development of modern science-based industries. There is no future for Britain as a backwater: we must be part of the mainstream of industrial advance and hence our emphasis, for example, on seeking new ways of promoting technological co-operation on a European scale. ...

Clearly major decisions on public expenditure must affect the shape of our economy, especially when these involve large sums of money and large amounts of scare resources, including highly-trained manpower. None the less – and here we come to a real difference between ourselves and our opponents – we do not believe that government intervention to shape the economy is as important as intervention to encourage growth. ... For one thing, we set a higher store by consumer preference which we believe should normally be paramount. Secondly, and more important in a period of rapid technological change, we do not believe that any government can forecast which firms, which industries or even which technologies will be most important to the nation in ten or even five years' time.

Sir Edward Boyle, *Conservatives and Economic Planning*, Conservative Political Centre, 1966, pp. 11–14.

## 6.9 **Market forces**

The virtues of market forces, here given a cautious endorsement by Nigel Lawson in the mid-1960s, later became the central faith of the Party's economic ideas in the Thatcher era, during which Lawson served as Chancellor of the Exchequer from 1983 to 1989.

Certainly if there is such a thing as a Tory economic policy, the Tories themselves are keeping remarkably quiet about it. ... in the economic section of the [1966] Manifesto, which is apparently so important that it has to be put first in the whole document, there is little more in terms of policy than commitments to lower taxation, increased incentives for earning and saving, more competition and the reform of the trade unions. All of them doubtless worthy aims, but they hardly add up to an economic policy ...

It is perhaps an awareness of this void which leads a number of Conservatives to embrace the doctrines of Manchester School Liberalism. Uncertain as to what a Tory Government ought to do in the economic field, they fall back on the answer that it should do nothing at all – or at least as little as possible, leaving as much as possible to the free play of market forces. There are undoubtedly attractions in this type of approach. In the first place it is quite clear that Socialists distrust the working of the market and advocate an ever-increasing role for the state, while Tories, like old-style Liberals, believe that in present conditions there is more cause to distrust the state and to leave a far greater share of the load to the free economy. There is, thus, a clear distinction between the parties. ...

But convenient and natural as this approach to Conservative economic policy is, it is plainly an inadequate one. ... The slumps of the past have shown all too clearly that complete laissez-faire leads to anything but the optimum solution to the nation's – indeed, the world's – economic problems. This is one reason why governments are forced to intervene and take a positive role in economic policy. And another reason is that they are directly responsible for a large sector of the economy themselves – defence, education, welfare and so on, not to mention the less direct relationship with the nationalised industries – which must not only be run efficiently but whose activities inevitably have a profound bearing on the rest of the economy and on the economic problems of the nation as a whole.

171

So therefore it is not enough, valid as it is as far as it goes, for Conservatives to stand on the liberal platform of less state interference. They can say, certainly, that the state's role should be smaller than is advocated and practised by the present Government. They might even legitimately hold the view that it should be smaller than it was in the last days of the last Conservative administration. But whatever happens there remains a major government role left, and the important question in the formulation of Conservative economic policy is what that role should be. That is the heart of the matter.

Nigel Lawson, in *Conservatism Today: Four Personal Points of View*, Conservative Political Centre, 1966, pp. 48–51.

### 6.10 The foundations of Thatcherism

The first major policy statement prepared after Thatcher became Leader in 1975 laid the foundations of the Party's aims and principles in the 1980s. The new tone which it struck, especially on taxation and public spending, was shaped by two influences. The first was Thatcher's conversion to the monetarist and libertarian views advocated by her mentor, Sir Keith Joseph, and promoted by influential 'think-tanks' such as the Institute of Economic Affairs and the Centre for Policy Studies. The second was the economic problems and financial crisis which Britain was experiencing acutely, especially during the humiliating 'IMF crisis' in 1976.

The Conservative approach entails living within our means, paying our way in the world, mastering inflation, reviving the wealth-creating part of the economy and encouraging all those on whom it depends. This approach means less bureaucracy and less legislation, lower taxes and borrowing, higher profits leading to more investment and more employment, and rewards for enterprise and hard work. To gain the consent and support which will be essential if we are going to meet all these objectives, we shall have to encourage a wider understanding of the free enterprise system and greater participation in it, and also to secure from all sections of society a broader acceptance and understanding of economic reality. ...

The first essential in economic management is the conquest of inflation. This must be the foundation of a more stable economic environment. To this end, a steady and disciplined monetary policy is vital. Monetary policy will be neither stable nor disciplined unless the State's own finances are swiftly put in order. As things are, the Government's expenditure far outruns its revenue. ...A reduction in government borrowing is thus essential to proper control of the money supply. In addition, it would now be right to announce clear targets for monetary expansion as one of the objectives of economic management. ... The Conservative Party's view that public spending cuts are essential if we are to bring the economy back into balance, and avoid an explosion in the money supply and an acceleration of the rise in prices, has now been accepted by politicians and informed opinion across a very wide political spectrum. ... it is clear that very large reductions will be unavoidable. The days of high spending politics are at an end. ... Frightening examples of serious waste and extravagance are well known to every citizen, and are now reported widely and regularly in the press.

Regaining control of public expenditure, and steadily reducing the share of national income absorbed by government, is not a narrow, restrictive policy. ... We do not argue that all public spending is bad and that only private spending is good. But too much public spending that the nation cannot afford is bad. It saddles an increasing number of people with a growing burden of tax. It throttles initiative at every level. It destroys jobs. We shall only have a chance of breaking out of the closing Socialist circle of tax, subsidy, controls, debt and unemployment if we succeed in cutting the overload of public spending. ...

Much of our present and future prosperity and expansion depends on the health and growth of smaller businesses. They provide a vital element in the free enterprise system. They ensure a wide range of choice for consumers, employ many millions of people, and are a major source of inventions and new products. Small businesses have faced exceptionally difficult conditions recently. They have had to grapple not only with the recession and inflation but also with a hostile government. ... We shall therefore be announcing in a few months a detailed programme for the revival of smaller businesses. ...

Our policies are designed to restore and defend individual freedom and responsibility. We mean to protect the individual from excessive interference by the State or by organisations licensed by the State, to stop the drift of power away from the people and their democratic institutions, and to give them more power as citizens, as owners and as consumers. We shall do this by better financial management, by reducing the proportion of the nation's wealth consumed by the State, by steadily easing the burden of Britain's debts, by lowering taxes when we can, by encouraging home ownership, by taking the first steps towards making this country a nation of worker owners, by giving parents a greater say in the better education of their children.

*The Right Approach: A Statement of Conservative Aims*, Conservative Central Office, October 1976, pp. 23–7, 35, 71.

### 6.11 The pragmatic approach

Sir Ian Gilmour's analysis of Conservative history and principles, *Inside Right*, was an influential and eloquent argument for a moderate and pragmatic approach. In 1981, as a leading cabinet 'wet', he was dismissed from the first Thatcher government.

British Conservatism then is not an '-ism'. It is not an idea. Still less is it a system of ideas. It cannot be formulated in a series of propositions, which can be aggregated into a creed. It is not an ideology or a doctrine. It is too much bound up with British history and with the Conservative Party. Yet equally it is not merely a practice, the practice of the Conservative Party. ...

The Conservative attitude to change must clearly often be purely responsive. Necessary change is often unpredictable, and Conservatives are the last people to favour change which is unnecessary. ... How much the Tories should attempt to initiate is a matter of judgement at the time. That judgement should be formed by the needs of the country, the temper of the people, and the behaviour of the party's opponents. It cannot merely be formed by a judgement of what the party would like to do. ...

To build upon experience, rather than to attempt to overturn it, to pay attention to the available evidence, is the way to effect change in accordance with 'the manners, the customs, the laws, and the traditions of a people' ... Conservatives favour the development of old institutions and customs and the grafting of the new onto the old rather than outright abolition and brand-new creation. ... Britain is not an organism. But it is much more like an organism than a piece of

Conservatism, the state and society

machinery or a random memoryless collection of atomized individuals. Hence the path of wisdom is to treat it as though it were an organism, and to avoid causing it pain or giving shocks to its system.

Anticipatory change is not only likely to help the Tory Party to stay in power and therefore to lead to less change of the sort that Conservatives think is undesirable. By removing grievances before they fester it is also likely to lead to greater moderation by Labour Governments. ... In the British two-party system, moderation in one party is likely to engender moderation in the other, and extremism is likely to breed extremism. The true Conservative course therefore is to stick as closely as possible to the centre with a slight Right incline. This may well produce acceptance and consensus, and at most only a Left incline in response. A sharp Right turn on the other hand is likely to be followed by an even sharper Left turn. Hence Conservative moderation brings its own reward. The best way of safeguarding the future is by not trying to return to the past. ...

Conservatives avoid ideology because they have seen that all ideologies are wrong. They strongly suspect, too, that the adoption of an ideology would make them a party based on class. Ideology seems inseparable from class; hence the Tories can only remain a national party if they remain free from ideological infection.

Ian Gilmour, *Inside Right: A Study of Conservatism*, London, 1977, pp. 121–32.

## 6.12 'One nation' Toryism

The Disraelian theme of 'one nation' Toryism became the emblem of the traditional and pragmatic Conservatives – the 'wets' on monetarism and economic policy – who were concerned by the divisive and confrontational aspects of Thatcherism. Their case was put by Francis Pym, Foreign Secretary from the Falklands crisis of 1982 to the election victory of 1983, in a book written after he was dropped from the cabinet.

I believe in a particular approach to politics which is variously described as 'the Disraelian tradition' or 'One Nation Conservatism'. This approach has characterised the party at its greatest moments

175

and has ensured its survival as a broad party of government rather than as a narrow and dogmatic faction. The first quality of this tradition is to welcome and then to synthesise a wide spectrum of opinion. It is founded on the need to listen to people, whether one agrees with them or not. It demands a constant attempt to win their consent. It believes in building on the things that unite people and not exaggerating the things that divide them. It has become quite unfashionable.

... At the moment, the only options for a Conservative Member of Parliament are to be praised as an echo, to be castigated as a rebel, or to say nothing. That is what I dislike about the current state of affairs. It promotes narrow-mindedness and intolerance. It adopts the principle that to veer even one degree off the true course is to miss the harbour. It ignores the fact that the coast is graced by many harbours, none of them perfect.

But fashions change. ... In the meantime, my concern is that the flag of traditional Conservatism is kept flying ... The values of this tradition are as much to do with the approach to politics as with specific policies. ... The politics of consent ... are based on the proposition that it is both more attractive and more effective if Governments attempt to win the consent of the nation as a whole, rather than railroad people into partisan decisions. In that way, the policies are more acceptable at the time and are less likely to be reversed later.

Such an approach calls for an understanding of people and of circumstances. It calls for a harmony between individual ambition and wider social considerations. It calls for a recognition that we are all interdependent. It calls for tolerance and humour. It calls for leadership that responds to people in the present and anticipates their needs in the future. It precludes dogma, ideology, inflexibility, shortsightedness and intolerance. It asserts that life itself is a balance and that politics must reflect this fact. That is why my main political concern, now as always, is not to be the permanent protagonist of a fixed point of view, but to make a positive effort to redress whatever imbalance currently exists.

Francis Pym, *The Politics of Consent*, London, 1984, pp. ix–xi.

## 6.13 **Property, inequality and class**

The defence of property has always been a fundamental element in British Conservatism. In presenting the Conservative case before the 1983 general election, Chris Patten explains the benefits that property brings and argues that inequality is a natural state.

The private possession of property also helps to spread power and to assure individual liberty. A society in which there is private property, distributed among many different individuals and institutions, will not necessarily be a free society, but it is much more likely to be free than a society in which most things are owned by the State. Property not only supports liberty, its possession also provides a reasonable objective for every individual and a safeguard for the family; working and saving to acquire property helps to fuel the engine of the economy and to make it more prosperous. The failures of Soviet agriculture are far from being the only example of the economic consequences of collectivised ownership.

The unequal distribution of property is in part a result of the unequal distribution of talent among individuals, in part of the random operation of chance and in part of heredity. Since Conservatives do not believe that absolute equality is attainable, and that its pursuit is debilitating and wasteful, they are not motivated by the desire to equalise wherever they can; but since they believe in fairness, there are extremes of inequality which they would not be prepared to tolerate. Man is equal in two ways: he is equal to his fellows in the eyes of God and he is equal as a citizen – one man's vote counts as much as the next man's. However, human beings do not have equal abilities and good fortune cannot be ladled out in precisely equal helpings. People should be given similar opportunities to make the best of those talents that they have. The State should not attempt to equalise those talents, hindering those with more in order to minimise the advantage which they inevitably possess. The pursuit of equality of result guarantees mediocrity and promotes unfairness; discrimination against ability is a particularly unattractive feature of much egalitarianism.

Differential advantages produce social inequalities and social inequalities in turn produce a class system. ... Conservatives are not obsessed by class. Some sort of class structure is inevitable; there has been no developed society without one. What is important is first that any class system should be fluid; secondly, that within it those who possess more should be prepared to discharge the greater responsibilities conferred by privilege; and thirdly, that class should not be allowed to divide the nation.

Chris Patten, *The Tory Case*, London, 1983, pp. 11–12.

### 6.14 The crusade of Thatcherism

At the height of her power, Margaret Thatcher summed up the outlook of her government in her speech to the 1986 Annual Conference.

But just now I want to speak about Conservative policies, policies which spring from deeply held beliefs. The charge is sometimes made that our policies are only concerned with money and efficiency. I am the first to acknowledge that morality is not and never has been the monopoly of any one party. Nor do *we* claim that it is. But we *do* claim that it is the foundation of our policies.

Why are we Conservatives so opposed to inflation? Only because it puts up prices? No, because it destroys the value of people's savings. Because it destroys jobs, and with it people's hopes. That's what the fight against inflation is all about. Why have we limited the power of trade unions? Only to improve productivity? No, because trade union members want to be protected from intimidation and to go about their daily lives in peace – like everyone else in the land. Why have we allowed people to buy shares in the nationalised industries? Only to improve efficiency? No, to spread the nation's wealth among as many people as possible. Why are we setting up new kinds of schools in our towns and cities? To create privilege? No, to give families in some of our inner cities greater choice in the education of their children, a choice denied them by their Labour councils. Enlarging choice is rooted in our Conservative tradition. Without choice, talk of morality is an idle and an empty thing. ...

Our opponents would have us believe that all problems can be solved by state intervention. But governments should not run business. Indeed, the weakness of the case for state ownership has become all too apparent. For state planners do not have to suffer the consequences of their mistakes. It's the taxpayers who have to pick up the bill. This government has rolled back the frontiers of the state, and will roll them back still further. So popular is our policy that it's being taken up all over the world. ... The policies we have pioneered are catching on in country after country. We Conservatives believe in popular capitalism – believe in a property-owning democracy. And it works! ...

The great political reform of the last century was to enable more and more people to have a vote. Now the great Tory reform of this century is to enable more and more people to own property. Popular capitalism is nothing less than a crusade to enfranchise the many in the economic life of the nation. We Conservatives are returning power to the people. That is the way to one nation, one people.

Margaret Thatcher, speech to the Annual Conference, 10 October 1986.

### 6.15 **John Major and the 'classless society'**

John Major's first speech as Leader to the Party Conference set out many of the themes of his leadership, not least in the evocation of his own humble origins in Brixton.

This is the first conference I have addressed as Leader of the Conservative Party. It is hard to explain quite how I feel about that. It is a long road from Coldharbour Lane to Downing Street. It is a tribute to the Conservative Party that that road can be travelled. Perhaps at the back of this hall today there is another young man or woman who stands where I did 30 years ago. Who knows few people here. Who feels it is a long road to this platform, too. They should remember the last two leaders were a builder's son from Broadstairs and a grocer's daughter from Grantham. We don't need lectures in the Conservative Party about opportunity. We are the Party of opportunity. This Party is open to all. And to all those who may be watching, wherever you come from, whatever your background, I say simply this: 'Come and join us.' There are no barriers in our Party, just as there will be no barriers in the Britain we are building together.

Some people ask whether we will have a different sort of Conservatism in future. Of course we will. We all bring our own beliefs, our own instincts, and our own experiences to politics. And I am no

179

exception. But the fundamental beliefs of the Conservative Party, those beliefs that brought me into this Party, ... remain as strong today as ever. Old though our Party is, the values behind it are older still. They are rooted in the instincts of every individual. And it is through our policies that we make them come alive.

What is it that we offer? A strong Britain, confident of its position; secure in its defence; firm in its respect for the law. A strong economy, free from the threat of inflation, in which taxes can fall, savings can grow, and independence is assured. I want to give individuals greater control over their own lives. Every mother, every father, a say over their child's education. Every schoolchild, a choice of routes to the world of work. Every patient, the confidence that their doctors can secure the best treatment for them. Every business, every worker, freedom from the destructive dictatorship of union militants. Every family, the right to have and to hold their own private corner of life; their own home, their own savings, their own security for the future – and for their children's future. Building the self-respect that comes from ownership. Showing the responsibility that follows from self-respect. That is our programme for the 90s. I will put it in a single phrase: the power to choose – and the right to own. ...

I spoke of a classless society. I don't shrink from that phrase. I don't mean a society in which everyone is the same, or thinks the same, or earns the same. But a tapestry of talents in which everyone from child to adult respects achievement; where every promotion, every certificate is respected, and each person's contribution is valued.

John Major, speech to the Annual Conference, 11 October 1991.

### 6.16 Conservatism and free markets

The free market became a central theme of Conservative thinking in the 1980s and 1990s. The limits on pure economic liberalism are here discussed by David Willetts, a prominent Conservative intellectual and a leading figure in the Thatcherite 'think-tank', the Centre for Policy Studies, from 1987 to 1992.[3]

---

3    After becoming an MP in 1992 he rose rapidly to ministerial office, but had to resign in 1996 after a criticism by Commons inquiry.

Modern conservatism aims to reconcile free markets (which deliver freedom and prosperity) with a recognition of the importance of community (which sustains our values). ... Some thinkers maintain that free markets and communities are irreconcilable – that free markets destroy communities. Free markets require the free movement of labour and of capital. Unemployed people are supposed to pull up sticks, 'get on their bikes', and move to where the new jobs are. ...

A conservative understands that, in Quintin Hogg's neat expression, economic liberalism is 'very nearly true'. It offers a host of valid insights into the operation of the economy, but it just will not do as a complete political philosophy. Free markets need conservatism. ...An understanding of our position in historic communities is essential to answer these deeper questions.

Secondly, the conservative understands the importance of the institutions and affiliations which sustain capitalism. There may be a universal instinct to 'truck, barter and exchange', but it only generates a modern advanced economy if it is expressed through a particular set of institutions such as private property, a law of contract, an independent judiciary, and legislation to ensure consumers have accurate information. These institutions need to be sustained by ties of loyalty and sentiment. ...

Thirdly, we do not accept markets and the price mechanism everywhere. You cannot sell your children. You cannot sell your vote. The state does not raise revenue by auctioning places on a jury. ...

If one turns to normal people's everyday experience, those fears about the destructive forces unloosed by free markets seem absurd and hysterical. The British suburb is not a place of rootless, miserable apathy. People, admittedly, do pursue their material aspirations – to own their house, to pay off the mortgage, to be able to afford a good holiday – but these are not immoral or shameful. And at the same time the latest sociological researchers confirm what one may anyway have suspected: that suburbs comprise rich networks of voluntary association, from Rotary Club to British Legion, from the rota for driving children to school to the firm's social club. Even that urge to home ownership, satisfied more successfully in the 1980s than in any other decade, has given people new and stronger ties to their neighbourhood. Ownership and belonging go together. Our civic culture is under greatest strain not in the suburbs but in the inner cities from where so many businesses have fled. It is the absence of a modern capitalist economy which brings the real problems, not its success. So conservatives can happily value both the historic traditions of this country and the values of freedom and the free market.

David Willetts, *Modern Conservatism*, Harmondsworth, 1992, pp. 92–4, 108.

## 6.17 The social agenda of the 1990s

In the 1990s, after the success of Thatcherism in reshaping the language of politics on the economic front, Conservative concerns about social matters – in particular the rising levels of crime and the threats to the traditional family – became more prominent and central.

Crime and the fear of crime are very real issues both to Conservative Party members and the electorate at large. The maintenance of law and order is a fundamental duty of government. For a society to be truly civilised people must feel secure in their own homes and not be frightened when they go out. Conservatives believe that this can only be achieved in a society which respects individual rights and common values and which ensures that those who flout the law are appropriately punished. Conservatives believe that individuals must be held responsible for their actions; social circumstances are no excuse for wrongdoing. Attitudes to law and order remain a crucial dividing line between the major political parties. Only the Conservatives can be trusted to be vigilant in the fight against lawlessness.

The consultation exercise clearly shows that Conservatives feel that one of the major causes of crime has been the breakdown of traditional families and communities. ... There is support for the view that broken homes can be a contributory factor to a life of crime. This is not to say that single mothers cannot bring up law-abiding children, who will succeed in what they do. After all tens of thousands of single mothers do just that. It is, however, felt that it is much more difficult for single mothers to bring up their children without support from others. For this reason it is seen as even more vital today than it was in the past for there to be a strong wider community which can inculcate and teach moral values. ...

Juvenile crime is seen as a major problem. The root causes of this can only be tackled through a strengthening of traditional structures.

The immediate criminal actions must, however, be tackled severely. Making parents take more responsibility for the actions of their children is seen as an important step. ...

More generally there is very strong support for the view that prison works and that the public must be protected from persistent and dangerous criminals. Punishment, as a concept, should be upheld. Prison sentences should be commensurate with the severity of the crime committed. Prisons themselves should be austere, while at the same time offering opportunities for genuine self-improvement and education. ... Among those who discussed the issue there was strong support for the return of the death penalty but it was raised in only a minority of the reports received.

It is widely felt that the victims of crime are too often ignored and that their concerns should be taken more into account. There is a general feeling that 'too much emphasis is placed on the rights of the accused rather than the victim' (Corby and East North Hants [association]). ...

There was widespread support for the police. ... Identity cards received considerable support but a number of constituencies reported 'strong feelings for and against' (Tunbridge Wells). ID cards are seen as a valuable tool in the fight against benefit fraud, and as a means to prevent the underage sale of alcohol and tobacco. ... Some groups were concerned about the civil liberties implications and saw them as a very un-British phenomenon, but most groups felt that only criminals have anything to fear from the introduction of compulsory ID cards.

*Our Nation's Future: Listening to the Conservative Party*, Conservative Central Office, 1996.

## 6.18 An unchanging faith

The essence of British Conservatism has remained unchanged during the half-century since 1945. Most Conservatives would recognise and support this definition, as relevant now as the twentieth century nears its close as it was nearly fifty years before.

A Conservative, then, is a man who holds fast to certain fundamental beliefs: to a belief in the religious basis of society, to a belief in our monarchical constitution, to a belief in the institution of private property, to a belief in the ancient virtues of patriotism, honesty, hard work and tolerance, to a belief in the authority attaching to the work of Time. Without these beliefs nations lose their essential cohesion and revert all too easily to barbarism. Combined with these fundamental beliefs is a scepticism about easy cures or solutions of the human dilemma, a refusal to worship fashionable idols ... and a determination to apply to the problems of the day an opportunism which is modified and controlled by principle, by respect for history, by good sense and by good manners.

Nigel Birch, *The Conservative Party*, London, 1949, p. 38.

# Appendix 1
# Leaders and leadership elections

## Leader of the Party

*date appointed*

Winston Churchill (created Knight of the Garter
in 1953)                                                9 Oct. 1940
Sir Anthony Eden                                       21 Apr. 1955
Harold Macmillan                                       22 Jan. 1957
Sir Alec Douglas-Home (renounced peerage,
previously 14th Earl of Home)                          11 Nov. 1963
Edward Heath                                            2 Aug. 1965
Margaret Thatcher                                      11 Feb. 1975
John Major                                             27 Nov. 1990
William Hague                                          19 June 1997

## Leadership elections

A leadership election system was introduced for the first time in 1965.

| *date and result* | | | *outcome* |
|---|---|---|---|
| 1965 | *First ballot* | (28 July) | Although Heath had not |
| | Edward Heath | 150 | secured the required margin (of |
| | Reginald Maudling | 133 | winning at least 15 per cent |
| | Enoch Powell | 15 | more of the vote than any other |
| | abstentions | 6 | candidate), Maudling and |
| | | | Powell both withdrew and |
| | | | there was no second ballot |

| date and result | outcome |
|---|---|

**1975**    *First ballot*    (4 Feb.)

| | | |
|---|---|---|
| Margaret Thatcher | 130 | |
| Edward Heath | 119 | |
| Hugh Fraser | 16 | |
| abstentions | 11 | |

Heath and Fraser withdrew; under the rules new candidates were nominated and entered the contest for the second ballot

*Second ballot*    (11 Feb.)

| | |
|---|---|
| Margaret Thatcher | 146 |
| William Whitelaw | 79 |
| James Prior | 19 |
| Sir Geoffrey Howe | 19 |
| John Peyton | 11 |
| abstentions | 2 |

Thatcher was elected as Leader

**1989**    *First ballot*    (5 Dec.)

| | |
|---|---|
| Margaret Thatcher | 314 |
| Sir Anthony Meyer | 33 |
| abstentions | 27 |

Thatcher was re-elected as Leader

**1990**    *First ballot*    (20 Nov.)

| | |
|---|---|
| Margaret Thatcher | 204 |
| Michael Heseltine | 152 |
| abstentions | 16 |

Thatcher failed to secure the 15 per cent margin (by 4 votes, the required majority being 56); a second ballot was therefore needed, and Thatcher decided to withdraw

*Second ballot*    (27 Nov.)

| | |
|---|---|
| John Major | 185 |
| Michael Heseltine | 131 |
| Douglas Hurd | 56 |
| abstentions | 0 |

Major was 2 votes short of an overall majority, but the other candidates then withdrew and there was no third ballot

**1995**    *First ballot*    (4 July)

| | |
|---|---|
| John Major | 218 |
| John Redwood | 89 |
| spoilt papers | 12 |
| abstentions | 8 |

Major was re-elected as Leader

*Appendix 1: Leaders and leadership elections*

| date and result | | | outcome |
|---|---|---|---|
| 1997 | *First ballot* | (10 June) | Lilley and Howard withdrew, |
| | Kenneth Clarke | 49 | and endorsed Hague for the |
| | William Hague | 41 | second ballot |
| | John Redwood | 27 | |
| | Peter Lilley | 24 | |
| | Michael Howard | 23 | |
| | abstentions | 0 | |
| | | | |
| | *Second ballot* | (17 June) | Redwood was eliminated under |
| | Kenneth Clarke | 64 | the rules, and the next day |
| | William Hague | 62 | endorsed Clarke |
| | John Redwood | 38 | |
| | abstentions | 0 | |
| | | | |
| | *Third ballot* | (19 June) | Hague was elected as Leader |
| | William Hague | 92 | |
| | Kenneth Clarke | 70 | |
| | abstentions | 2 | |

1997: one MP died shortly after polling day and before the first ballot, leaving 164 MPs

## Deputy Leader

| | *period of office* |
|---|---|
| Reginald Maudling | 4 Aug. 1965–18 July 1972 |
| William Whitelaw | 12 Feb. 1975–4 Aug. 1991 |

(Michael Heseltine was Deputy Prime Minister July 1995–May 1997, but not Deputy Leader)

# Appendix 2
# Party Chairmen and Chief Whips

## Chairman of the Party Organisation

| | *date appointed* |
|---|---|
| Ralph Assheton | 29 Oct. 1944 |
| 1st Baron Woolton (elevated to 1st Viscount, 1953) | 1 July 1946 |
| Oliver Poole (later created 1st Baron Poole, 1958) | 1 Nov. 1955 |
| 2nd Viscount Hailsham | 18 Sep. 1957 |
| Richard Austen Butler | 14 Oct. 1959 |
| Iain Macleod | 10 Oct. 1961 |
| 1st Baron Poole / Iain Macleod (joint) | 17 Apr. 1963 |
| 1st Viscount Blakenham | 21 Oct. 1963 |
| Edward du Cann | 21 Jan. 1965 |
| Anthony Barber | 11 Sep. 1967 |
| Peter Thomas | 31 July 1970 |
| 6th Baron Carrington | 7 Apr. 1972 |
| William Whitelaw | 11 June 1974 |
| Lord Thorneycroft (life peer) | 27 Feb. 1975 |
| Cecil Parkinson | 14 Sep. 1981 |
| John Selwyn Gummer | 14 Sep. 1983 |
| Norman Tebbit | 2 Sep. 1985 |
| Peter Brooke | 2 Nov. 1987 |
| Kenneth Baker | 24 July 1989 |
| Christopher Patten | 28 Nov. 1990 |
| Sir Norman Fowler | 10 May 1992 |
| Jeremy Hanley | 20 July 1994 |
| Brian Mawhinney | 5 July 1995 |
| Lord Parkinson (formerly Cecil Parkinson, created a life peer in 1992) | 20 June 1997 |

## Chief Whip in the House of Commons

|  | *date appointed* |
|---|---|
| James Stuart | 14 Jan. 1941 |
| Patrick Buchan-Hepburn | 4 July 1948 |
| Edward Heath | 30 Dec. 1955 |
| Martin Redmayne | 14 Oct. 1959 |
| William Whitelaw | 26 Nov. 1964 |
| Francis Pym | 20 June 1970 |
| Humphrey Atkins | 2 Dec. 1973 |
| Michael Jopling | 5 May 1979 |
| John Wakeham | 10 June 1983 |
| David Waddington | 13 June 1987 |
| Timothy Renton | 27 Oct. 1989 |
| Richard Ryder | 28 Nov. 1990 |
| Alastair Goodlad | 5 July 1995 |
| James Arbuthnot | 20 June 1997 |

# Appendix 3
# General elections and European elections

## The Conservative performance in general elections

| date of election | candidates nominated | MPs elected | total votes received | % share of vote |
|---|---|---|---|---|
| 5 July 1945 | 618 | 210 | 9,972,010 | 39.6 |
| 23 Feb. 1950 | 619 | 298 | 12,492,404 | 43.5 |
| 25 Oct. 1951 | 617 | 321 | 13,718,199 | 48.0 |
| 26 May 1955 | 624 | 345 | 13,310,891 | 49.7 |
| 8 Oct. 1959 | 625 | 365 | 13,750,876 | 49.3 |
| 15 Oct. 1964 | 630 | 304 | 12,002,642 | 43.4 |
| 31 Mar. 1966 | 629 | 253 | 11,418,455 | 41.0 |
| 18 June 1970 | 628 | 330 | 13,145,123 | 46.4 |
| 28 Feb. 1974 | 623 | 297 | 11,872,180 | 37.9 |
| 10 Oct. 1974 | 622 | 277 | 10,462,565 | 35.8 |
| 3 May 1979 | 622 | 339 | 13,697,923 | 43.9 |
| 9 June 1983 | 633 | 397 | 13,012,316 | 42.4 |
| 11 June 1987 | 633 | 376 | 13,760,583 | 42.3 |
| 9 Apr. 1992 | 645 | 336 | 14,092,891 | 41.9 |
| 1 May 1997 | 648 | 165 | 9,602,989 | 31.4 |

## The Conservative performance in European elections

| date of election | total no. of seats | % national* turnout | Con. MPs elected | % share of vote* |
|---|---|---|---|---|
| 7 June 1979 | 81 | 32.1 | 60 | 50.6 |
| 7 June 1984 | 81 | 31.8 | 45 | 40.8 |
| 15 June 1989 | 81 | 35.9 | 32 | 34.7 |
| 9 June 1994 | 89 | 36.2 | 18 | 27.9 |

* excluding Northern Ireland

# Guide to further reading

## General

With the appearance in the mid-1990s of a considerable number of works which deal with the post-war Conservative Party, there is now a choice of approaches. There are two general narratives: Brendan Evans and Andrew Taylor, *From Salisbury to Major: Continuity and Change in Conservative Politics*, Manchester, 1996, is most useful for the period 1945–70; John Charmley, *A History of Conservative Politics 1900–1996*, Basingstoke, 1996, gives a more even coverage but is lighter and concerned mainly with the leading personalities. A thematic structure was adopted in the substantial volume edited by Anthony Seldon and Stuart Ball, *Conservative Century: The Conservative Party since 1900*, Oxford, 1994 (see further references below). The essays in Anthony Seldon (ed.), *How Tory Governments Fall: The Tory Party in Power since 1783*, London, 1996, examine each of the periods when the Conservatives were in office and the reasons for their downfall, whilst Andrew Davies, *We, the Nation: The Conservative Party and the Pursuit of Power*, London, 1995, takes a more discursive look at the Party's nature and methods. Finally, a new edition is in preparation of Robert Blake's classic survey (the present version of which is entitled *The Conservative Party from Peel to Thatcher*, London, 1985).

For an introduction and background to the period, see Stuart Ball, *The Conservative Party and British Politics 1902–1951*, London, 1995. The fullest and most authoritative examination of the post-war years will be found in the final two volumes of the Longman series, A History of the Conservative Party, both of which were written by John Ramsden: *The Age of Churchill and Eden 1940–1957*, London, 1995, and *The Winds of Change: Macmillan to Heath, 1957–1975*, London, 1996. Another important aspect is dealt with in John Turner, '"A land fit for Tories to live in": the political ecology of the British Conservative Party 1944–1994', *Contemporary European History*,

4, 2, 1995. Philip Norton (ed.), *The Conservative Party*, Hemel Hempstead, 1996, and Steve Ludlam and Martin Smith (eds), *Contemporary British Conservatism*, Basingstoke, 1996, are principally concerned with the Thatcher and Major era, but the former ranges back over a wider period.

## Leaders and leadership

The selection of the Party Leader is discussed in Vernon Bogdanor's essay in Seldon and Ball (eds) *Conservative Century* (details above). Four case studies are Mark Wickham-Jones, 'Right turn: a revisionist account of the 1975 Conservative Party leadership election', *20th Century British History*, 8, 1, 1997; N. G. Jesse, 'Thatcher's rise and fall: an institutional analysis of the Tory leadership selection process', *Electoral Studies*, 15, 2, 1996; Philip Norton: 'Choosing the Leader: the 1989 Conservative contest', *Contemporary Record*, 4, 1990–91 (and see further works on the fall of Thatcher, below), and Keith Alderman, 'The Conservative Party leadership election of 1995', *Parliamentary Affairs*, 49, 2, 1996.

The following are the most useful and significant studies of the Party Leaders. For Churchill after 1945, see Paul Addison, *Churchill on the Home Front 1900–1955*, London, 1992, and John Ramsden, 'Winston Churchill and the leadership of the Conservative Party', *Contemporary Record*, 9, 1, 1995. David Dutton, *Anthony Eden: A Life and Reputation*, London, 1997, gives more attention than previous lives to his role in domestic politics. John Turner, *Macmillan*, London, 1994, provides a clear summary, whilst the 'authorised biography' by Alistair Horne, *Macmillan: Volume 2, 1957–1986*, London, 1989, is much more detailed. Home's succession and period as leader are covered in D. R. Thorpe, *Alec Douglas-Home*, London, 1996, whilst John Campbell, *Edward Heath*, London, 1993, lucidly analyses Heath's personality and the fortunes of his government. There are valuable essays on Conservative Premiers from Churchill to Heath in J. P. Mackintosh (ed.), *British Prime Ministers in the 20th Century, Volume 2: Churchill to Callaghan*, London, 1978. The most revealing study of Margaret Thatcher is Hugo Young, *One of Us: A Biography of Margaret Thatcher*, London, 'final edition' 1991; Kenneth Harris, *Thatcher*, London, 1988, is less critical and complete; whilst Peter Clarke, 'Margaret Thatcher's leadership in historical perspective',

*Parliamentary Affairs*, 45, 1992, places this seminal figure in a wider context. The essential study of her successor is Anthony Seldon, *Major: A Political Life*, London, 1997, but see also P. Jones and J. Hudson, 'The quality of political leadership: a case study of John Major', *British Journal of Political Science*, 26, 2, 1996.

There are also valuable studies of a number of other key figures: Anthony Howard, *Rab: The Life of R. A. Butler*, London, 1987; Robert Shepherd, *Iain Macleod*, London, 1994, and the same author's *Enoch Powell*, London, 1996; Morrison Halcrow, *Keith Joseph: A Single Mind*, London, 1989; Bruce Anderson, *Whitelaw: On the Right Track*, London, 1988; Michael Crick, *Michael Heseltine*, London, 1997; and in several of the chapters in Edmund Dell, *The Chancellors: A History of the Chancellors of the Exchequer 1945–1990*, London, 1996.

### The Parliamentary Party

The organisation of the Parliamentary Party and its social composition are discussed in the essays by Philip Norton and Byron Criddle in Seldon and Ball (eds) *Conservative Century* (details above). On the backgrounds of Conservative MPs, see also the essay in Ludlam and Smith (eds), *Contemporary British Conservatism* (details above), and D. Baker, A. Gamble and S. Ludlam, 'More "classless" and less "Thatcherite"? Conservative MPs after the 1992 election', *Parliamentary Affairs*, 45, 1992. Material on the 1922 Committee can be found in Philip Goodhart and Ursula Branston, *The 1922: The Story of the Conservative Backbenchers' Parliamentary Committee*, London, 1973. Issues of discipline and rebellion are dealt with in Jorgen Rasmussen, *The Relations of the Profumo Rebels with their Local Parties*, Tuscon, 1966; Philip Norton, *Conservative Dissidents: Dissent within the Parliamentary Conservative Party 1970–1974*, London, 1978; and D. Baker et al., 'Backbench Conservative attitudes towards European integration', *Political Quarterly,* 66, 2, 1995.

### The Party organisation

For an account of the national and local organisation and the role of the Annual Conference, consult the chapters by Stuart Ball and Richard Kelly in Seldon and Ball (eds) *Conservative Century* (details above).

The sensitive area of Party funds is dealt with in Michael Pinto-Duschinsky, *British Political Finance 1830–1980*, Washington, 1982, and the more recent J. Fisher, 'Political donations to the Conservative Party', *Parliamentary Affairs*, 47, 1, 1994.

The relationship between the central organisation and the constituencies is analysed in Michael Pinto-Duschinsky, 'Central Office and "power" in the Conservative Party', *Political Studies*, 20, 1972; D. J. Wilson, 'Constituency Party autonomy and central control', *Political Studies*, 21, 1973; Zig Layton-Henry, 'Constituency autonomy in the Conservative Party', *Parliamentary Affairs*, 29, 1976; and Philip Tether, 'Recruiting Conservative Party members: a changing role for Central Office', *Parliamentary Affairs*, 44, 1991, which also has some useful data on local numbers.

The Party membership are discussed in the essay by Seyd and Whiteley in Ludlam and Smith (eds), *Contemporary British Conservatism*, and their views are explored in M. Wilson, 'Grass roots Conservatism: motions to the Party Conference', in Neill Nugent and Roger King (eds), *The British Right: Conservative and Right Wing Politics in Britain*, Farnborough, 1977. More detailed material may be found in Richard Kelly, *Conservative Party Conferences*, Manchester, 1989, a case study of the round of gatherings held in 1986, and Paul Whiteley, Patrick Seyd and Jeremy Richardson, *True Blues: The Politics of Conservative Party Membership*, Oxford, 1994, which analyses the composition and opinions of the rank and file from evidence collected in 1992; Rupert Morris, *Tories: From Village Hall to Westminster*, Edinburgh, 1991, is an anecdotal picture from a similar period.

Particular aspects of organisation and support are examined in Beatrix Campbell, *The Iron Ladies: Why Do Women Vote Tory?*, London, 1987; Zig Layton-Henry, 'The Young Conservatives 1945–1970', *Journal of Contemporary History*, 8, 1973; and Timothy Evans, *Conservative Radicalism: A Sociology of Conservative Party Youth Structures and Libertarianism 1970–1992*, Oxford, 1996. The problems which the Party has faced since the 1950s in two particular areas are dealt with by D. J. Wilson and M. Pinto-Duschinsky, 'Conservative city machines: the end of an era', *British Journal of Political Science*, 6, 1976; S. Kendrick and D. McCrone, 'Politics in a cold climate: the Conservative decline in Scotland', *Political Studies*, 37, 1989; and D. Seawright and J. Curtice, 'The decline of the Scottish Conservative and Unionist Party 1950–1992: religion, ideology or economics?', *Contemporary Record*, 9, 2, 1995.

## Policies and ideas

The shaping of policy is described in the chapter by John Barnes and Richard Cockett in Seldon and Ball (eds) *Conservative Century* (details above), which also contains an essay on Conservative ideas and studies of key areas of government and domestic policy. For an insider's account of the process, see Michael Wolff, 'Policy-making within the Conservative Party', in J. P. Mackintosh (ed.), *People and Parliament*, Farnborough, 1978. John Ramsden, *The Making of Conservative Party Policy: The Conservative Research Department since 1929*, London, 1980, is a lucid analysis which perhaps inevitably puts the CRD too much at the centre of the picture.

On Conservatism, see the general survey by John Fair and J. A. Hutcheson, 'British Conservatism in the twentieth century: an emerging ideological tradition', *Albion*, 19, 1987. Andrew Gamble, *The Conservative Nation*, London, 1974, is a critical analysis of Conservative thought and policy between 1945 and 1974, whilst later developments are summarised in I. Crewe and D. Searing, 'Ideological change in the British Conservative Party', *American Political Science Review*, 82, 1988. For the context of the Thatcher era, see P. F. Whiteley, P. Seyd, J. Richardson and P. Bissell, 'Thatcherism and the Conservative Party', *Political Studies*, 42, 2, 1994; Arthur Aughey, 'Mrs Thatcher's political philosophy', *Parliamentary Affairs*, 36, 1983; Brian Harrison, 'Mrs Thatcher and the intellectuals', *20th Century British History*, 5, 2, 1994; D. Marsh, 'Explaining "Thatcherite" policies: beyond unidimensional explanation', *Political Studies*, 43, 4, 1995; Charles Covell, *The Redefinition of Conservatism: Politics and Doctrine*, Basingstoke, 1986; and Richard Cockett, *Thinking the Unthinkable: Think-Tanks and the Economic Counter-Revolution 1931–1983*, London, 1994.

For particular areas of policy, see Martin Francis and Ina Zweiniger-Bargielowska (eds), *The Conservatives and British Society 1880–1990*, Cardiff, 1996, which includes several essays on economic and social policy dealing in particular with the period 1945–70; Nigel Harris, *Competition and the Corporate Society: British Conservatives, the State and Industry 1945–1964*, London, 1972; Peter Dorey, *The Conservative Party and the Trade Unions*, London, 1995; Timothy Raison, *Tories and the Welfare State: A History of Conservative Social Policy since the Second World War*, Basingstoke, 1990; Christopher Knight, *The Making of Tory Education Policy in Postwar Britain 1950–1986*,

Guide to further reading

London, 1990; James Mitchell, *Conservatives and the Union: A Study of Conservative Party Attitudes to Scotland*, Edinburgh, 1990; and M. Cunningham, 'Conservative dissidents and the Irish question: the "pro-integrationist" lobby 1973–1994', *Irish Political Studies*, 10, 1995. There is much less on the Party and external affairs, but see Dan Horowitz: 'Attitudes of British Conservatives towards decolonisation in Africa', *African Affairs*, 59, 1970, and Wolfram Kaiser, 'Using Europe and abusing the Europeans: the Conservatives and the European Community 1957–1994', *Contemporary Record*, 8, 2, 1994.

## Post-war revival and success, 1945–64

The history of the Conservative Party during this period is surveyed with clarity and depth in John Ramsden's volumes in the Longman series (see above): *The Age of Churchill and Eden 1940–1957* and *The Winds of Change: Macmillan to Heath, 1957–1975*.

On the defeat and after, see M. D. Kandiah, 'The Conservative Party and the 1945 election', *Contemporary Record*, 9, 1, 1995; the early but still informative study by J. D. Hoffman, *The Conservative Party in Opposition 1945–1951*, London, 1964; and the reappraisal by John Ramsden, '"A Party for owners or a Party for earners": how far did the British Conservative Party really change after 1945?', *Royal Historical Society, Transactions*, fifth series, 37, 1987. The post-war Conservative revival and the theme of 'consensus' in the period 1945–64 are discussed in the contributions of the two editors in Harriet Jones and Michael Kandiah (eds), *The Myth of Consensus: New Views on British History 1945–1964*, Basingstoke, 1996; in E. H. H. Green, 'The Conservative Party, the state and the electorate 1945–1964', in Jon Lawrence and Miles Taylor (eds), *Party, State and Society: Electoral Behaviour in Britain since 1920*, Aldershot, 1997; and in two articles by Ina Zweiniger-Bargielowska: 'Rationing, austerity, and the Conservative Party recovery after 1945', *Historical Journal*, 37, 1, 1994, and 'Explaining the gender gap: the Conservative Party and the women's vote 1945–1964', in the volume which she co-edited with Francis, *The Conservatives and British Society 1880–1990* (details above).

The governments of the 1950s are examined briefly in Andrew Boxer, *The Conservative Governments 1951–1964*, London, 1996, and more fully in Kevin Jefferys, *Retreat from New Jerusalem: British Politics 1951-1964*, Basingstoke, 1997; see also Michael Pinto-Duschinsky, 'Bread and circuses? The Conservatives in office 1951–1964', in Vernon Bogdanor and Robert Skidelsky (eds), *The Age of Affluence 1951–1964*, London, 1970, and the essays in Peter Hennessy and Anthony Seldon (eds), *Ruling Performance: British Governments from Attlee to Thatcher*, Oxford, 1987. Particular governments are analysed in Anthony Seldon, *Churchill's Indian Summer: The Conservative Government 1951–1955*, London, 1981, which was based on extensive interviewing, and Henry Pelling, *Churchill's Peacetime Ministry 1951–1955*, Basingstoke, 1996, written after the files in the Public Record Office became available; L. A. Siedentop, 'Mr. Macmillan and the Edwardian style', in Bogdanor and Skidelsky (eds), *Age of Affluence*; and Keith Alderman, 'Harold Macmillan's "night of the long knives"', *Contemporary Record*, 6, 1992–93.

Problems in external affairs are considered by Lord Beloff, 'The crisis and its consequences for the British Conservative Party', in W. R. Louis and R. Owen (eds), *Suez 1956: The Crisis and its Consequences*, Oxford, 1989; Philip Murphy, *Party Politics and Decolonization: The Conservative Party and British Colonial Policy in Tropical Africa 1951–1964*, Oxford, 1995; Ronald Butt, 'The Common Market and Conservative Party politics 1961–1962', *Government and Opposition*, 2, 1967; and David Dutton, 'Anticipating Maastricht: the Conservative Party and Britain's first application to join the European Community', *Contemporary Record*, 7, 3, 1993.

## Changes of course, 1964–79

Any consideration of this period should begin with Ramsden's *The Winds of Change: Macmillan to Heath, 1957–1975*. An earlier account which remains useful is M. Wilson and K. Phillips, 'The Conservative Party: from Macmillan to Thatcher', in Nugent and King (eds), *The British Right* (details above). For particular phases, see L. Johnman, 'The Conservative Party in opposition 1964–1970', in R. Coopey, S. Fielding and N. Tiratsoo (eds), *The Wilson Governments 1964–1970*, London, 1993; Stuart Ball and Anthony Seldon (eds), *The Heath Government 1970–1974: A Reappraisal*, London, 1996 (in particular Ball's essay, 'The Conservative Party and the Heath government'); Martin Holmes, *Political Pressure and Economic Policy:*

Guide to further reading

British Government 1970–1974, London, 1982; R. Behrens, *The Conservative Party from Heath to Thatcher: Policies and Politics 1974–1979*, Farnborough, 1980; and Zig Layton-Henry (ed.), *Conservative Party Politics*, London, 1980.

## The Thatcher and Major governments, 1979–97

Much has been written on the Thatcher governments, but as yet little on the period after 1990. On the 1980s generally, see the introductory survey by Richard Evans, *Thatcher and Thatcherism*, London, 1997, and Andrew Gamble, *The Free Economy and the Strong State: The Politics of Thatcherism*, London, 2nd edition, 1994. More detailed accounts are Peter Jenkins, *Mrs Thatcher's Revolution: The Ending of the Socialist Era*, London, revised edition, 1989; Peter Riddell, *The Thatcher Decade*, Oxford, 1989; Kenneth Minogue and Michael Biddiss (eds), *Thatcherism: Personality and Politics*, Basingstoke, 1987; Dennis Kavanagh, *Thatcherism and British Politics: The End of Consensus?*, Oxford, 1987; and Dennis Kavanagh and Anthony Seldon (eds), *The Thatcher Effect*, Oxford, 1989.

The conduct of particular governments is dealt with in Martin Holmes, *The First Thatcher Government 1979–1983*, Brighton, 1985; Martin Burch, 'Mrs Thatcher's approach to leadership in government, 1979–June 1983', *Parliamentary Affairs*, 36, 1983; D. Dolowitz, D. Marsh, F. O'Neill and D. Richards, 'Thatcherism and the 3 "Rs": radicalism, realism and rhetoric in the third term of the Thatcher government', *Parliamentary Affairs*, 49, 3, 1996; and David Butler, Andrew Adonis and Tony Travers, *Failure in British Government: The Politics of the Poll Tax*, Oxford, 1994.

For the fall of Thatcher, see the two related articles by Philip Norton, '"The Lady's not for turning" but what about the rest? Margaret Thatcher and the Conservative Party 1979–1989', and 'Choosing a leader: Margaret Thatcher and the Parliamentary Conservative Party 1989–90', both in *Parliamentary Affairs*, 43, 1990; R. K. Alderman and N. Carter, 'A very Tory coup: the ousting of Mrs Thatcher', *Parliamentary Affairs*, 44, 1991; Mark Wickham-Jones and Donald Shell, 'What went wrong? The fall of Mrs Thatcher', *Contemporary Record*, 5, 1991–92; Alan Watkins, *A Conservative Coup: The Fall of Margaret Thatcher*, London, 1991; and Robert Shepherd, *The Power Brokers: The Tory Party and its Leaders*, London, 1991, which focuses mainly

198

*Guide to further reading*

upon the fall of Thatcher but also provides a comparative background. For the Major governments, see Dennis Kavanagh and Anthony Seldon (eds), *The Major Effect*, London, 1994, and J. Andrew Brown, 'The Major effect: changes in party leadership and party popularity', *Parliamentary Affairs*, 45, 1992. For the troublesome issue of Europe, see M. Sowemimo, 'The Conservative Party and European integration 1988–1995', *Party Politics*, 2, 1, 1996, and two articles by D. Baker, A. Gamble and S. Ludlam: 'Whips or scorpions? The Maastricht vote and the Conservative Party', *Parliamentary Affairs*, 46, 1993, and 'The Parliamentary siege of Maastricht, 1993: Conservative divisions and British ratification', *Parliamentary Affairs*, 47, 1994.

### Sources and memoirs

In contrast to the Labour Party, there is a striking lack of published diaries or papers of post-war Conservatives; Alan Clark's *Diaries*, London, 1993, are the outstanding and entertaining exception, but unfortunately do not take us inside the cabinet. Douglas Hurd, then Heath's political secretary, gave an insight into the problems of that ministry in *An End to Promises: Sketch of a Government 1970–1974*, London, 1979.

Of the Party Leaders, two have written lengthy memoirs: Harold Macmillan produced six volumes in rapid succession (London, 1966–73), and Margaret Thatcher dealt with her Premiership in *The Downing Street Years*, London, 1993, before returning to the period up to 1979 in *The Path to Power*, London, 1995. Lord Home wrote more modestly in *The Way the Wind Blows*, London, 1976, whilst Eden's three volumes say almost nothing on domestic politics.

From the wide range of other memoirs, the following are the most helpful or detailed: Lord Butler, *The Art of the Possible*, London, 1971; Lord Woolton, *Memoirs*, London, 1959; Earl of Kilmuir (David Maxwell-Fyfe), *Political Adventure*, London, 1964; John Boyd-Carpenter, *Way of Life*, London, 1980; Lord Hailsham, *A Sparrow's Flight*, London, 1990; James Prior, *A Balance of Power*, London, 1986; Lord Carrington, *Reflect on Things Past*, London, 1988; Sir Geoffrey Howe, *Conflict of Loyalty*, London, 1994; Nigel Lawson, *The View from Number 11*, London, 1992; Norman Tebbit, *Upwardly Mobile*, London, 1988; and Kenneth Baker, *The Turbulent Years*, London, 1993. Other memoirs worth consulting are: Reginald Maudling, *Memoirs*,

*Guide to further reading*

London, 1978; Lord Whitelaw, *The Whitelaw Memoirs*, London, 1989; Peter Walker, *Staying Power: An Autobiography*, London, 1991; Norman Fowler, *Ministers Decide*, London, 1991; and Cecil Parkinson, *Right at the Centre*, London, 1992.

# Index

# Index

leadership elections 20–1,
29, 42–5
policies *see* defence; economic; foreign; imperial;
policy-making; social
politics (1945–51) 7, 21–2,
66–7, 105–6, 165–7;
(1951–64) 7–8, 107–16;
(1964–74) 116–23; (1979–
90) 124–31; (1990–97)
131–41
propaganda 112
*see also* Chief Whip; finance;
organisation, central;
organisation, local; Parliamentary Party;
Conservative Political Centre *see*
organisation, central
Conservative Research Department *see* organisation,
central
crime 182–3
Critchley, J. 17, 49–52, 56–7,
92–3

defence policy 151–2, 159–60
documents 12–19
Douglas, J. 113–14, 116–17
Du Cann, E. 31, 55

Eccles, D. 167–8
economic policy 107–8, 112,
115, 121–2, 130, 172–4
choice 105, 107–8, 125–6,
178–9
inflation 122–3, 173, 178
interventionism 169–70
market forces 119, 140,
171–2, 180–2
nationalisation 109, 112,
119–20
privatisation 125–6
Eden, A. 22–4, 103–4
European Community 154–6,

158–9
application to join 142–3,
150–1
entry into 154–5
relations with 126–7, 132,
135–8, 160–1
Evans, D. 139
Exchange Rate Mechanism 132,
138

Fell, A. 93
finance 64, 67, 94–6
Fookes, Dame J. 87
foreign policy 112, 143–4
Cold War 130–1, 157
Europe 126–7, 132, 135–8,
142–3, 150–1, 154–5,
160–1
Fowler, N. 69, 95
Fowler report 69–71, 95–6
Fox, Sir M. 42
freedom 105, 107–8, 125–6,
178–9
Fraser, Sir M. 16, 100–1,
111–14, 120, 121–3

Garel-Jones, T. 39–40
general elections (1945) 21,
102–3; (1950) 106; (1951)
166–7; (1955) 23–4; (1959)
111–12; (1970) 120; (1992)
40–1, 131–2, 139; (1997)
11, 135–41
Gilmour, I. 124–5, 155–6, 174–5
Gorman, T. 48–9
Grant, Sir A. 88

Hailsham, Lord 27–8, 110–11,
164–5
Hammersmith South 21, 93
Heath, E. 20, 28
character 30
government 8–9, 120–2
fall 30–1

202

# Index